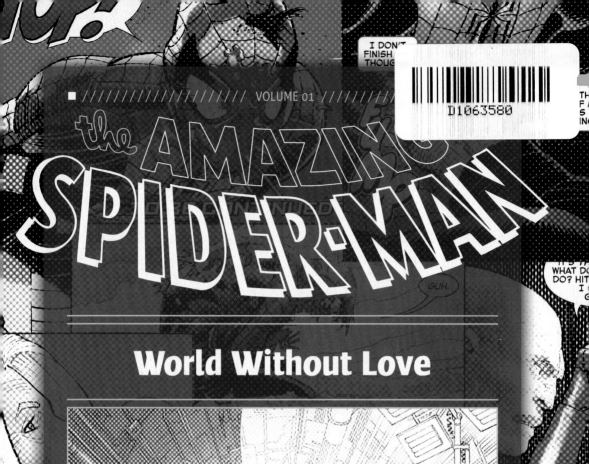

the AMAZING SPIDER-MAN

World Without Love

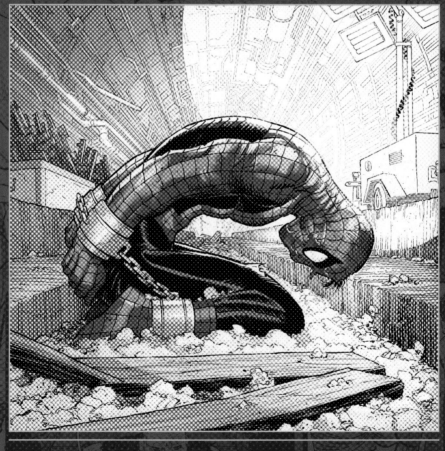

PETER PARKER has the proportional speed, strength and agility of a **SPIDER**; adhesive fingertips and toes; and the unique precognitive awareness of danger called **"SPIDER-SENSE"**! After the tragic death of his Uncle Ben, **PETER PARKER** understood that with great power there must also come great responsibility. He became the crimefighting super hero called...

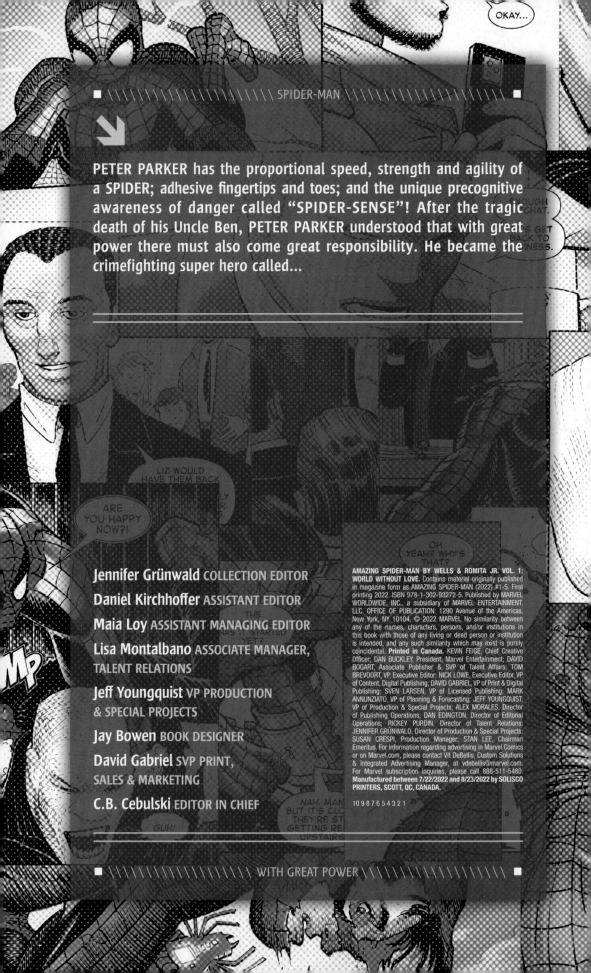

Jennifer Grünwald COLLECTION EDITOR

Daniel Kirchhoffer ASSISTANT EDITOR

Maia Loy ASSISTANT MANAGING EDITOR

Lisa Montalbano ASSOCIATE MANAGER, TALENT RELATIONS

Jeff Youngquist VP PRODUCTION & SPECIAL PROJECTS

Jay Bowen BOOK DESIGNER

David Gabriel SVP PRINT, SALES & MARKETING

C.B. Cebulski EDITOR IN CHIEF

AMAZING SPIDER-MAN BY WELLS & ROMITA JR. VOL. 1: WORLD WITHOUT LOVE. Contains material originally published in magazine form as AMAZING SPIDER-MAN (2022) #1-5. First printing 2022. ISBN 978-1-302-93272-5. Published by MARVEL WORLDWIDE, INC., a subsidiary of MARVEL ENTERTAINMENT, LLC. OFFICE OF PUBLICATION: 1290 Avenue of the Americas, New York, NY 10104. © 2022 MARVEL. No similarity between any of the names, characters, persons, and/or institutions in this book with those of any living or dead person or institution is intended, and any such similarity which may exist is purely coincidental. **Printed in Canada.** KEVIN FEIGE, Chief Creative Officer; DAN BUCKLEY, President, Marvel Entertainment; DAVID BOGART, Associate Publisher & SVP of Talent Affairs; TOM BREVOORT, VP, Executive Editor; NICK LOWE, Executive Editor, VP of Content, Digital Publishing; DAVID GABRIEL, VP of Print & Digital Publishing; SVEN LARSEN, VP of Licensed Publishing; MARK ANNUNZIATO, VP of Planning & Forecasting; JEFF YOUNGQUIST, VP of Production & Special Projects; ALEX MORALES, Director of Publishing Operations; DAN EDINGTON, Director of Editorial Operations; RICKEY PURDIN, Director of Talent Relations; JENNIFER GRÜNWALD, Director of Production & Special Projects; SUSAN CRESPI, Production Manager; STAN LEE, Chairman Emeritus. For information regarding advertising in Marvel Comics or on Marvel.com, please contact Vit DeBellis, Custom Solutions & Integrated Advertising Manager, at vdebellis@marvel.com. For Marvel subscription inquiries, please call 888-511-5480. **Manufactured between 7/22/2022 and 8/23/2022 by SOLISCO PRINTERS, SCOTT, QC, CANADA.**

10 9 8 7 6 5 4 3 2 1

VOLUME 01

the AMAZING SPIDER-MAN

World Without Love

Zeb Wells WRITER

John Romita Jr. PENCILER

Scott Hanna INKER

Marcio Menyz COLORIST

VC's **Joe Caramagna** LETTERER

John Romita Jr., **Scott Hanna** & **Marcio Menyz** COVER ART

Lindsey Cohick & **Kaeden McGahey** ASSISTANT EDITORS

Nick Lowe EDITOR

SPIDER-MAN CREATED BY STAN LEE & STEVE DITKO

THERE MUST ALSO COME GREAT RESPONSIBILITY

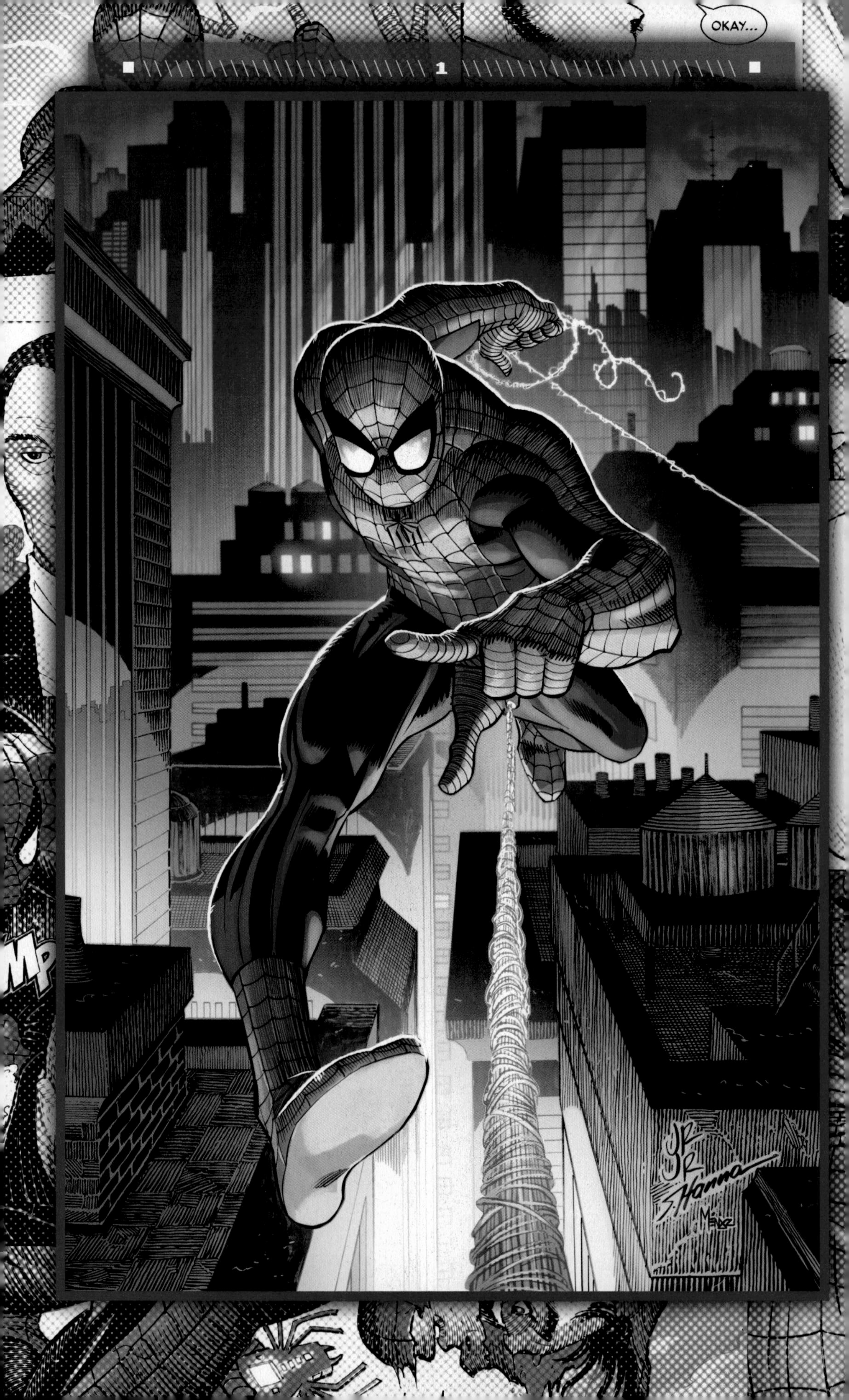
OKAY...
1

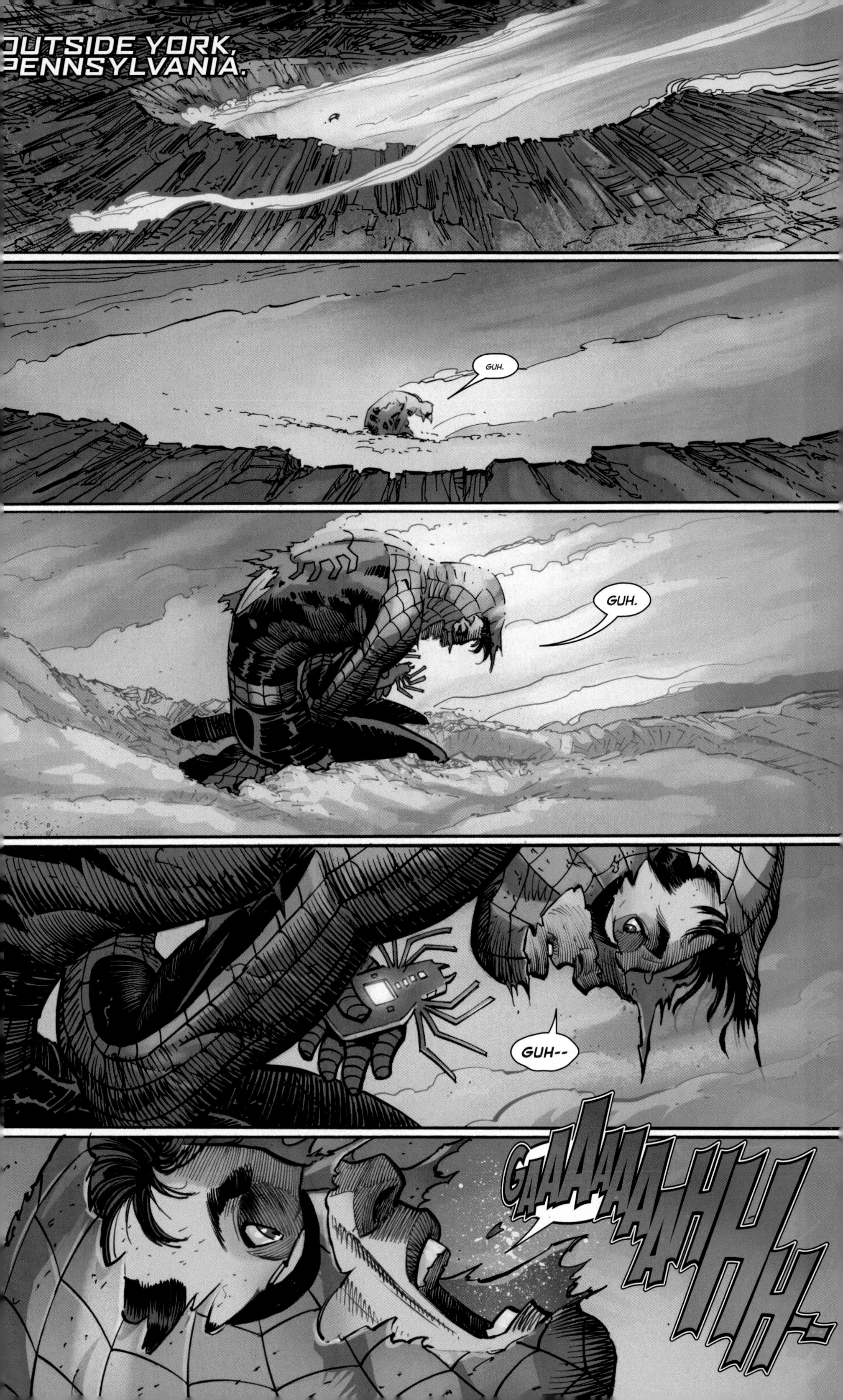
OUTSIDE YORK, PENNSYLVANIA.
GUH.
GUH.
GUH--
GAAAAAAHHHH--

SIX MONT

HS LATER

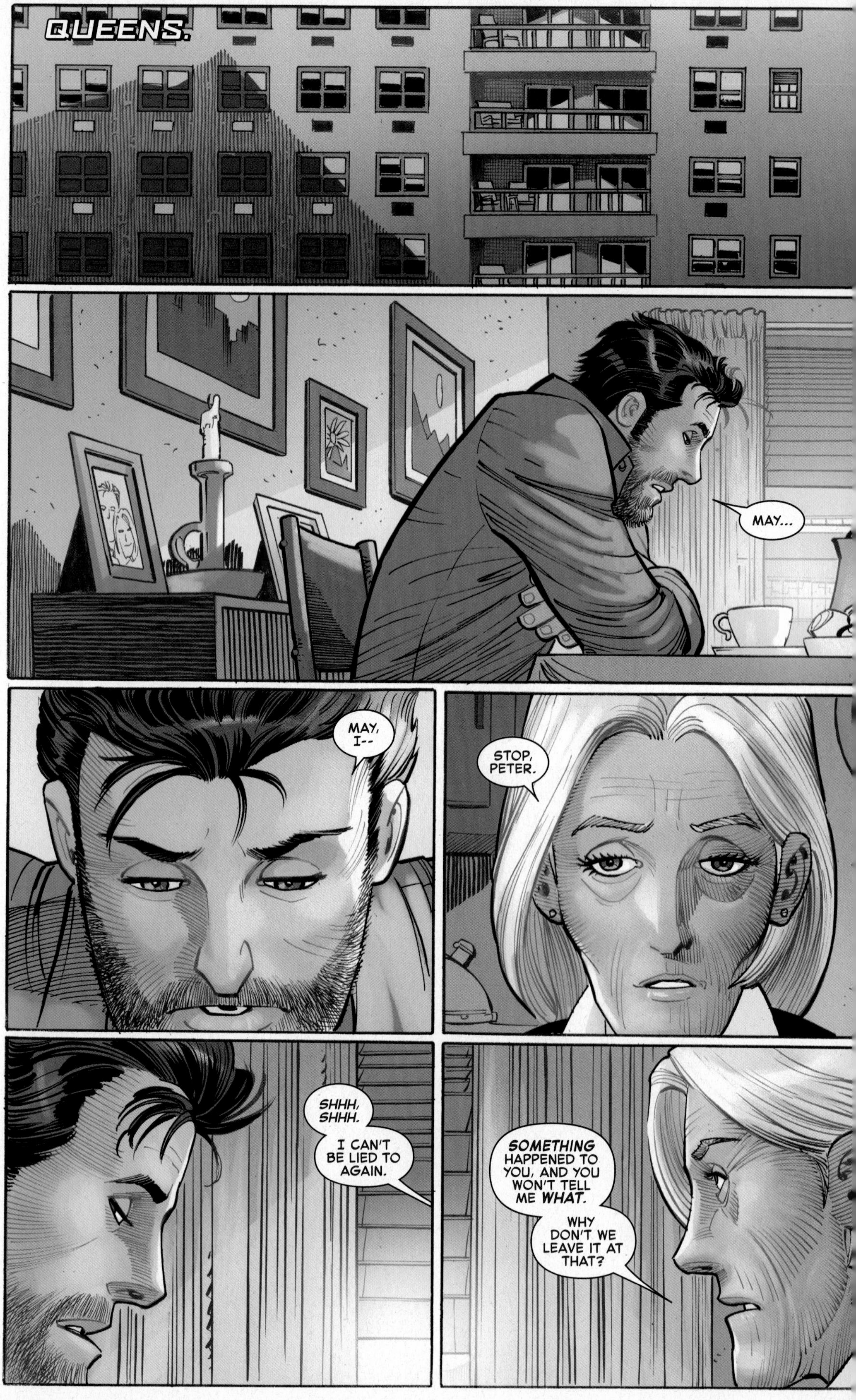
QUEENS.
MAY...
MAY, I--
STOP, PETER.
SHHH, SHHH.
I CAN'T BE LIED TO AGAIN.
SOMETHING HAPPENED TO YOU, AND YOU WON'T TELL ME WHAT.
WHY DON'T WE LEAVE IT AT THAT?

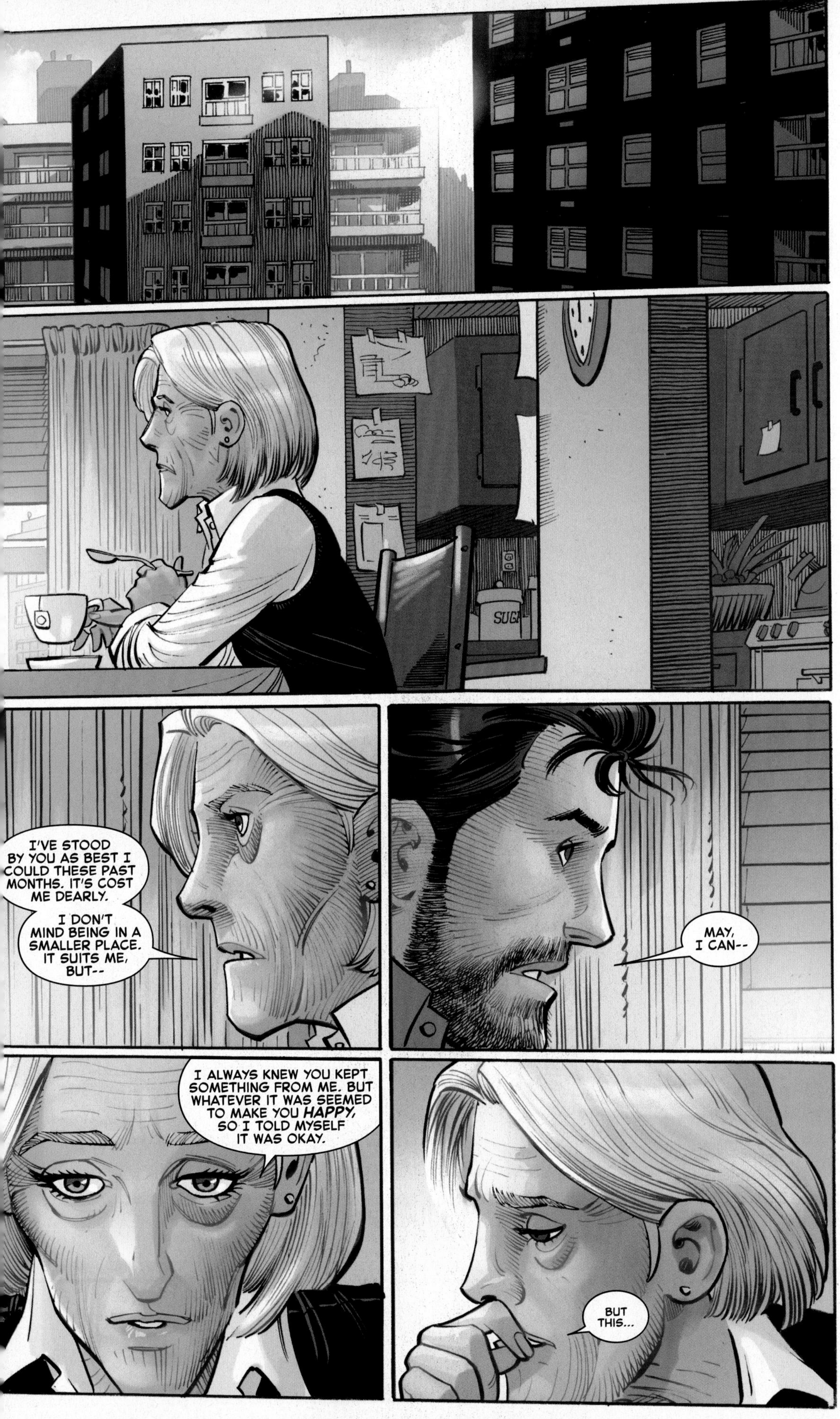

SUG
I'VE STOOD BY YOU AS BEST I COULD THESE PAST MONTHS. IT'S COST ME DEARLY.
I DON'T MIND BEING IN A SMALLER PLACE. IT SUITS ME, BUT--
MAY, I CAN--
I ALWAYS KNEW YOU KEPT SOMETHING FROM ME. BUT WHATEVER IT WAS SEEMED TO MAKE YOU HAPPY, SO I TOLD MYSELF IT WAS OKAY.
BUT THIS...

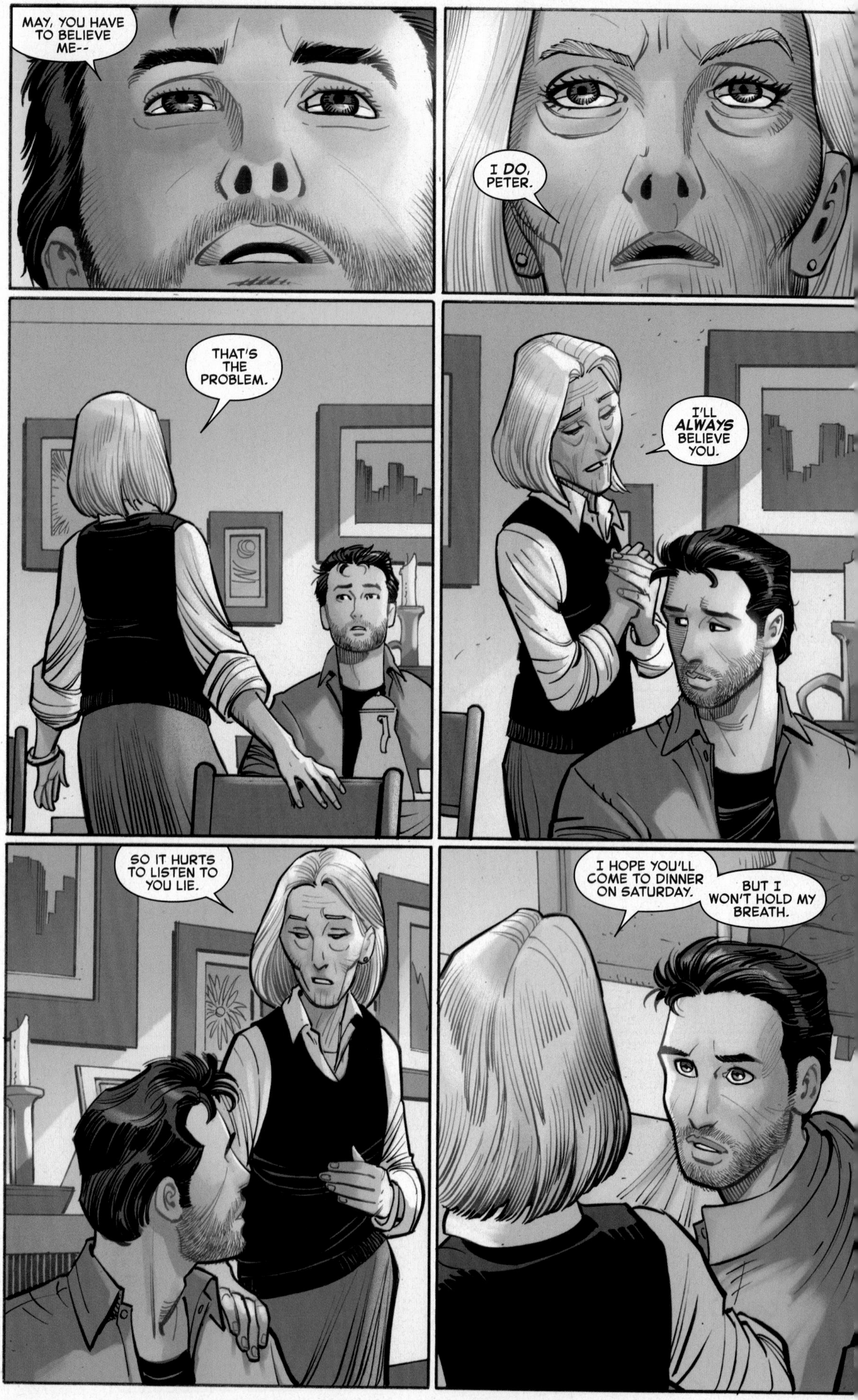
MAY, YOU HAVE TO BELIEVE ME--
I DO, PETER.
THAT'S THE PROBLEM.
I'LL ALWAYS BELIEVE YOU.
SO IT HURTS TO LISTEN TO YOU LIE.
I HOPE YOU'LL COME TO DINNER ON SATURDAY.
BUT I WON'T HOLD MY BREATH.

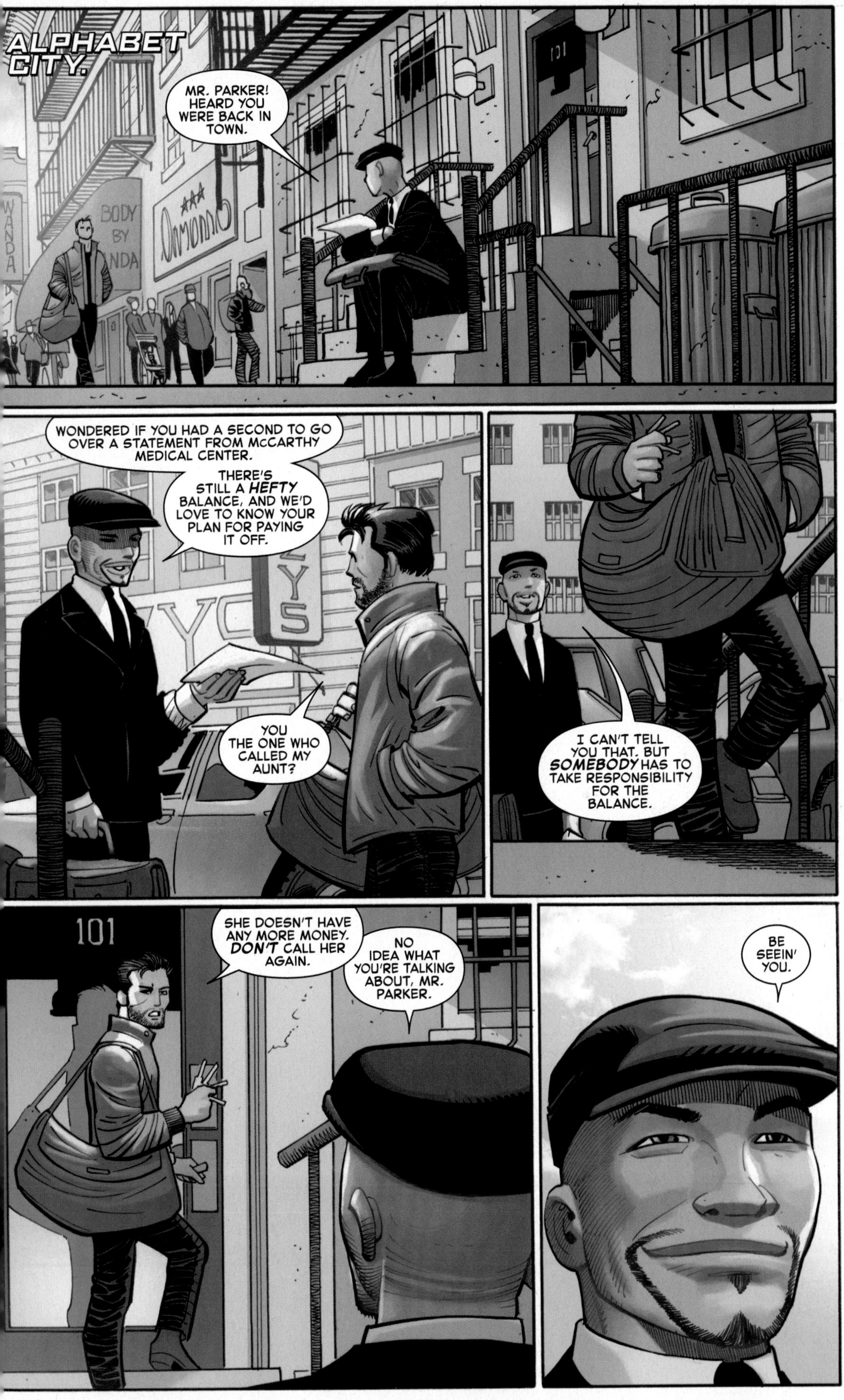
ALPHABET CITY.
MR. PARKER! HEARD YOU WERE BACK IN TOWN.
BODY BY WANDA
101
WONDERED IF YOU HAD A SECOND TO GO OVER A STATEMENT FROM McCARTHY MEDICAL CENTER.
THERE'S STILL A HEFTY BALANCE, AND WE'D LOVE TO KNOW YOUR PLAN FOR PAYING IT OFF.
YOU THE ONE WHO CALLED MY AUNT?
I CAN'T TELL YOU THAT. BUT SOMEBODY HAS TO TAKE RESPONSIBILITY FOR THE BALANCE.
101
SHE DOESN'T HAVE ANY MORE MONEY. DON'T CALL HER AGAIN.
NO IDEA WHAT YOU'RE TALKING ABOUT, MR. PARKER.
BE SEEIN' YOU.

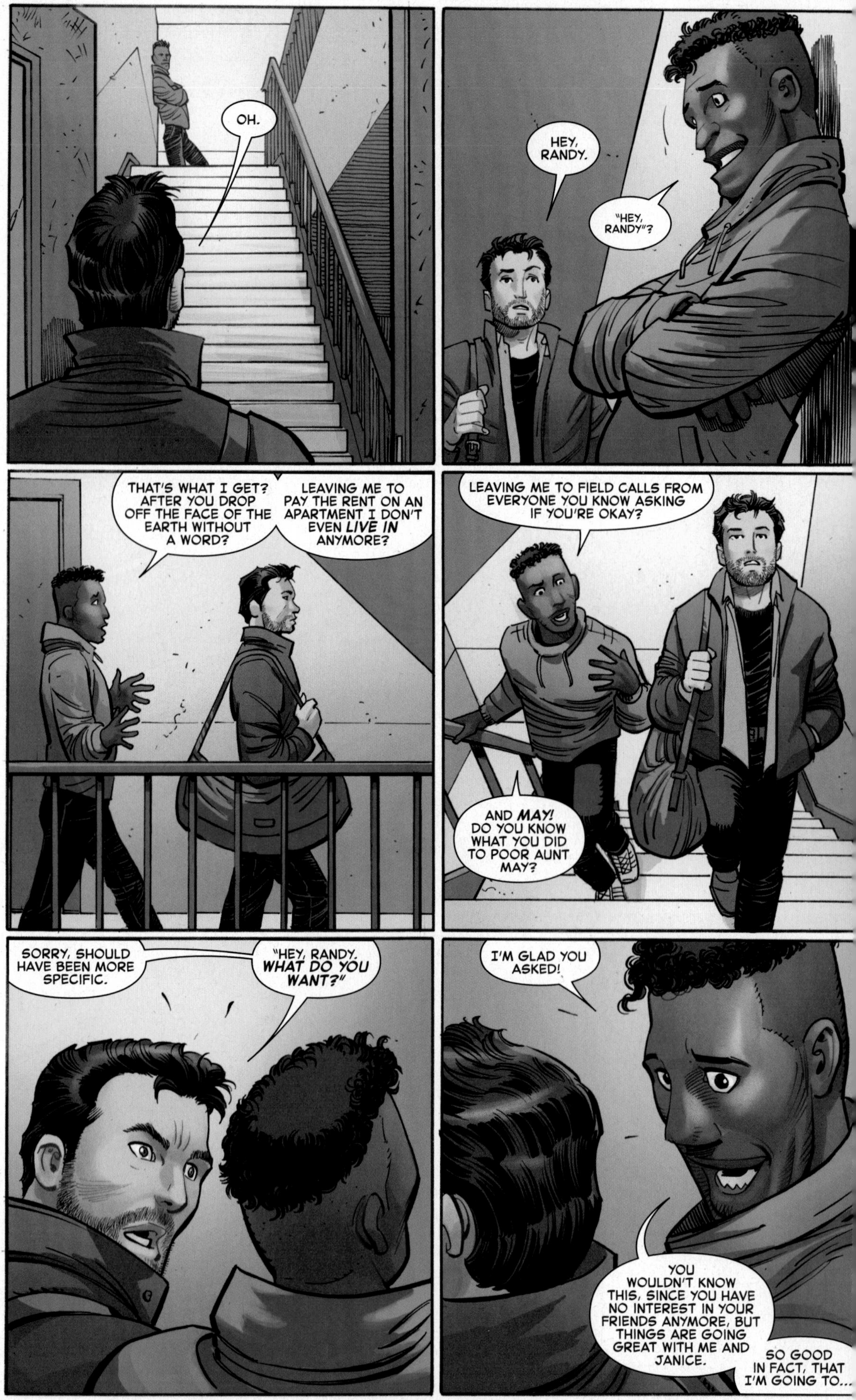

OH.
HEY, RANDY.
"HEY, RANDY"?
THAT'S WHAT I GET? AFTER YOU DROP OFF THE FACE OF THE EARTH WITHOUT A WORD?
LEAVING ME TO PAY THE RENT ON AN APARTMENT I DON'T EVEN LIVE IN ANYMORE?
LEAVING ME TO FIELD CALLS FROM EVERYONE YOU KNOW ASKING IF YOU'RE OKAY?
AND MAY! DO YOU KNOW WHAT YOU DID TO POOR AUNT MAY?
SORRY, SHOULD HAVE BEEN MORE SPECIFIC.
"HEY, RANDY. WHAT DO YOU WANT?"
I'M GLAD YOU ASKED!
YOU WOULDN'T KNOW THIS, SINCE YOU HAVE NO INTEREST IN YOUR FRIENDS ANYMORE, BUT THINGS ARE GOING GREAT WITH ME AND JANICE.
SO GOOD IN FACT, THAT I'M GOING TO...

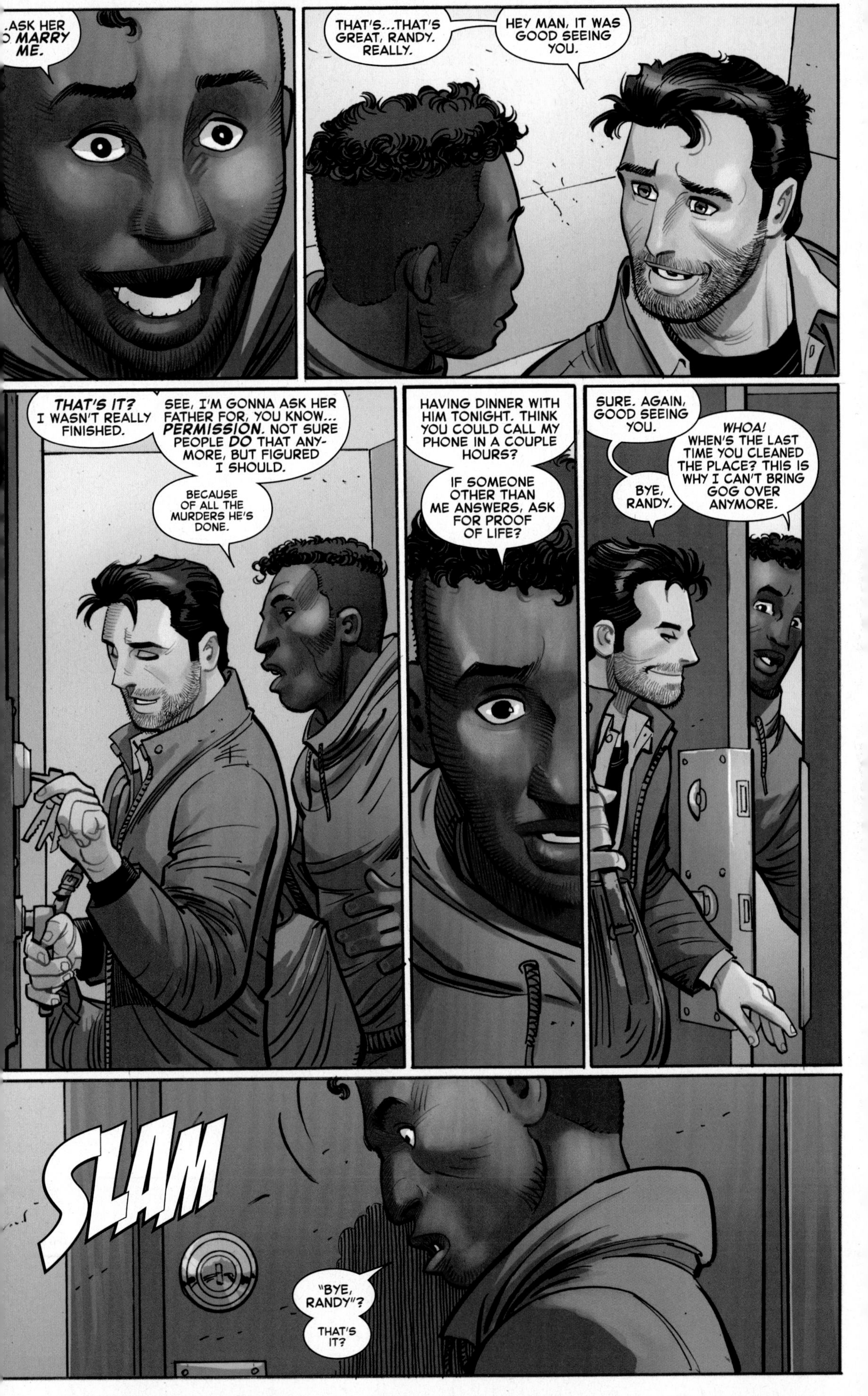
...ASK HER TO MARRY ME.
THAT'S...THAT'S GREAT, RANDY. REALLY.
HEY MAN, IT WAS GOOD SEEING YOU.
THAT'S IT? I WASN'T REALLY FINISHED.
SEE, I'M GONNA ASK HER FATHER FOR, YOU KNOW... PERMISSION. NOT SURE PEOPLE DO THAT ANYMORE, BUT FIGURED I SHOULD.
BECAUSE OF ALL THE MURDERS HE'S DONE.
HAVING DINNER WITH HIM TONIGHT. THINK YOU COULD CALL MY PHONE IN A COUPLE HOURS?
IF SOMEONE OTHER THAN ME ANSWERS, ASK FOR PROOF OF LIFE?
SURE. AGAIN, GOOD SEEING YOU.
BYE, RANDY.
WHOA! WHEN'S THE LAST TIME YOU CLEANED THE PLACE? THIS IS WHY I CAN'T BRING GOG OVER ANYMORE.
SLAM
"BYE, RANDY"?
THAT'S IT?

WHATEVER! SOMETHING'S NOT RIGHT WITH YOU, PETER. GET HELP, MAN!

AND THE BEARD ISN'T WORKING, BY THE WAY!

RANDY, ONE OF MY BEST FRIENDS, TAKING POTSHOTS AT ME. THINKS I LET HIM DOWN.

THE WORST PART IS, HE'S RIGHT. MAY, RANDY, NORMAN...

...THEY'RE ALL RIGHT.

BUT MJ...

MARY JANE WATSON

CALL

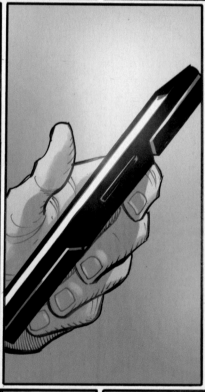

BZZT

RR

Yo, Pete! Come on, man. This is ridiculous.
Jan 13

WHERE ARE YOU?
Jan 29

Some guy looking for you. Collections? Where you at?
Mar 2

52 W 136th. 8 p.m. In case I DISAPPEAR.

You remember who my gf's dad is, right?
Today

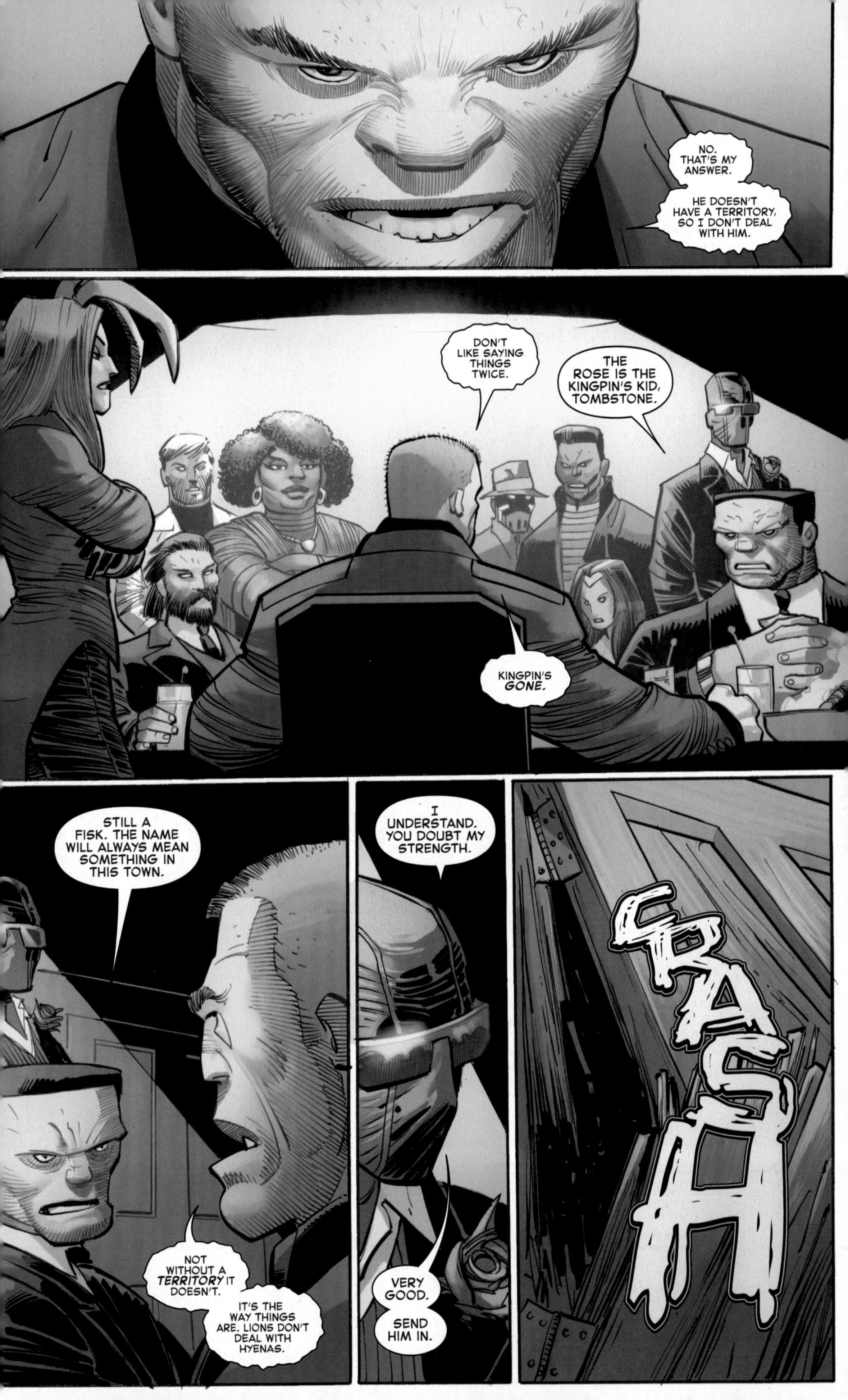
NO. THAT'S MY ANSWER.
HE DOESN'T HAVE A TERRITORY, SO I DON'T DEAL WITH HIM.
DON'T LIKE SAYING THINGS TWICE.
THE ROSE IS THE KINGPIN'S KID, TOMBSTONE.
KINGPIN'S *GONE.*
STILL A FISK. THE NAME WILL ALWAYS MEAN SOMETHING IN THIS TOWN.
NOT WITHOUT A *TERRITORY* IT DOESN'T.
IT'S THE WAY THINGS ARE. LIONS DON'T DEAL WITH HYENAS.
I UNDERSTAND. YOU DOUBT MY STRENGTH.
VERY GOOD.
SEND HIM IN.
CRASH

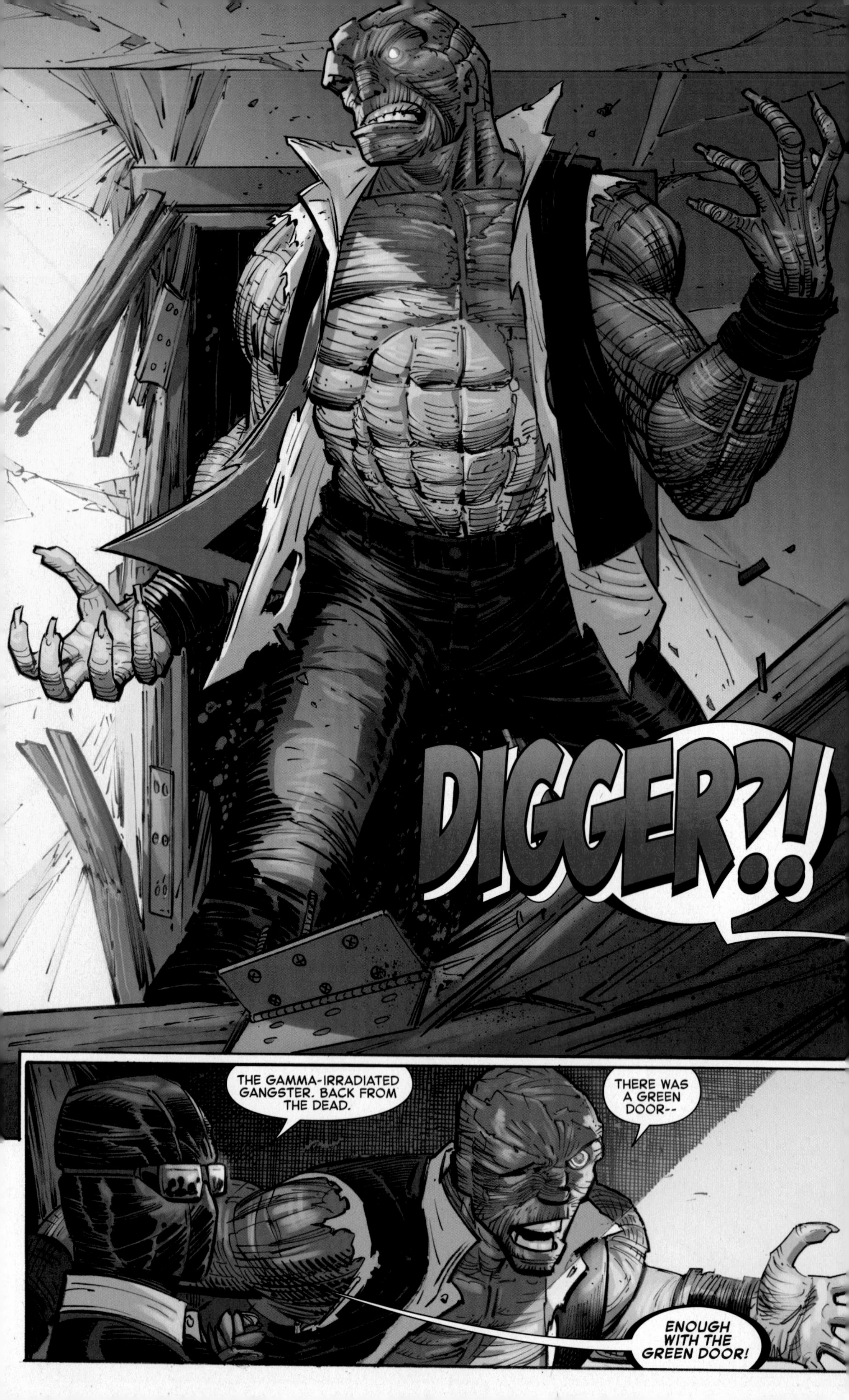
DIGGER?!
THE GAMMA-IRRADIATED GANGSTER. BACK FROM THE DEAD.
THERE WAS A GREEN DOOR--
ENOUGH WITH THE GREEN DOOR!

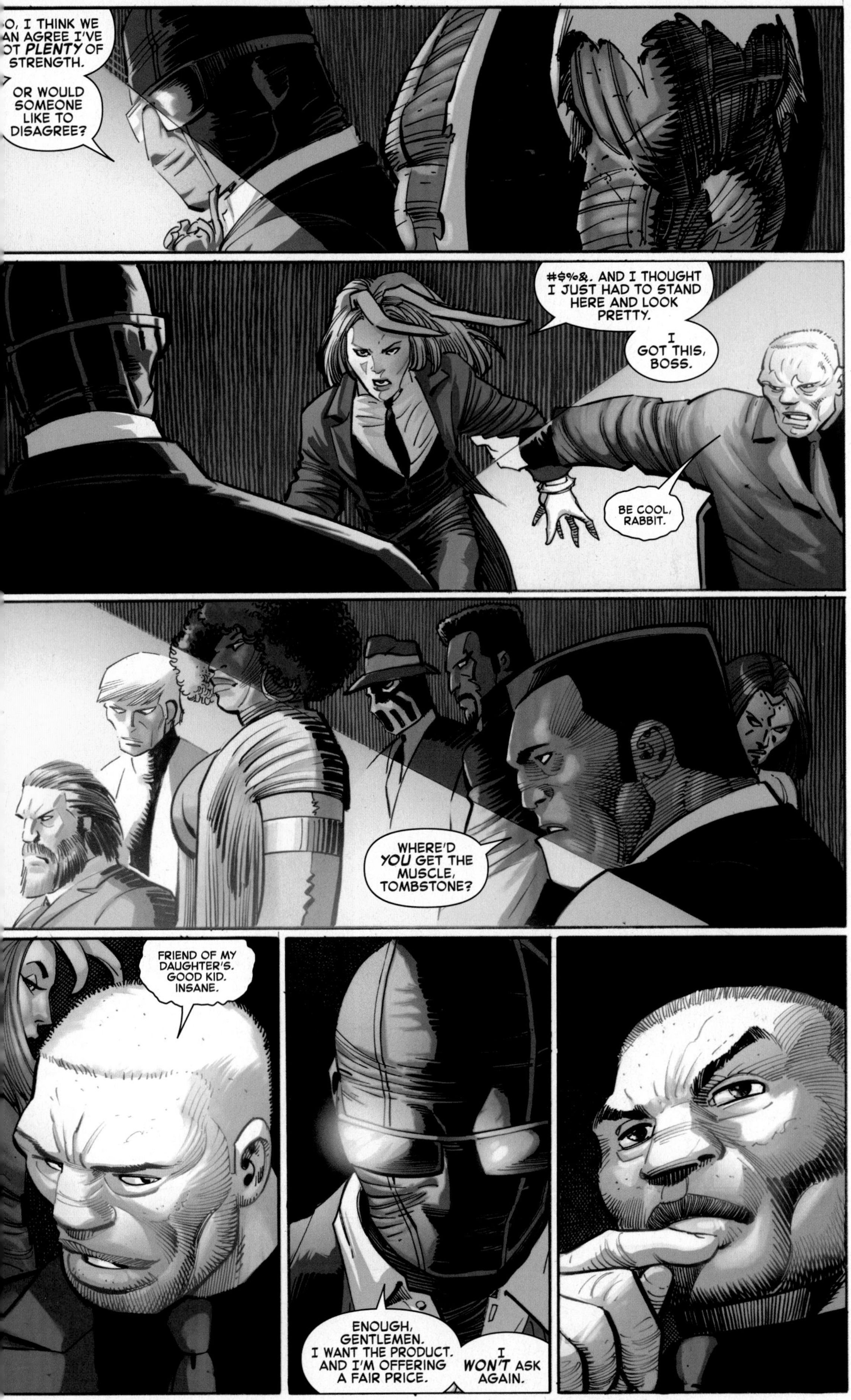
O, I THINK WE AN AGREE I'VE OT PLENTY OF STRENGTH.
OR WOULD SOMEONE LIKE TO DISAGREE?
#$%&. AND I THOUGHT I JUST HAD TO STAND HERE AND LOOK PRETTY.
I GOT THIS, BOSS.
BE COOL, RABBIT.
WHERE'D YOU GET THE MUSCLE, TOMBSTONE?
FRIEND OF MY DAUGHTER'S. GOOD KID. INSANE.
ENOUGH, GENTLEMEN. I WANT THE PRODUCT. AND I'M OFFERING A FAIR PRICE.
I WON'T ASK AGAIN.

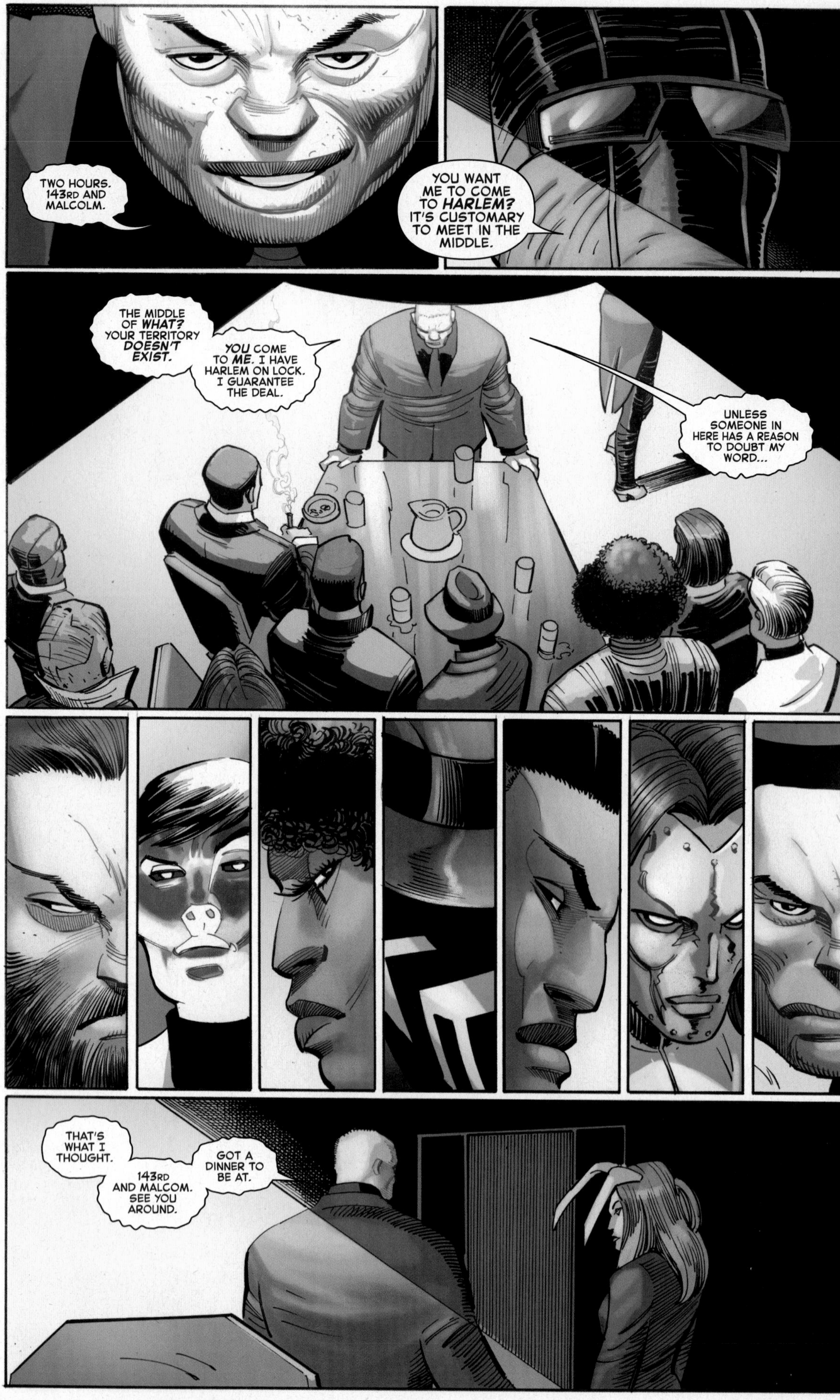
TWO HOURS. 143RD AND MALCOLM.
YOU WANT ME TO COME TO HARLEM? IT'S CUSTOMARY TO MEET IN THE MIDDLE.
THE MIDDLE OF WHAT? YOUR TERRITORY DOESN'T EXIST.
YOU COME TO ME. I HAVE HARLEM ON LOCK. I GUARANTEE THE DEAL.
UNLESS SOMEONE IN HERE HAS A REASON TO DOUBT MY WORD...
THAT'S WHAT I THOUGHT.
143RD AND MALCOM. SEE YOU AROUND.
GOT A DINNER TO BE AT.

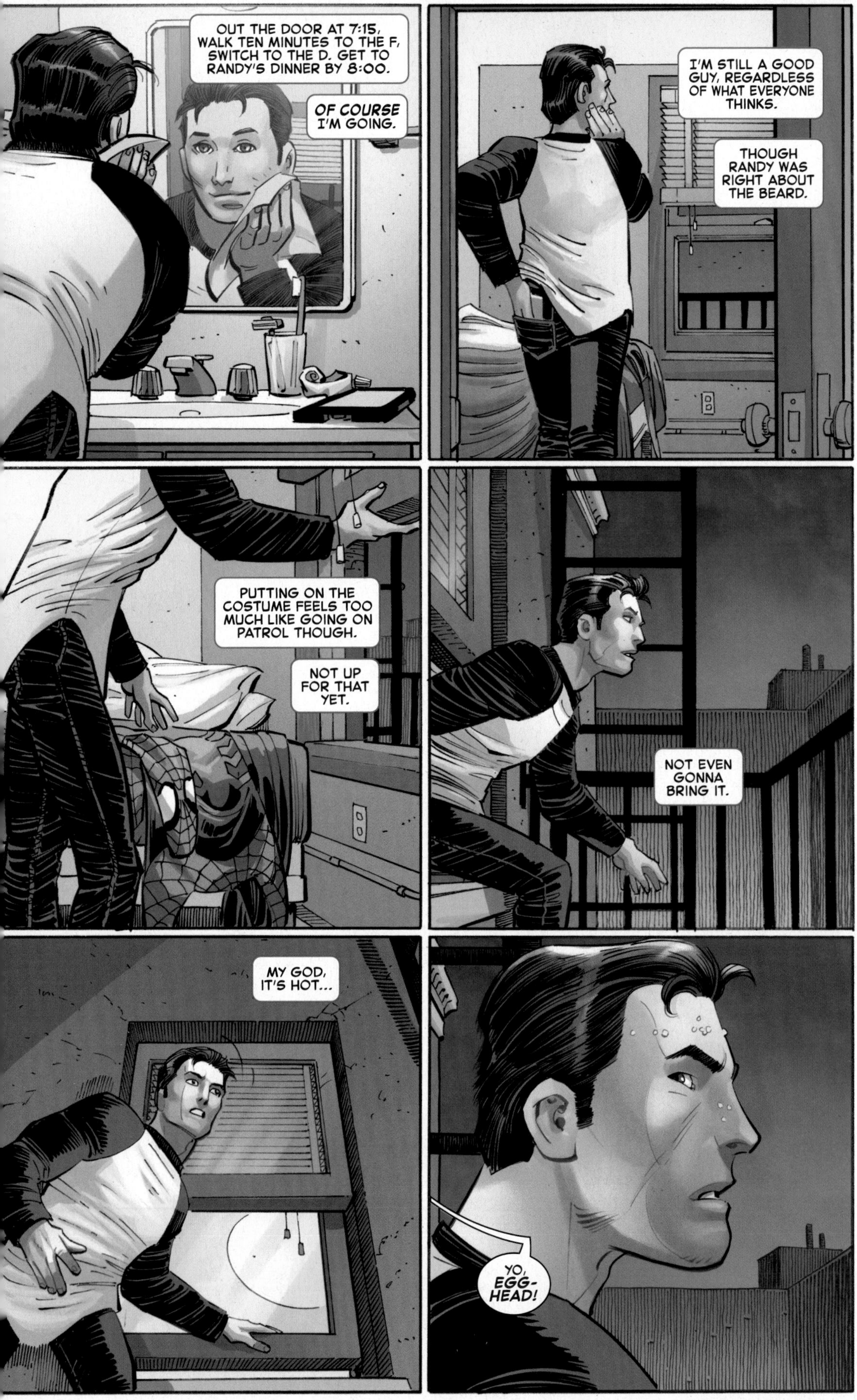
OUT THE DOOR AT 7:15, WALK TEN MINUTES TO THE F, SWITCH TO THE D. GET TO RANDY'S DINNER BY 8:00.
OF COURSE I'M GOING.
I'M STILL A GOOD GUY, REGARDLESS OF WHAT EVERYONE THINKS.
THOUGH RANDY WAS RIGHT ABOUT THE BEARD.
PUTTING ON THE COSTUME FEELS TOO MUCH LIKE GOING ON PATROL THOUGH.
NOT UP FOR THAT YET.
NOT EVEN GONNA BRING IT.
MY GOD, IT'S HOT...
YO, *EGG-HEAD!*

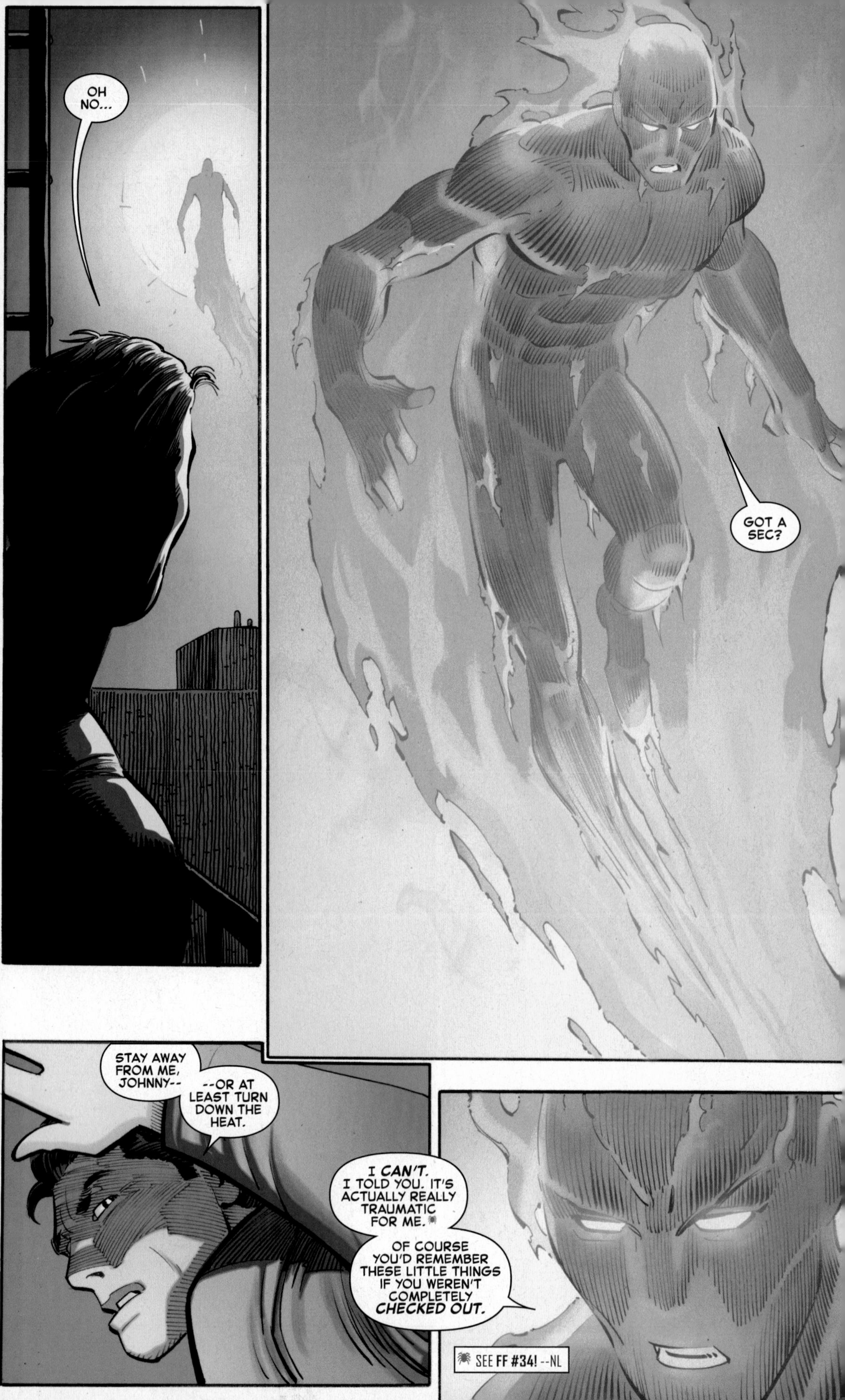

OH NO...
GOT A SEC?
STAY AWAY FROM ME, JOHNNY--
--OR AT LEAST TURN DOWN THE HEAT.
I CAN'T. I TOLD YOU. IT'S ACTUALLY REALLY TRAUMATIC FOR ME.
OF COURSE YOU'D REMEMBER THESE LITTLE THINGS IF YOU WEREN'T COMPLETELY CHECKED OUT.
SEE FF #34! --NL

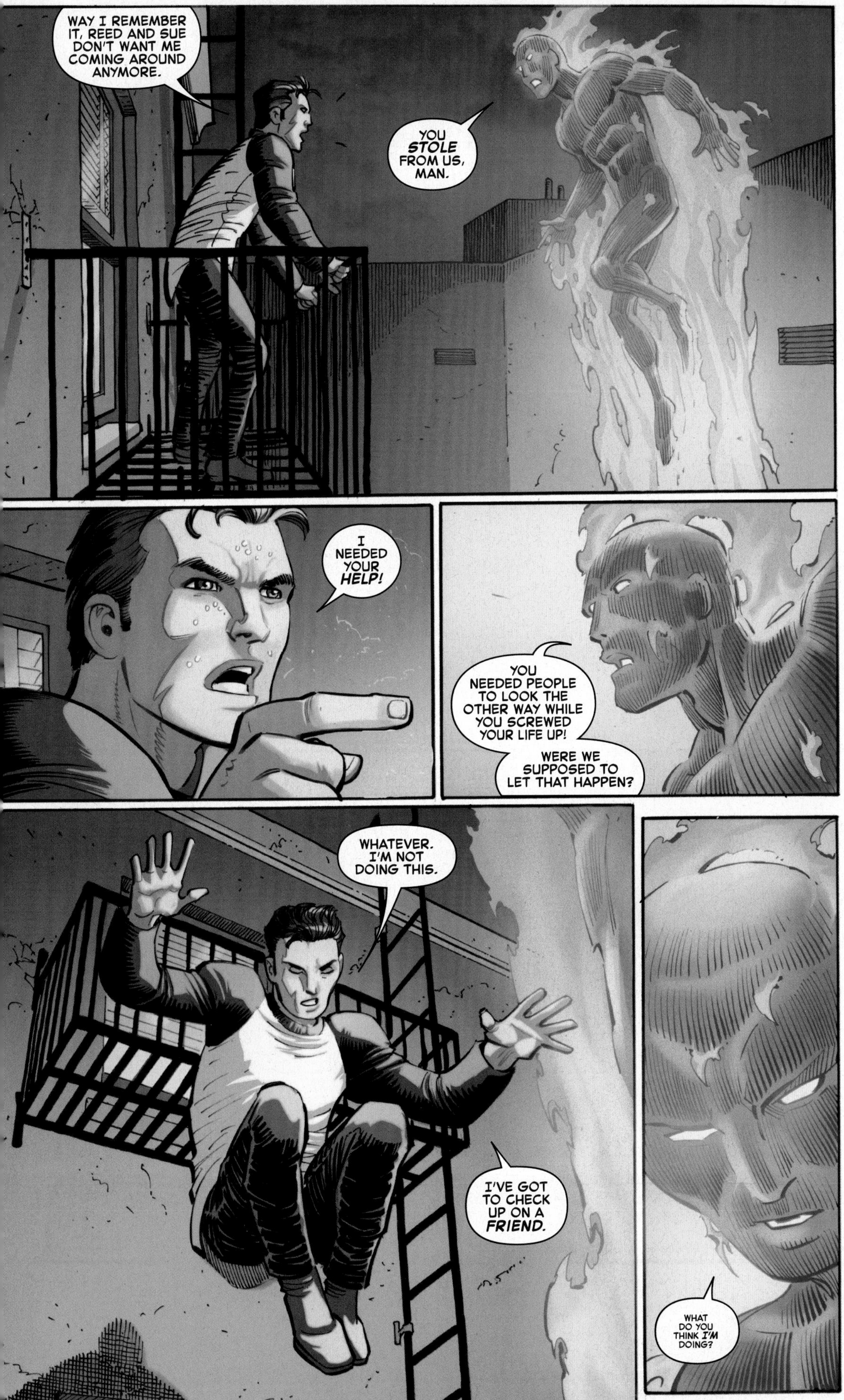
WAY I REMEMBER IT, REED AND SUE DON'T WANT ME COMING AROUND ANYMORE.
YOU *STOLE* FROM US, MAN.
I NEEDED YOUR *HELP!*
YOU NEEDED PEOPLE TO LOOK THE OTHER WAY WHILE YOU SCREWED YOUR LIFE UP!
WERE WE SUPPOSED TO LET THAT HAPPEN?
WHATEVER. I'M NOT DOING THIS.
I'VE GOT TO CHECK UP ON A *FRIEND.*
WHAT DO YOU THINK *I'M* DOING?

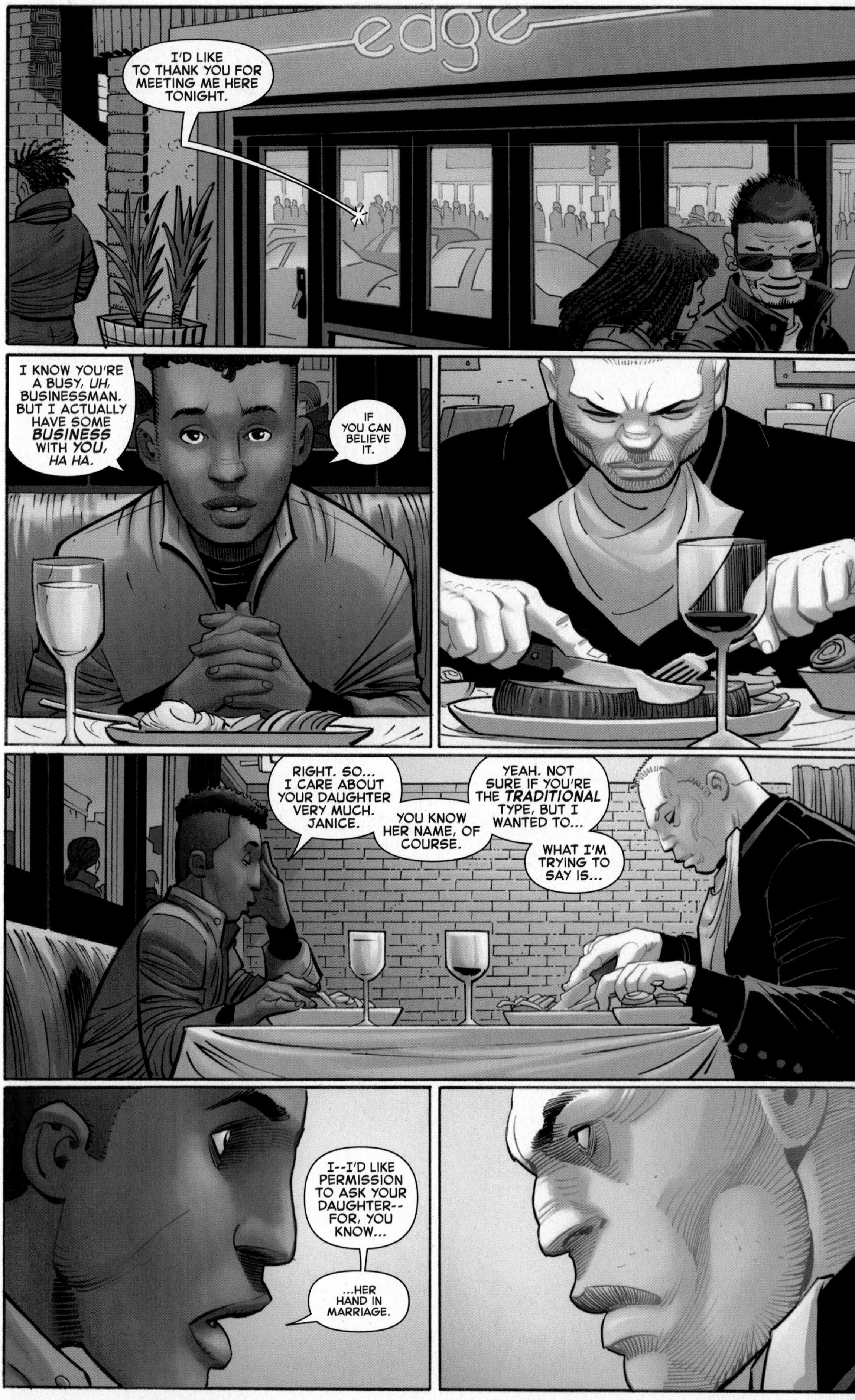

edge
I'D LIKE TO THANK YOU FOR MEETING ME HERE TONIGHT.
I KNOW YOU'RE A BUSY, *UH,* BUSINESSMAN. BUT I ACTUALLY HAVE SOME ***BUSINESS*** WITH ***YOU,*** *HA HA.*
IF YOU CAN BELIEVE IT.
RIGHT. SO... I CARE ABOUT YOUR DAUGHTER VERY MUCH. JANICE.
YOU KNOW HER NAME, OF COURSE.
YEAH. NOT SURE IF YOU'RE THE ***TRADITIONAL*** TYPE, BUT I WANTED TO...
WHAT I'M TRYING TO SAY IS...
I--I'D LIKE PERMISSION TO ASK YOUR DAUGHTER-- FOR, YOU KNOW...
...HER HAND IN MARRIAGE.

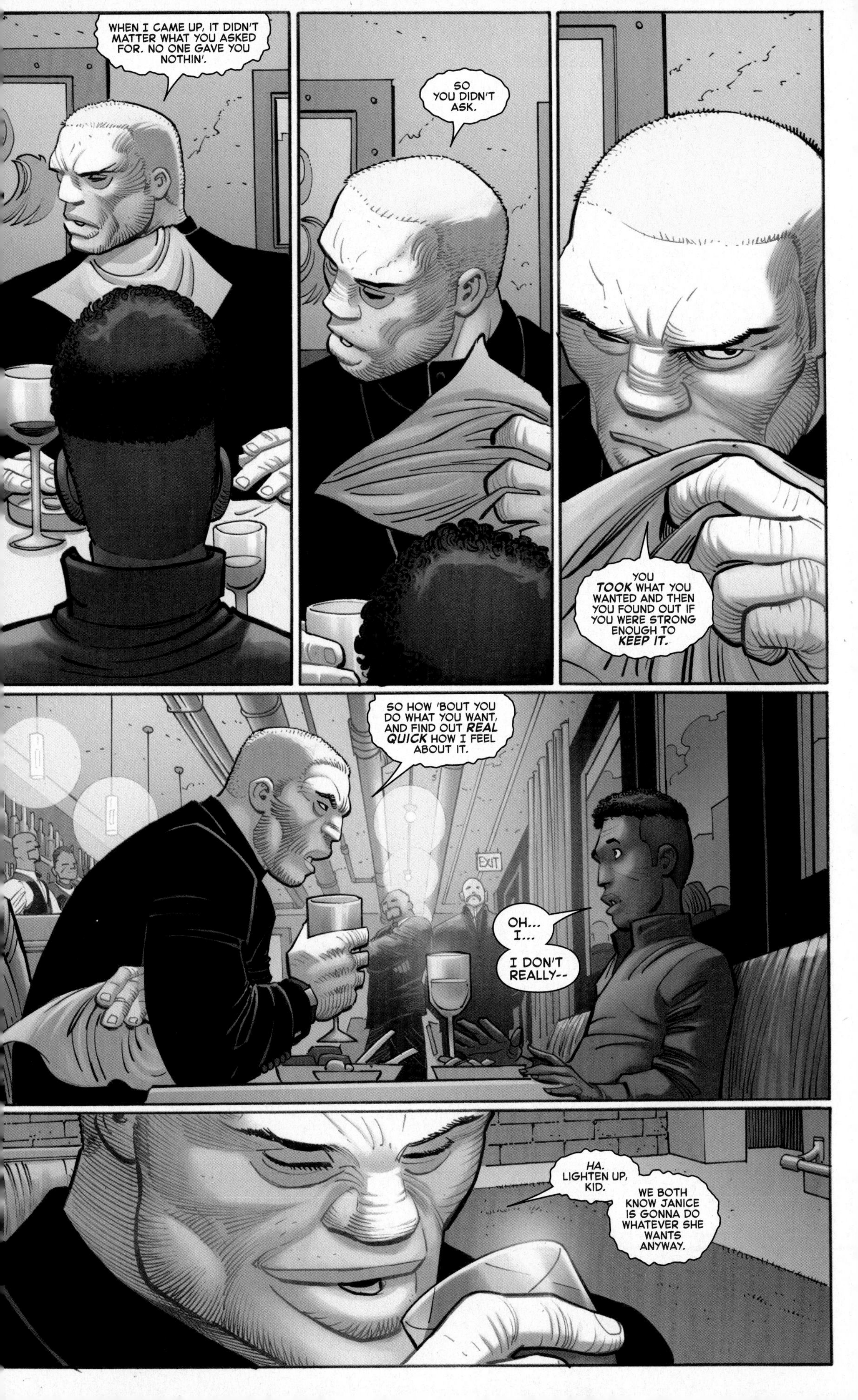
WHEN I CAME UP, IT DIDN'T MATTER WHAT YOU ASKED FOR. NO ONE GAVE YOU NOTHIN'.
SO YOU DIDN'T ASK.
YOU TOOK WHAT YOU WANTED AND THEN YOU FOUND OUT IF YOU WERE STRONG ENOUGH TO KEEP IT.
SO HOW 'BOUT YOU DO WHAT YOU WANT, AND FIND OUT REAL QUICK HOW I FEEL ABOUT IT.
EXIT
OH... I...
I DON'T REALLY--
HA. LIGHTEN UP, KID.
WE BOTH KNOW JANICE IS GONNA DO WHATEVER SHE WANTS ANYWAY.

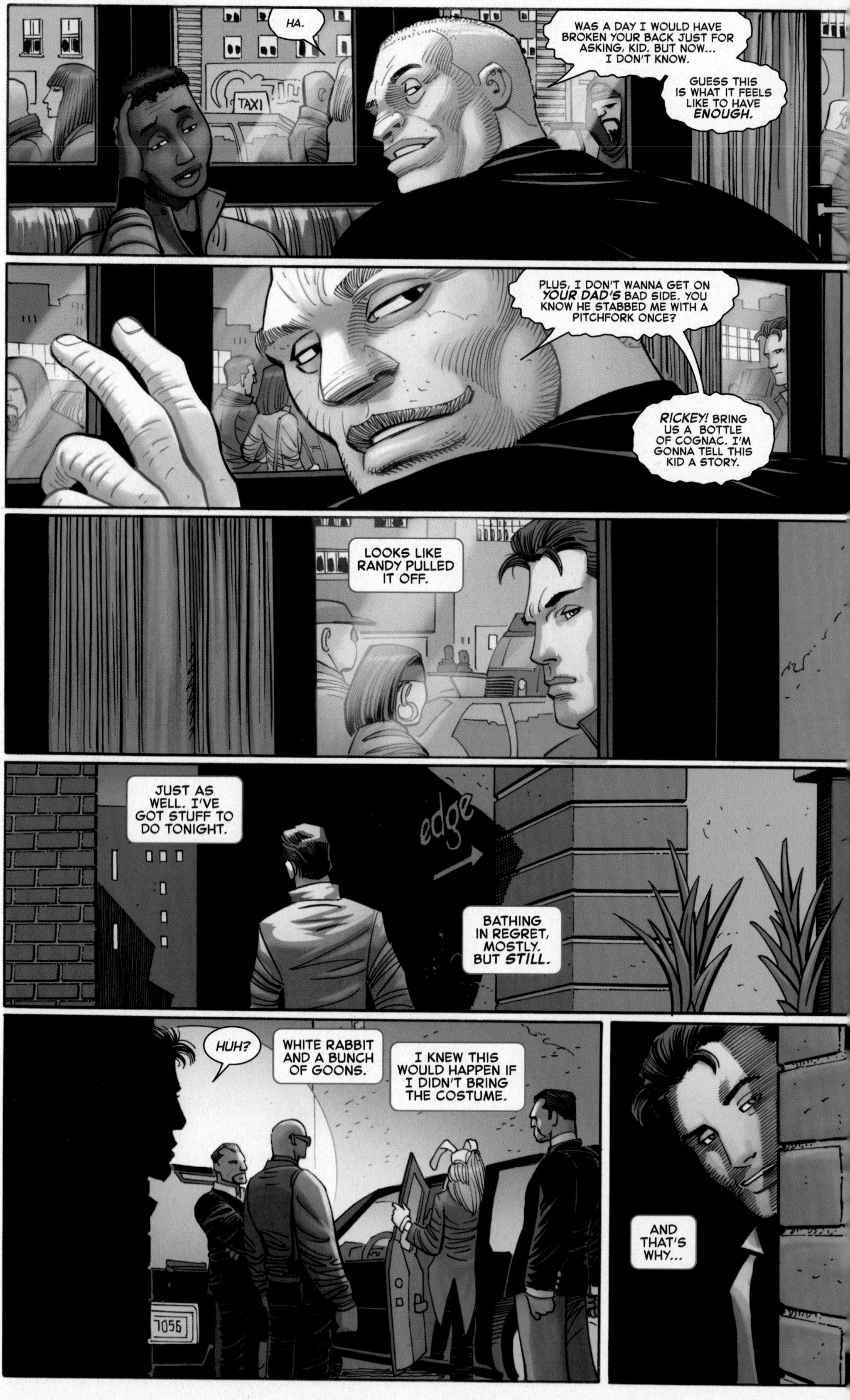

HA.
WAS A DAY I WOULD HAVE BROKEN YOUR BACK JUST FOR ASKING, KID. BUT NOW... I DON'T KNOW.
GUESS THIS IS WHAT IT FEELS LIKE TO HAVE ENOUGH.
TAXI
PLUS, I DON'T WANNA GET ON YOUR DAD'S BAD SIDE. YOU KNOW HE STABBED ME WITH A PITCHFORK ONCE?
RICKEY! BRING US A BOTTLE OF COGNAC. I'M GONNA TELL THIS KID A STORY.
LOOKS LIKE RANDY PULLED IT OFF.
JUST AS WELL. I'VE GOT STUFF TO DO TONIGHT.
edge
BATHING IN REGRET, MOSTLY. BUT STILL.
HUH?
WHITE RABBIT AND A BUNCH OF GOONS.
I KNEW THIS WOULD HAPPEN IF I DIDN'T BRING THE COSTUME.
7056
AND THAT'S WHY...

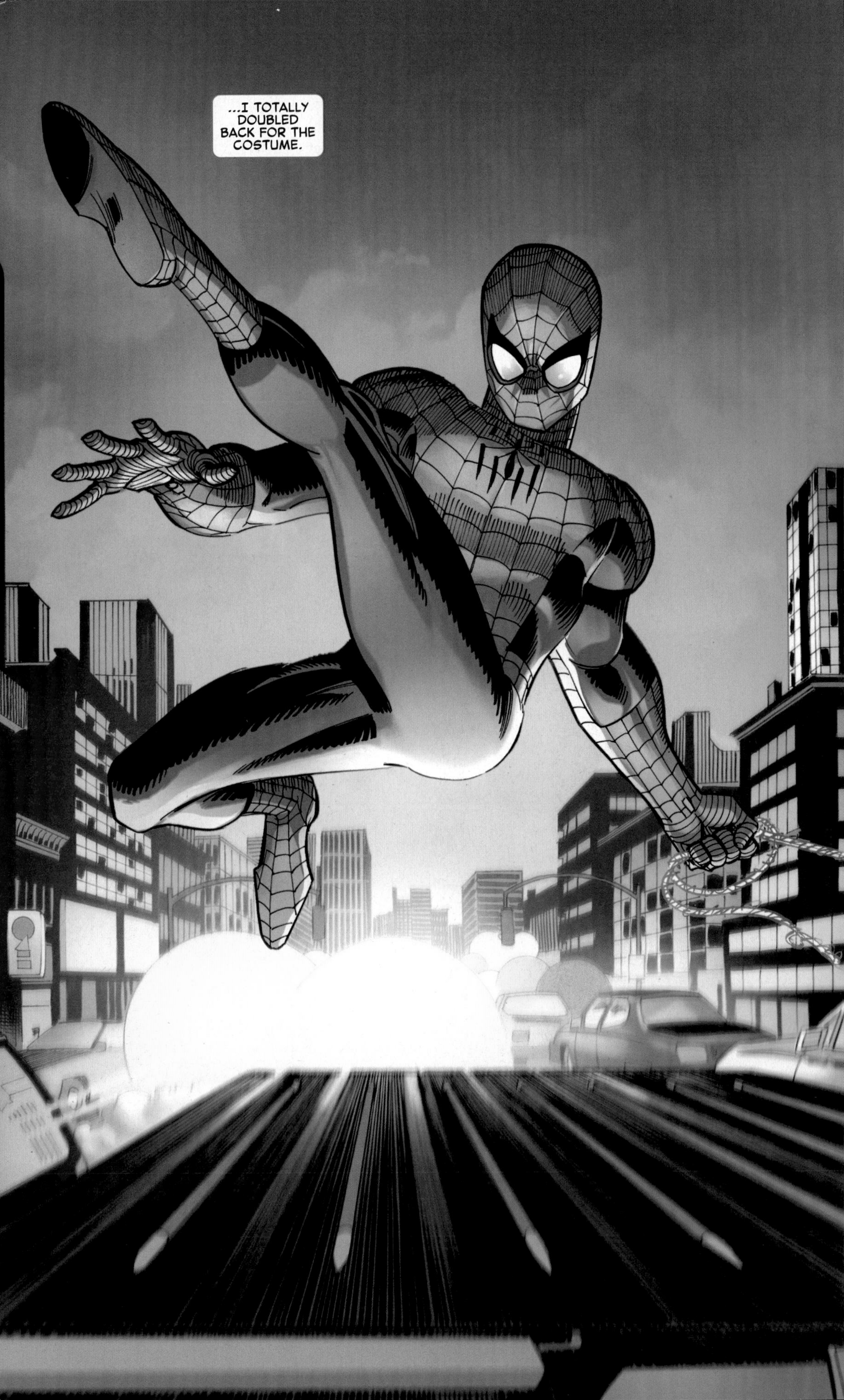
...I TOTALLY DOUBLED BACK FOR THE COSTUME.

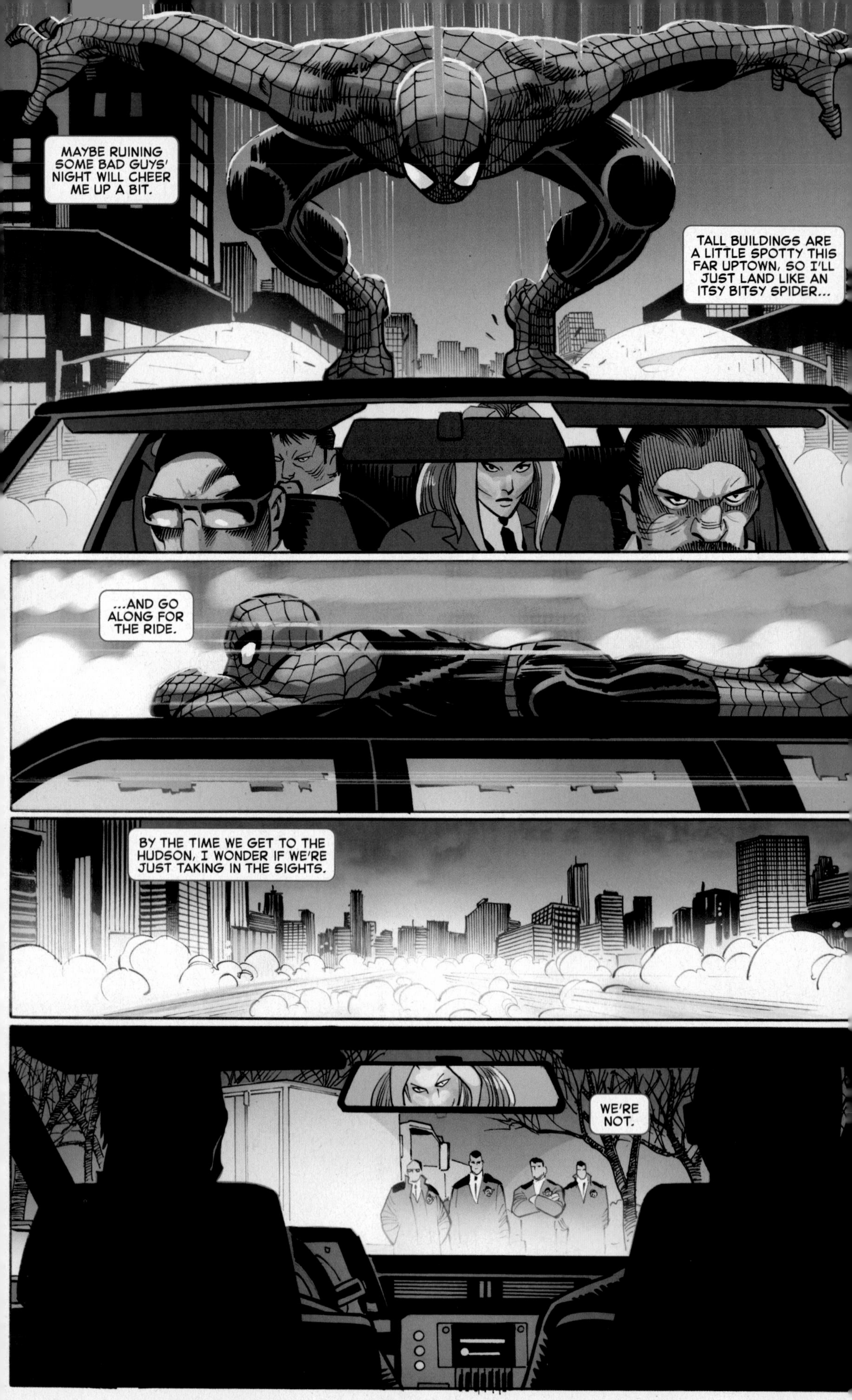
MAYBE RUINING SOME BAD GUYS' NIGHT WILL CHEER ME UP A BIT.
TALL BUILDINGS ARE A LITTLE SPOTTY THIS FAR UPTOWN, SO I'LL JUST LAND LIKE AN ITSY BITSY SPIDER...
...AND GO ALONG FOR THE RIDE.
BY THE TIME WE GET TO THE HUDSON, I WONDER IF WE'RE JUST TAKING IN THE SIGHTS.
WE'RE NOT.

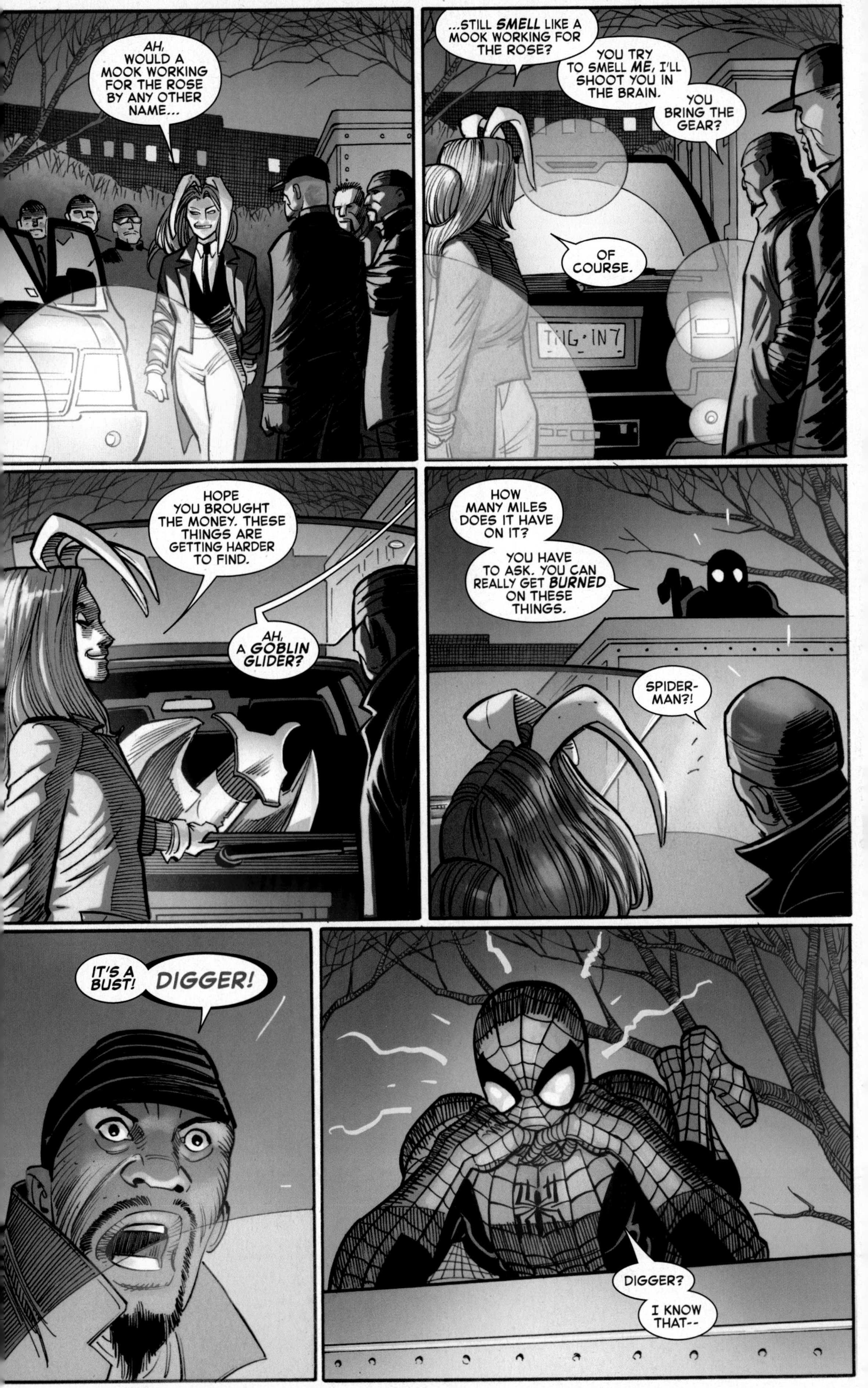
AH, WOULD A MOOK WORKING FOR THE ROSE BY ANY OTHER NAME...
...STILL SMELL LIKE A MOOK WORKING FOR THE ROSE?
YOU TRY TO SMELL ME, I'LL SHOOT YOU IN THE BRAIN.
YOU BRING THE GEAR?
OF COURSE.
THG-IN7
HOPE YOU BROUGHT THE MONEY. THESE THINGS ARE GETTING HARDER TO FIND.
AH, A GOBLIN GLIDER?
HOW MANY MILES DOES IT HAVE ON IT?
YOU HAVE TO ASK. YOU CAN REALLY GET BURNED ON THESE THINGS.
SPIDER-MAN?!
IT'S A BUST!
DIGGER!
DIGGER?
I KNOW THAT--

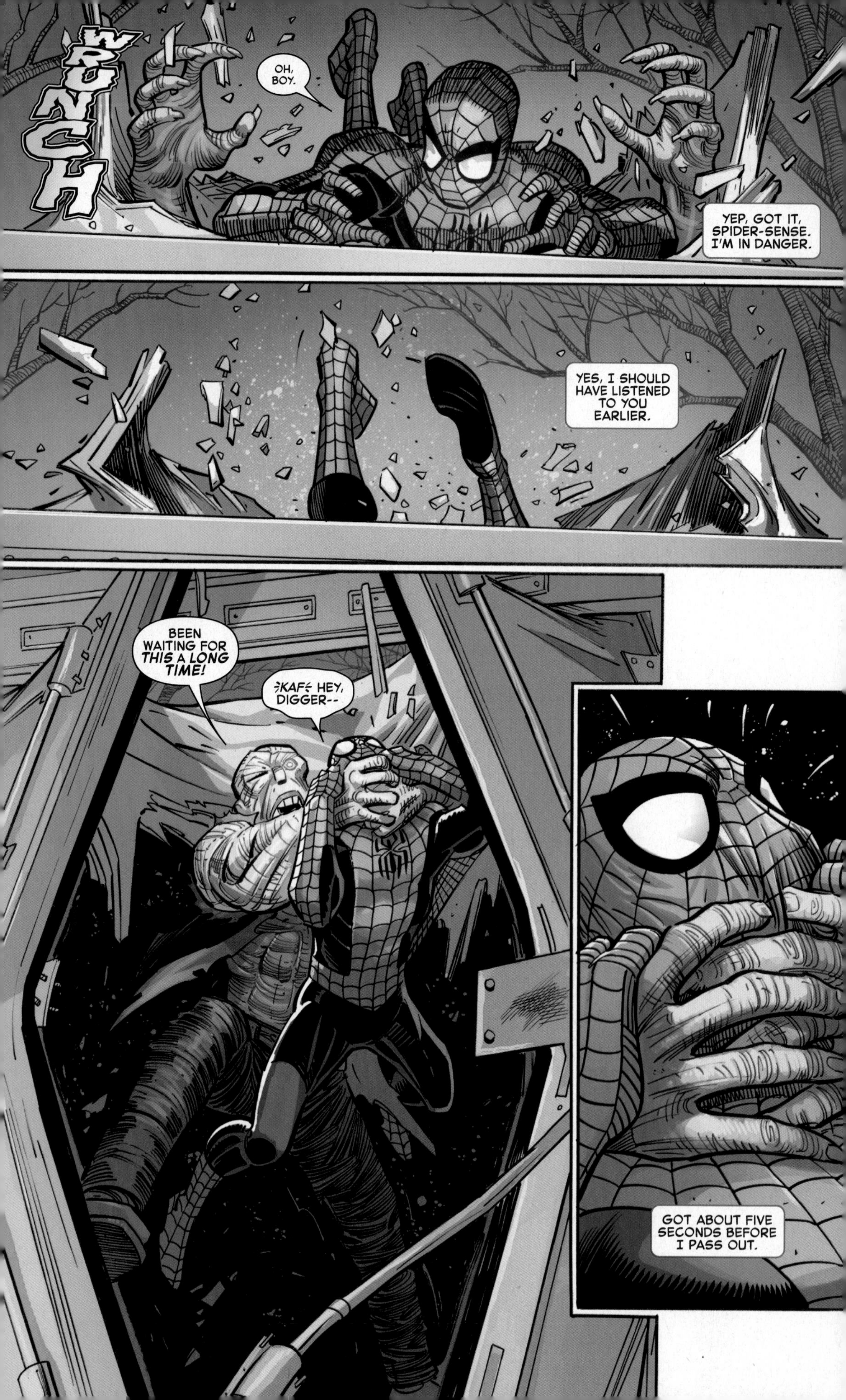

WRUNCH
OH, BOY.
YEP, GOT IT, SPIDER-SENSE. I'M IN DANGER.
YES, I SHOULD HAVE LISTENED TO YOU EARLIER.
BEEN WAITING FOR THIS A LONG TIME!
KAF HEY, DIGGER--
GOT ABOUT FIVE SECONDS BEFORE I PASS OUT.

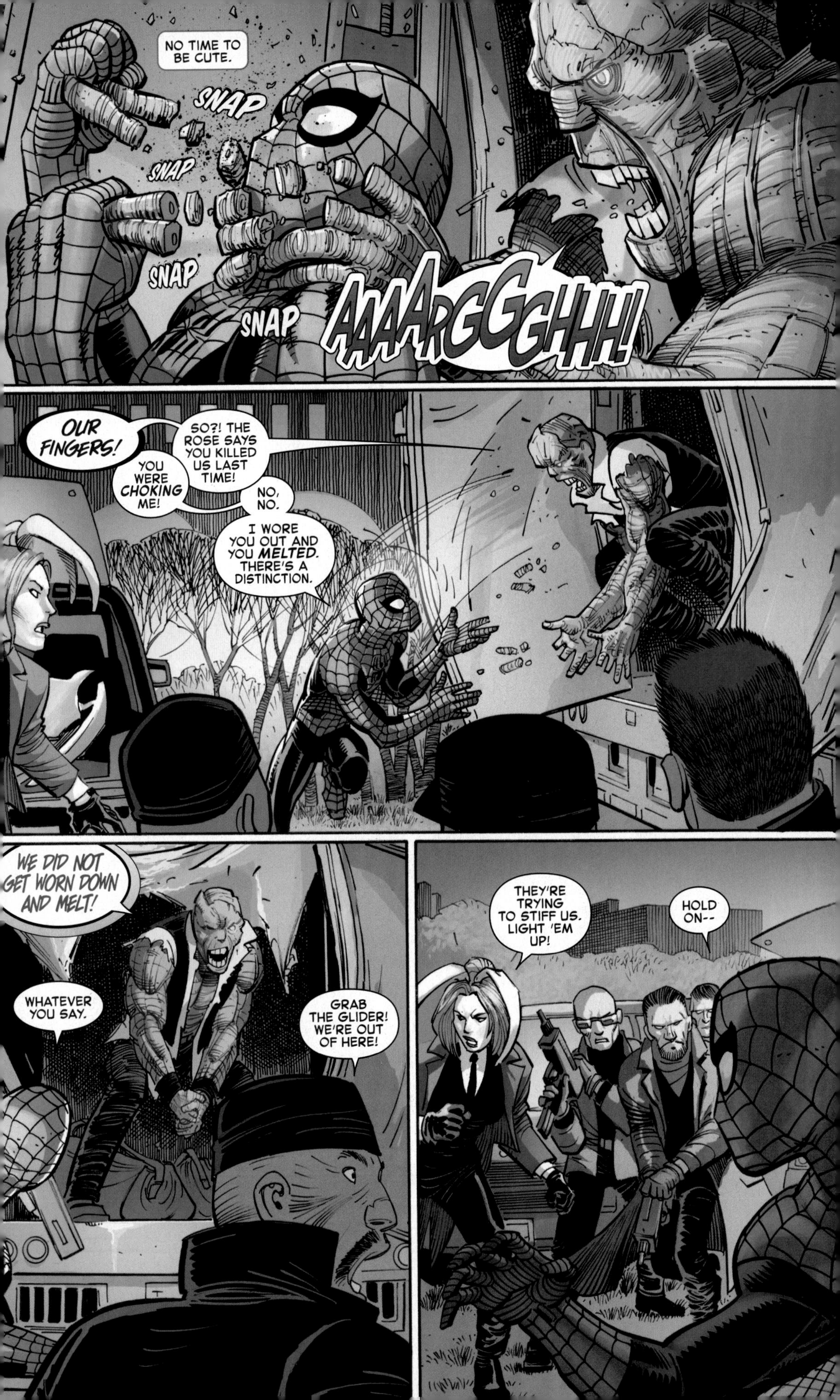
NO TIME TO BE CUTE.
SNAP
SNAP
SNAP
SNAP
AAAARGGGHHH!
OUR FINGERS!
SO?! THE ROSE SAYS YOU KILLED US LAST TIME!
YOU WERE CHOKING ME!
NO, NO.
I WORE YOU OUT AND YOU MELTED. THERE'S A DISTINCTION.
WE DID NOT GET WORN DOWN AND MELT!
WHATEVER YOU SAY.
GRAB THE GLIDER! WE'RE OUT OF HERE!
THEY'RE TRYING TO STIFF US. LIGHT 'EM UP!
HOLD ON--

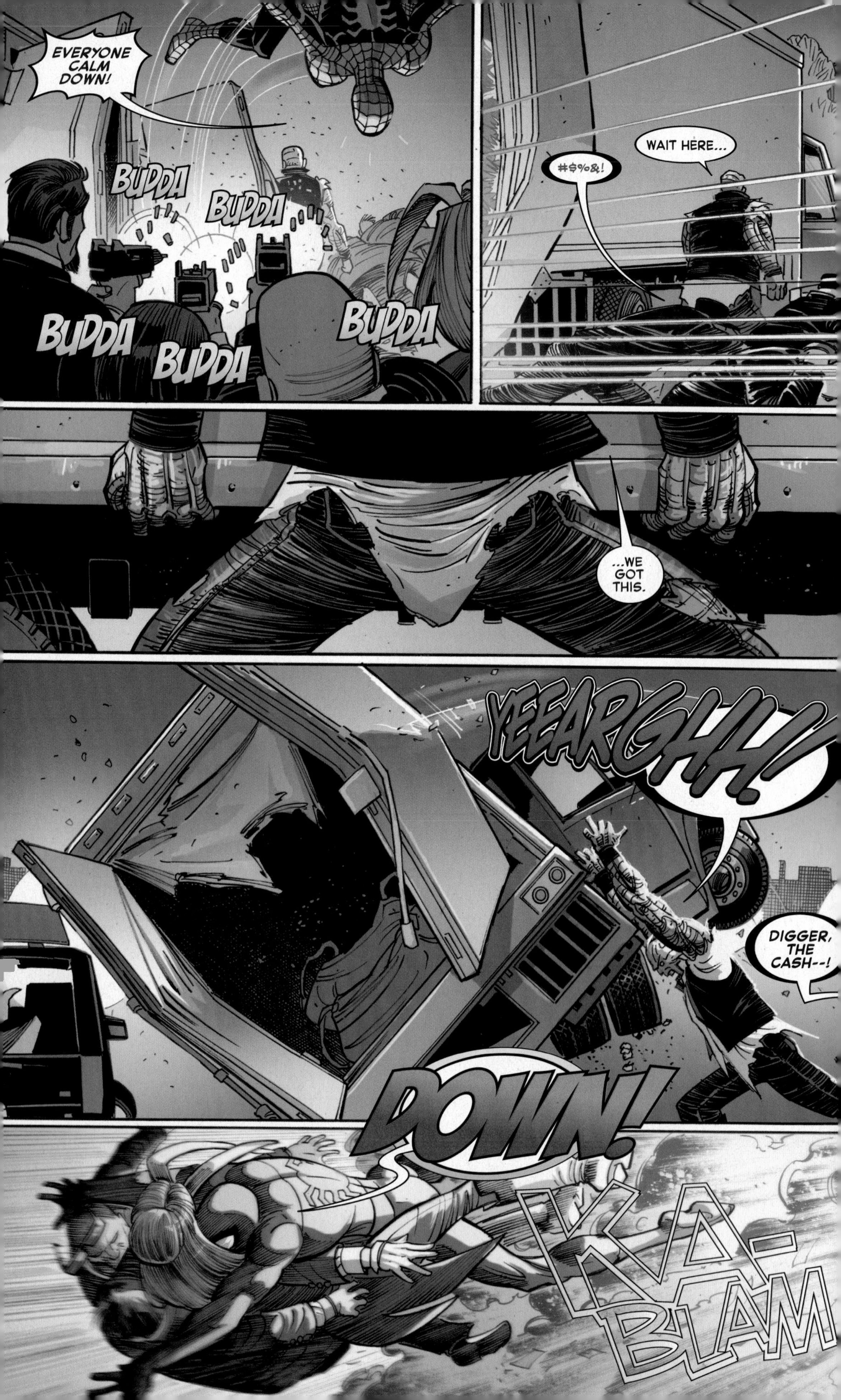
EVERYONE CALM DOWN!
BUDDA
BUDDA
BUDDA
BUDDA
BUDDA
WAIT HERE...
#$%&!
...WE GOT THIS.
YEEARGHH!
DIGGER, THE CASH--!
DOWN!
KA-BLAM

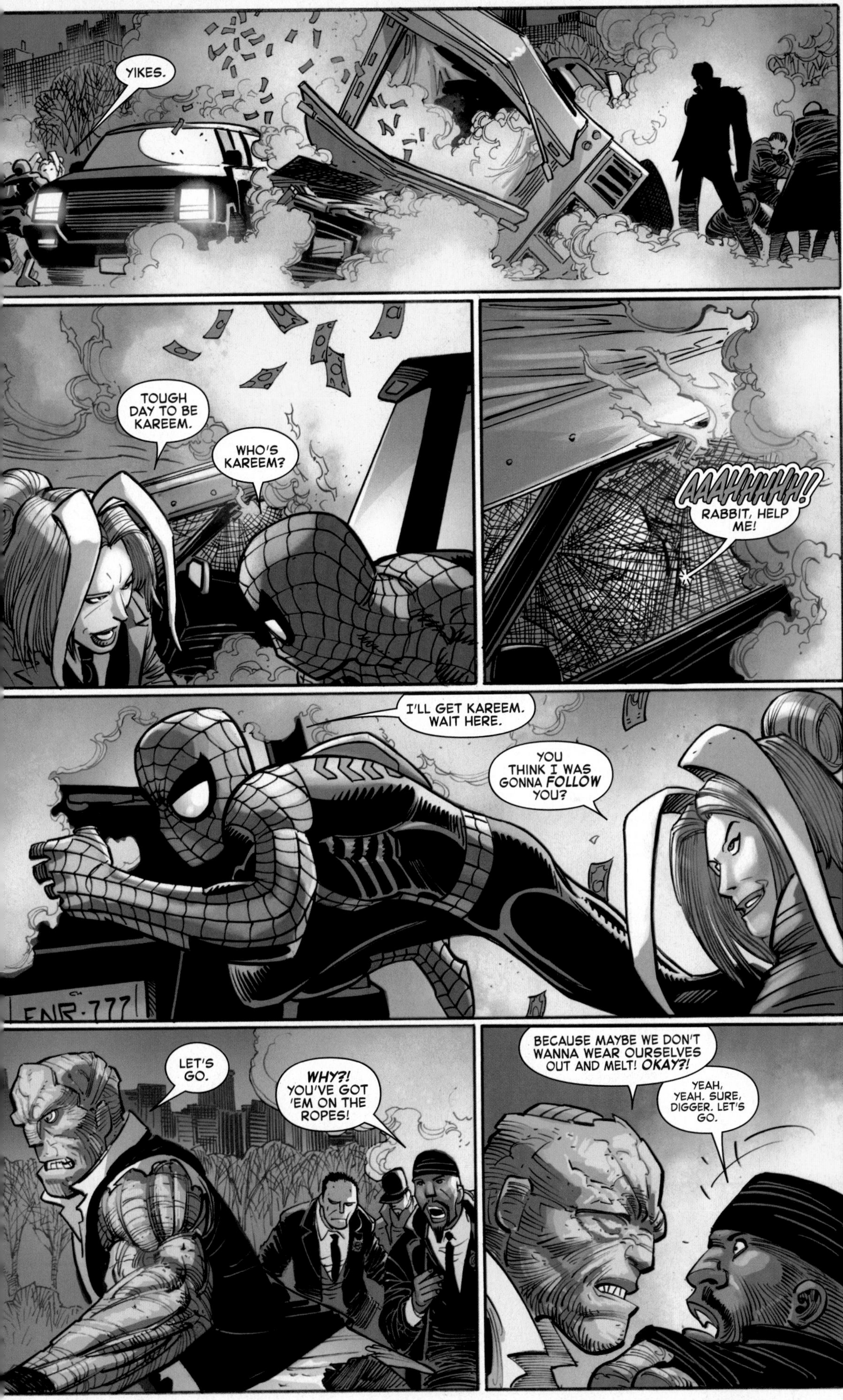
YIKES.
TOUGH DAY TO BE KAREEM.
WHO'S KAREEM?
AAAHHHHH!
RABBIT, HELP ME!
I'LL GET KAREEM. WAIT HERE.
YOU THINK I WAS GONNA *FOLLOW* YOU?
ENR-777
LET'S GO.
WHY?! YOU'VE GOT 'EM ON THE ROPES!
BECAUSE MAYBE WE DON'T WANNA WEAR OURSELVES OUT AND MELT! *OKAY?!*
YEAH, YEAH. SURE, DIGGER. LET'S GO.

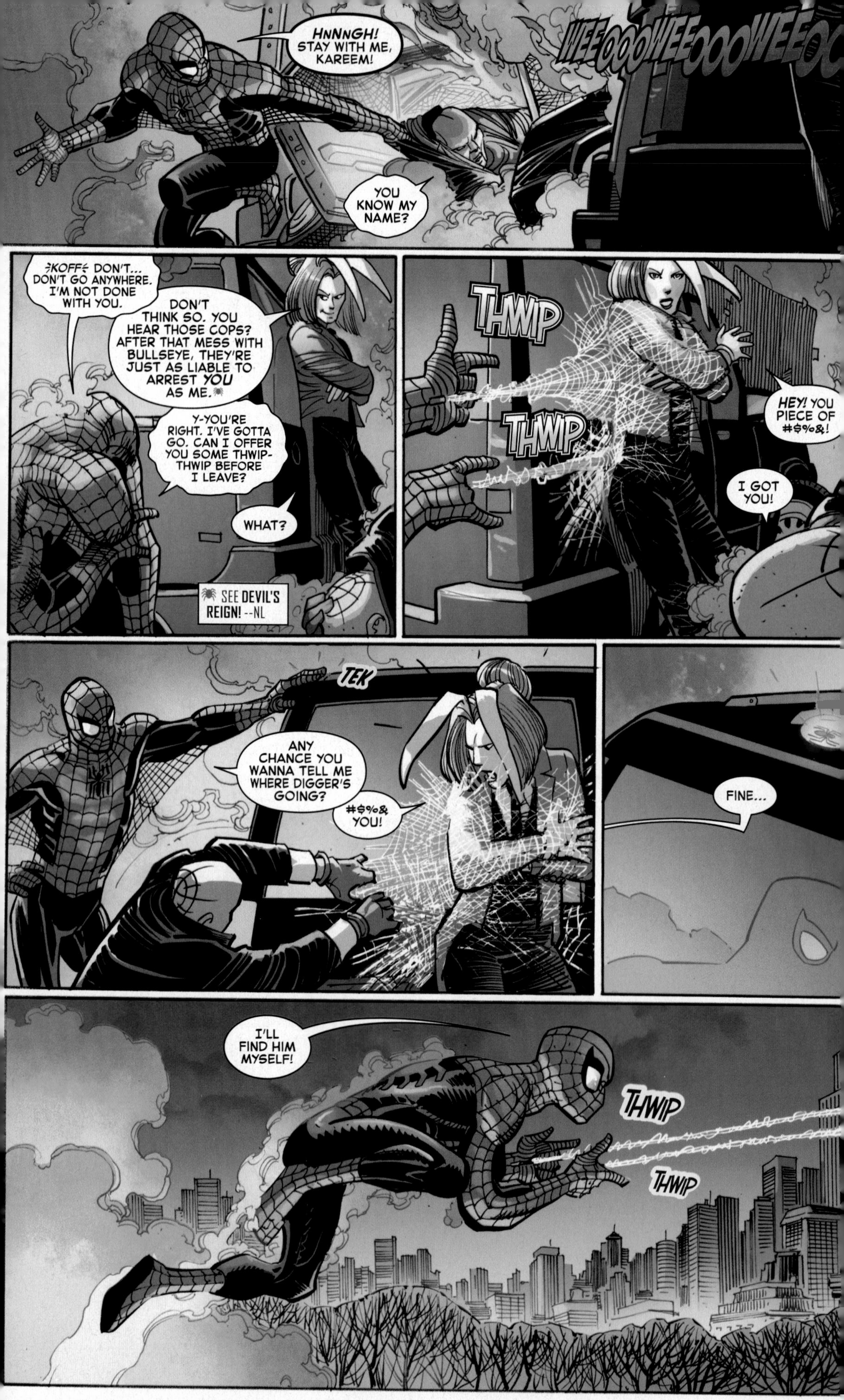

HNNNGH! STAY WITH ME, KAREEM!
WEEOOOWEEOOOWEEOO
YOU KNOW MY NAME?
KOFF DON'T... DON'T GO ANYWHERE. I'M NOT DONE WITH YOU.
DON'T THINK SO. YOU HEAR THOSE COPS? AFTER THAT MESS WITH BULLSEYE, THEY'RE JUST AS LIABLE TO ARREST YOU AS ME.
Y-YOU'RE RIGHT. I'VE GOTTA GO. CAN I OFFER YOU SOME THWIP-THWIP BEFORE I LEAVE?
WHAT?
SEE DEVIL'S REIGN! --NL
THWIP
THWIP
HEY! YOU PIECE OF #$%&!
I GOT YOU!
TEK
ANY CHANCE YOU WANNA TELL ME WHERE DIGGER'S GOING?
#$%& YOU!
FINE...
I'LL FIND HIM MYSELF!
THWIP
THWIP

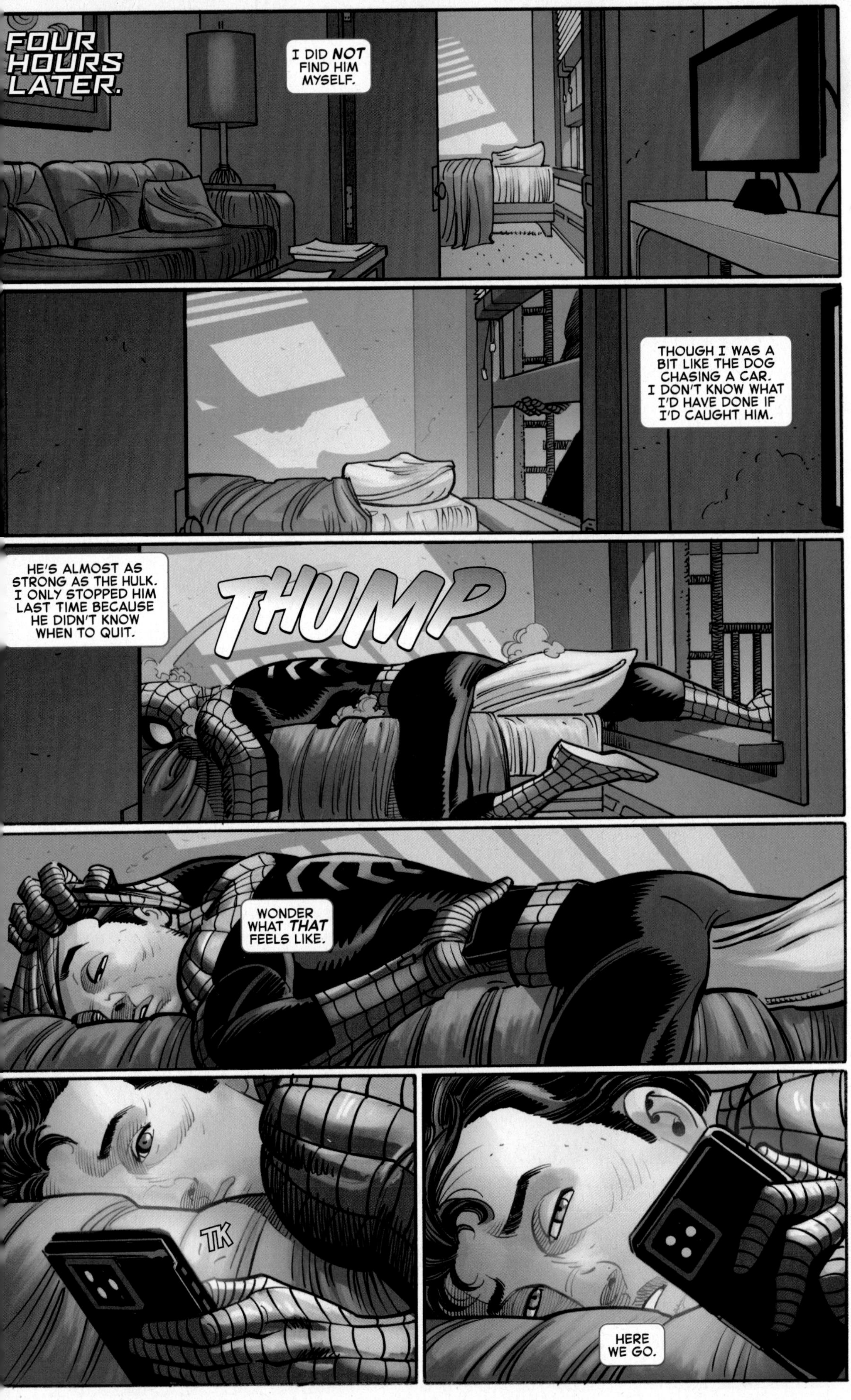
FOUR HOURS LATER.
I DID NOT FIND HIM MYSELF.
THOUGH I WAS A BIT LIKE THE DOG CHASING A CAR. I DON'T KNOW WHAT I'D HAVE DONE IF I'D CAUGHT HIM.
HE'S ALMOST AS STRONG AS THE HULK. I ONLY STOPPED HIM LAST TIME BECAUSE HE DIDN'T KNOW WHEN TO QUIT.
THUMP
WONDER WHAT THAT FEELS LIKE.
TK
HERE WE GO.

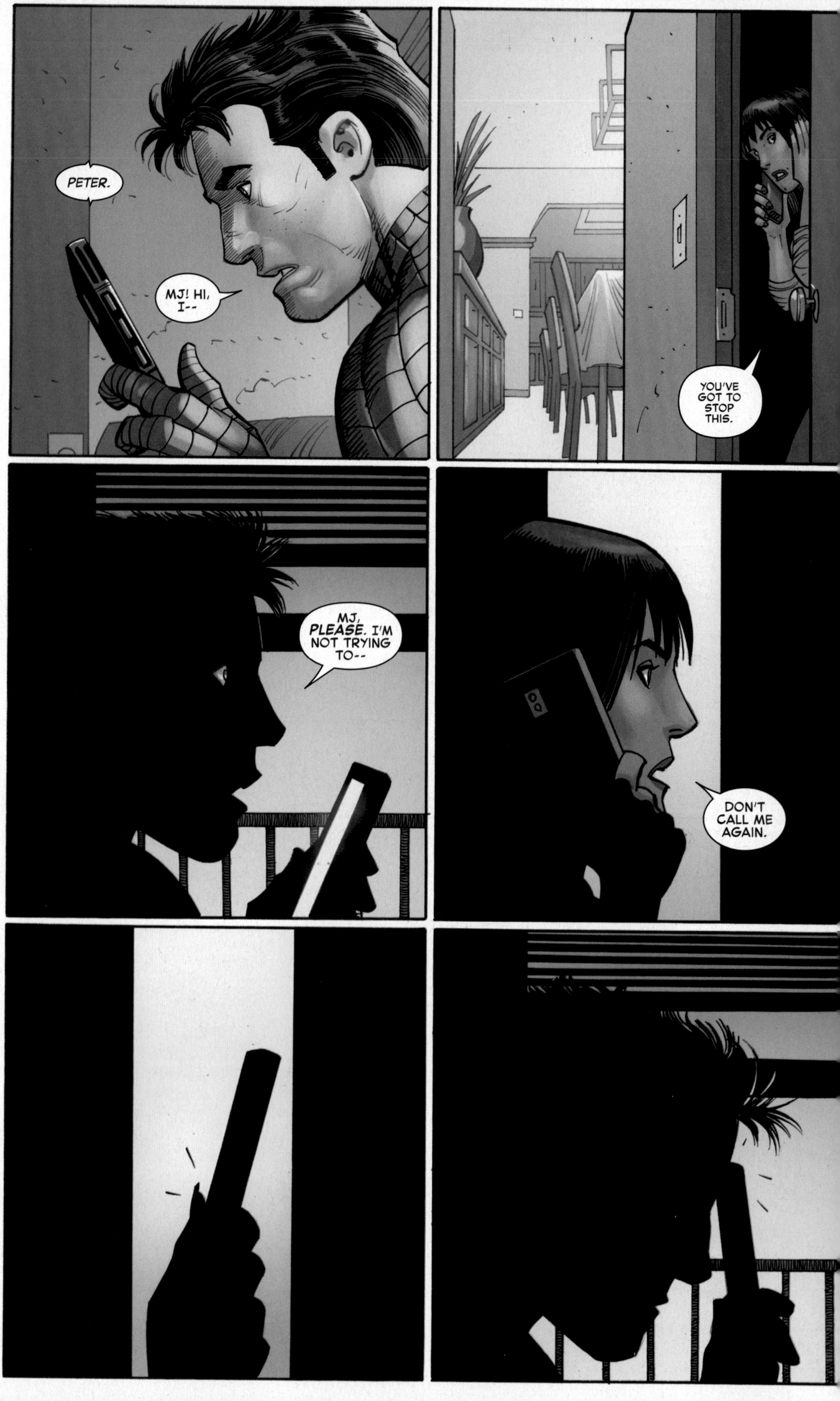
PETER.
MJ! HI, I--
YOU'VE GOT TO STOP THIS.
MJ, PLEASE. I'M NOT TRYING TO--
DON'T CALL ME AGAIN.

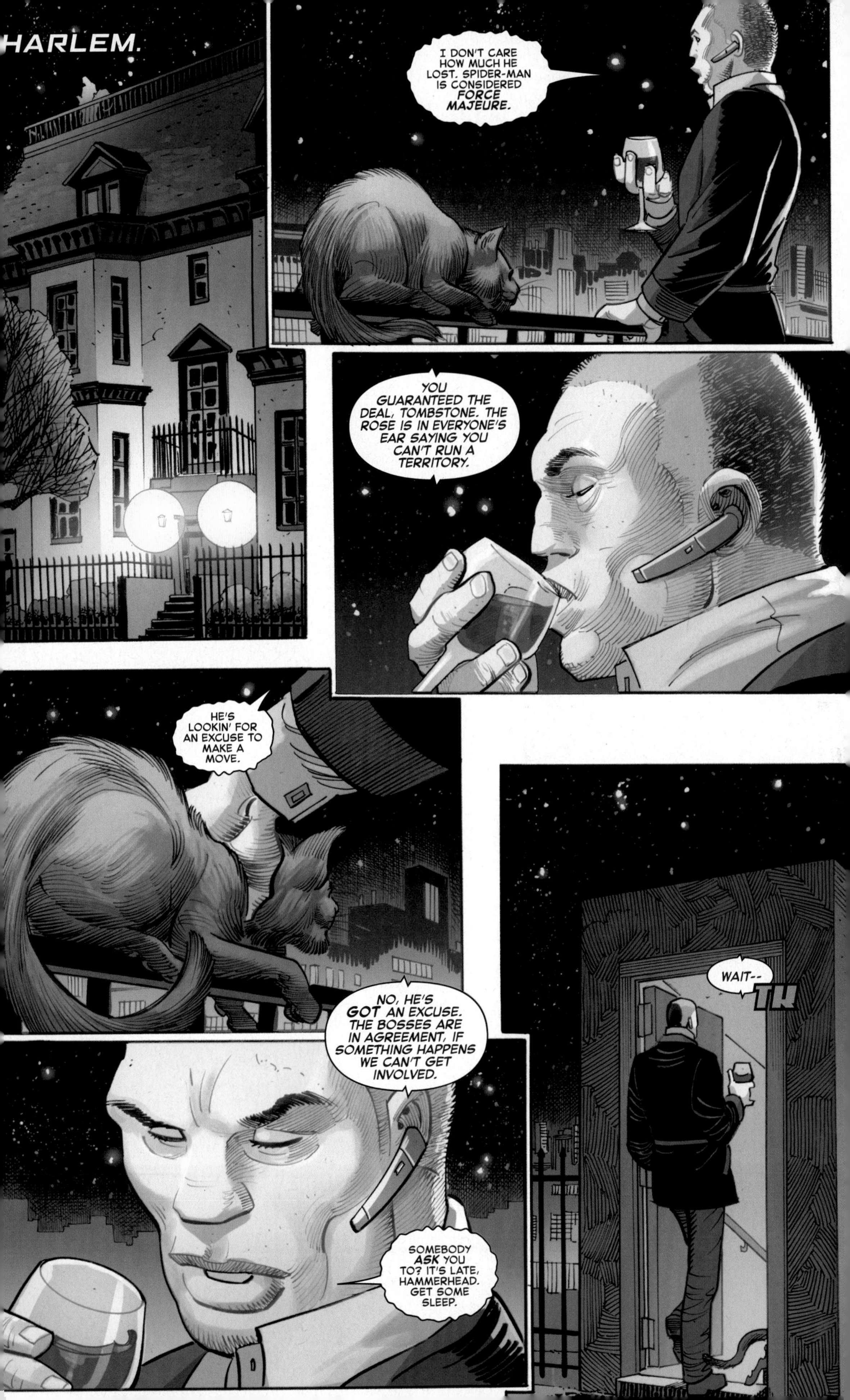
HARLEM.
I DON'T CARE HOW MUCH HE LOST. SPIDER-MAN IS CONSIDERED FORCE MAJEURE.
YOU GUARANTEED THE DEAL, TOMBSTONE. THE ROSE IS IN EVERYONE'S EAR SAYING YOU CAN'T RUN A TERRITORY.
HE'S LOOKIN' FOR AN EXCUSE TO MAKE A MOVE.
NO, HE'S GOT AN EXCUSE. THE BOSSES ARE IN AGREEMENT, IF SOMETHING HAPPENS WE CAN'T GET INVOLVED.
SOMEBODY ASK YOU TO? IT'S LATE, HAMMERHEAD. GET SOME SLEEP.
WAIT--
TK

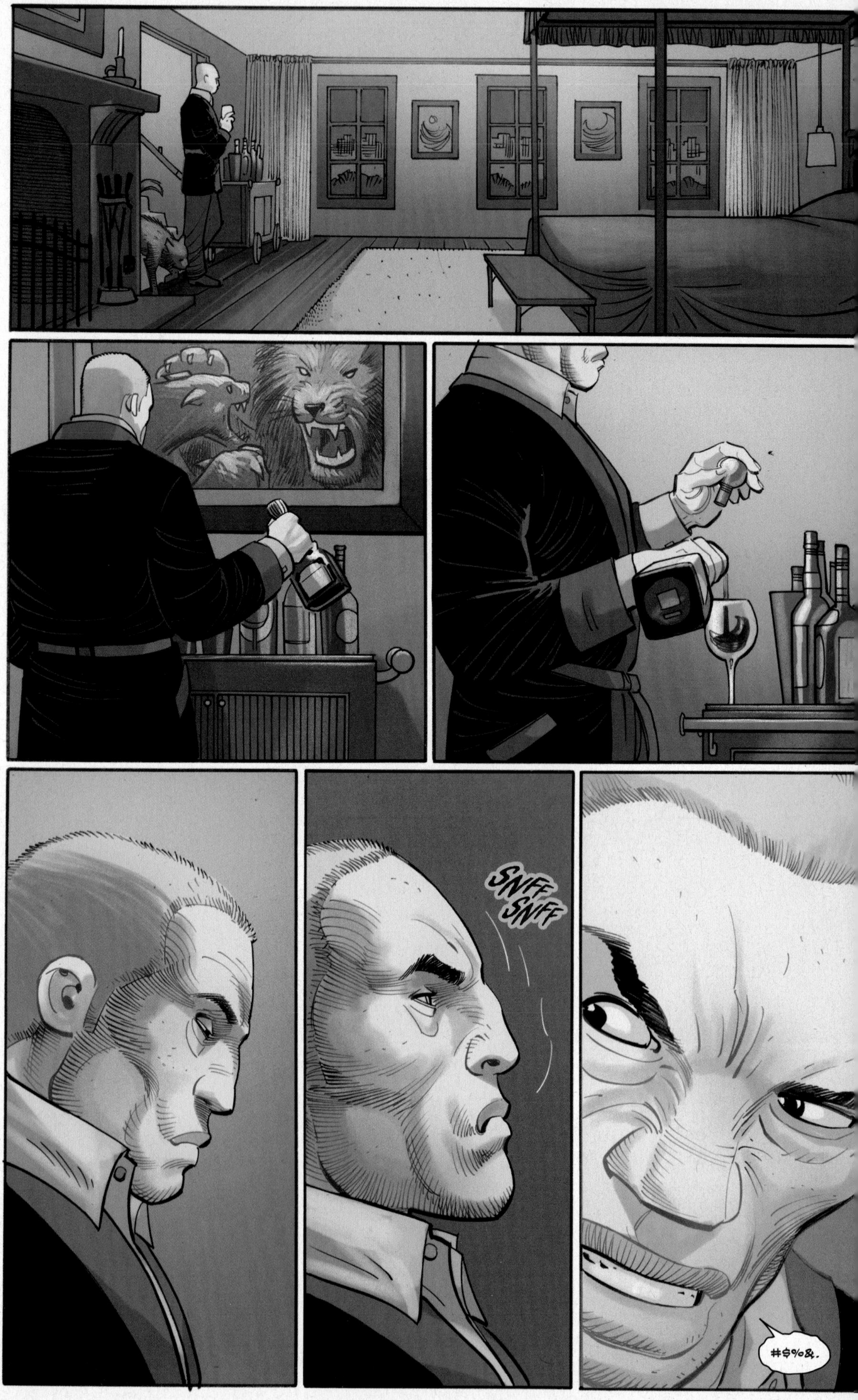
SNFF SNFF
#$%&.

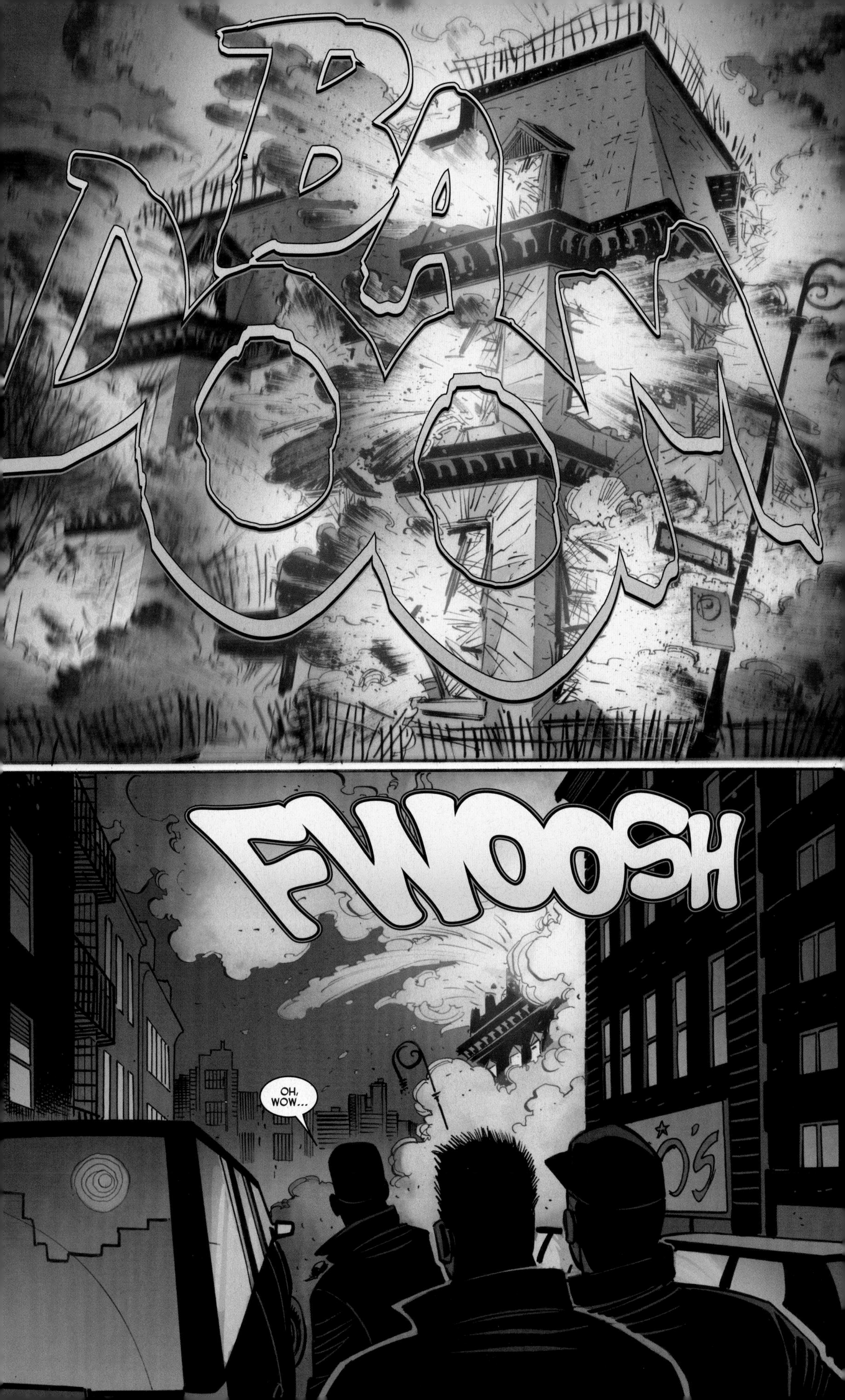
BADOOM
FWOOSH
OH, WOW...

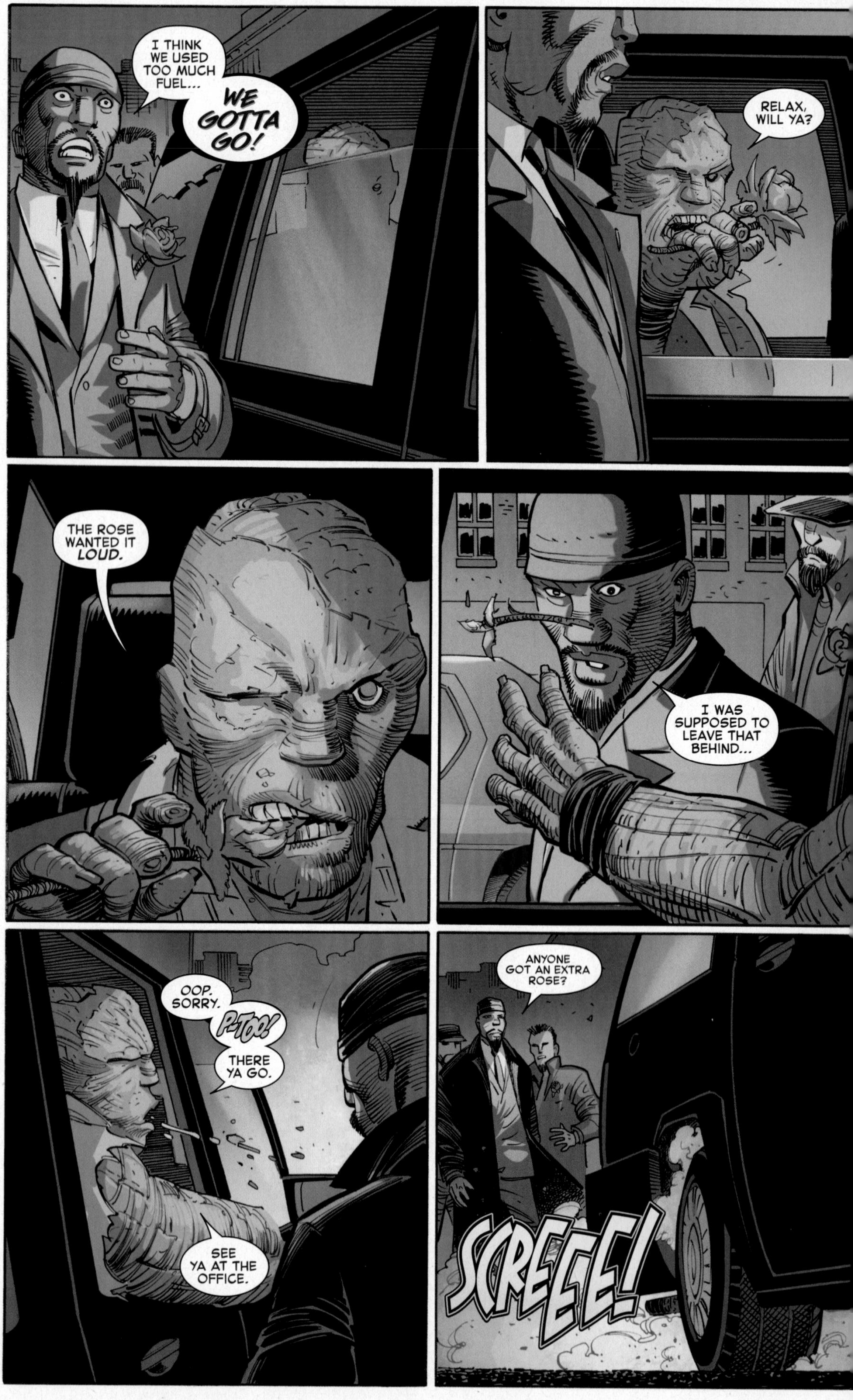
I THINK WE USED TOO MUCH FUEL...
WE GOTTA GO!
RELAX, WILL YA?
THE ROSE WANTED IT LOUD.
I WAS SUPPOSED TO LEAVE THAT BEHIND...
OOP. SORRY.
P-TOO!
THERE YA GO.
SEE YA AT THE OFFICE.
ANYONE GOT AN EXTRA ROSE?
SCREEE!

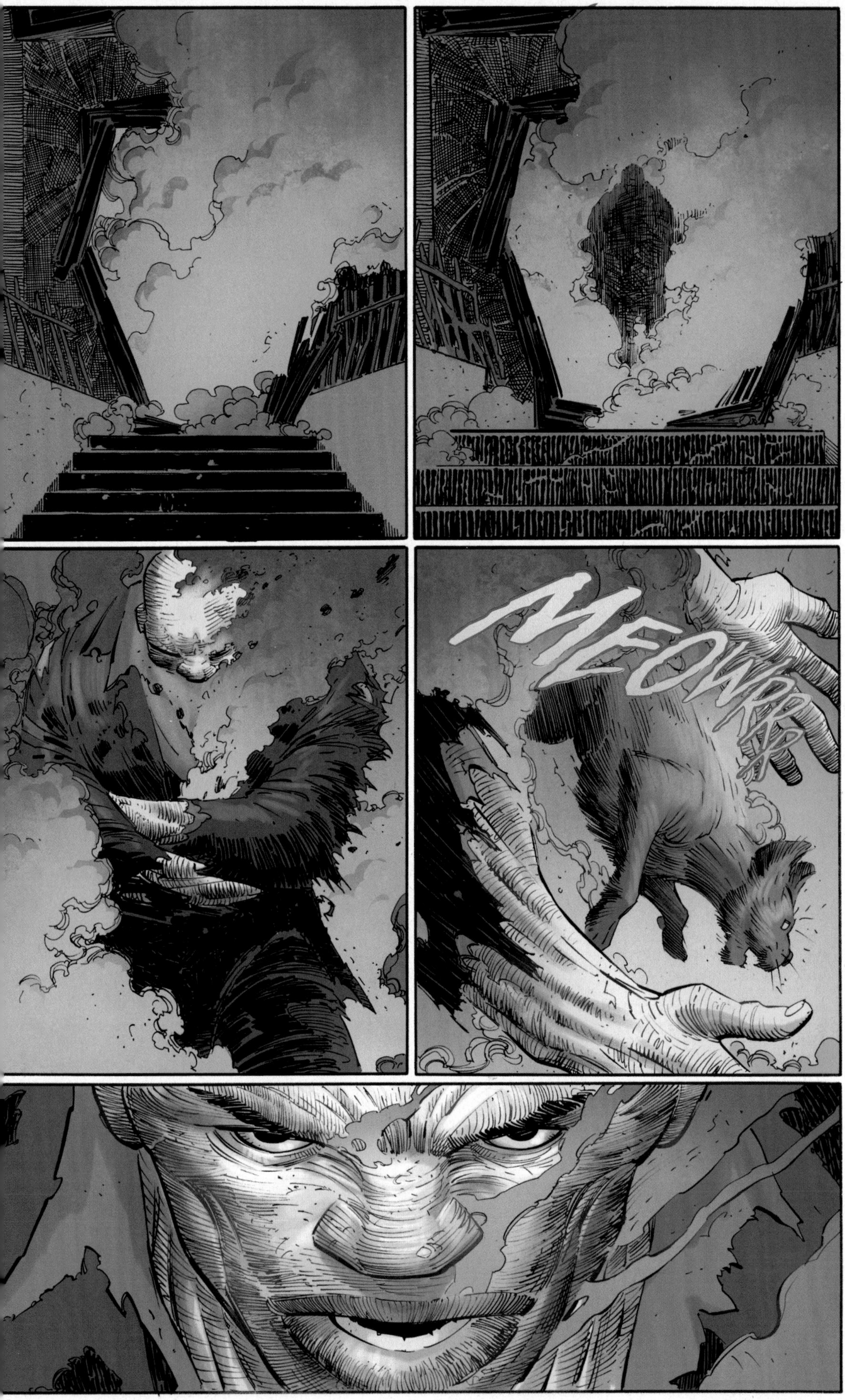
MEOWRRR

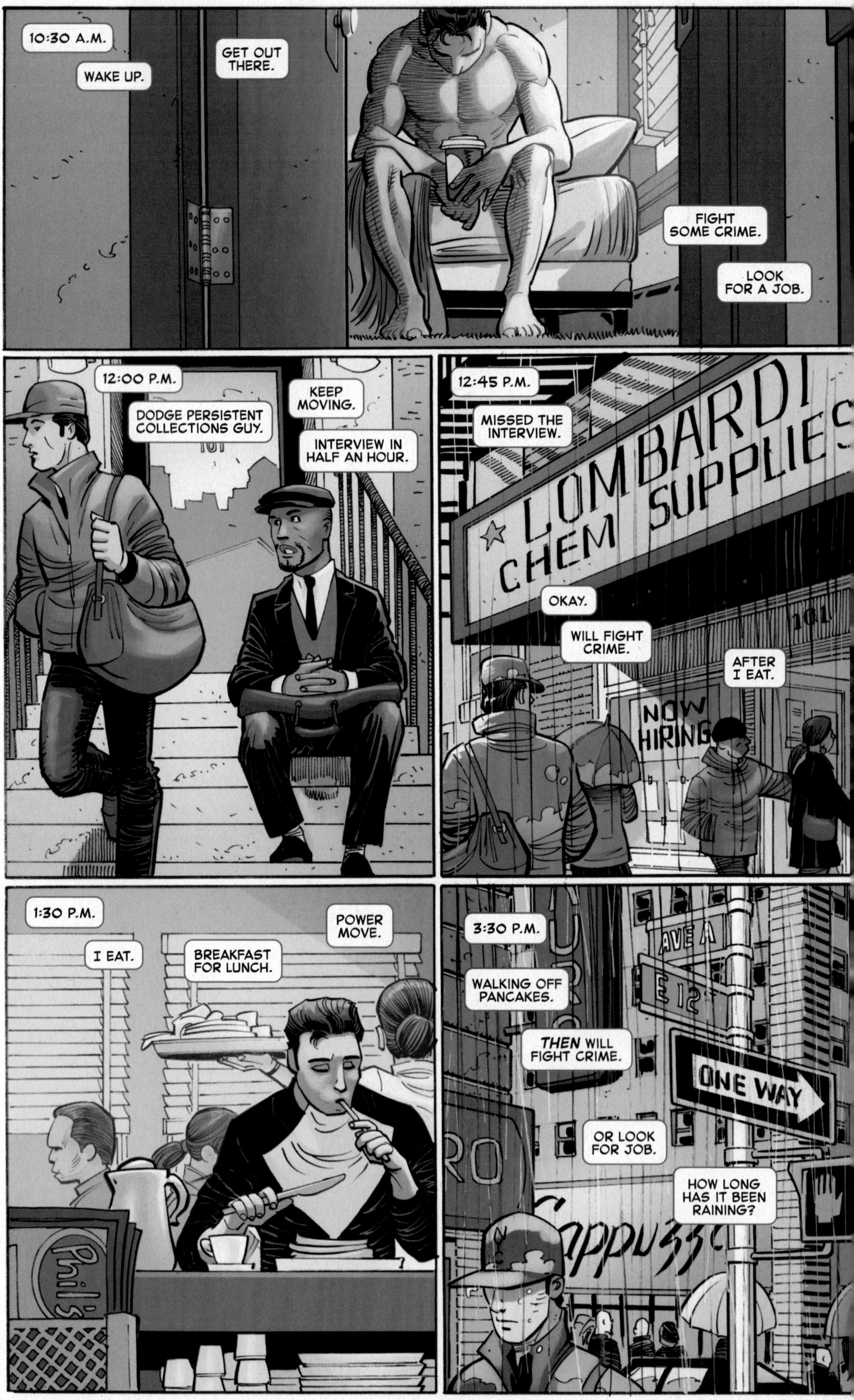
10:30 A.M.
WAKE UP.
GET OUT THERE.
FIGHT SOME CRIME.
LOOK FOR A JOB.
12:00 P.M.
DODGE PERSISTENT COLLECTIONS GUY.
KEEP MOVING.
INTERVIEW IN HALF AN HOUR.
12:45 P.M.
MISSED THE INTERVIEW.
LOMBARDI CHEM SUPPLIES
OKAY.
WILL FIGHT CRIME.
AFTER I EAT.
NOW HIRING
1:30 P.M.
I EAT.
BREAKFAST FOR LUNCH.
POWER MOVE.
Phil's
3:30 P.M.
AVE A
E 12
WALKING OFF PANCAKES.
THEN WILL FIGHT CRIME.
ONE WAY
OR LOOK FOR JOB.
HOW LONG HAS IT BEEN RAINING?

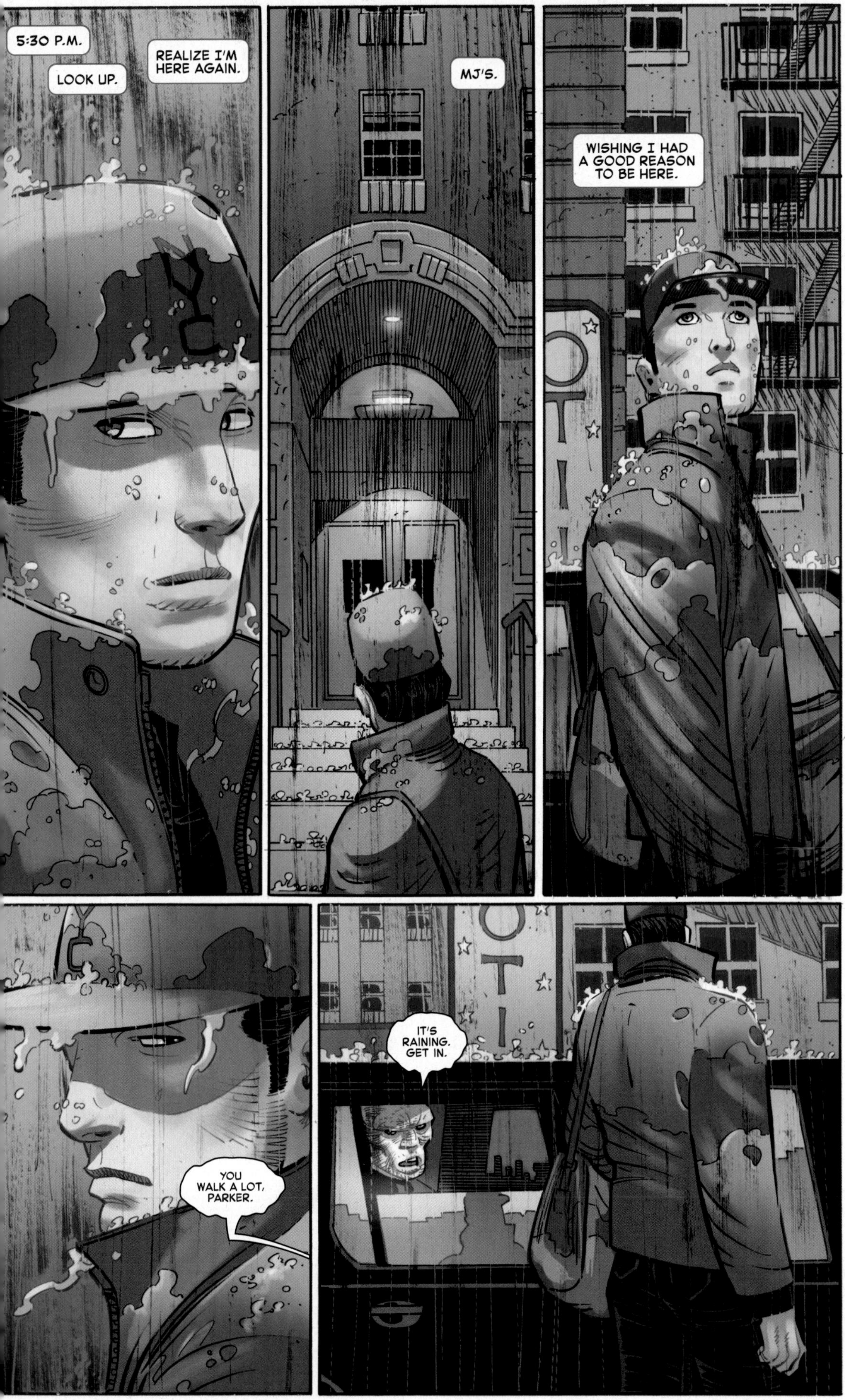
5:30 P.M.
LOOK UP.
REALIZE I'M HERE AGAIN.
MJ'S.
WISHING I HAD A GOOD REASON TO BE HERE.
YOU WALK A LOT, PARKER.
IT'S RAINING. GET IN.

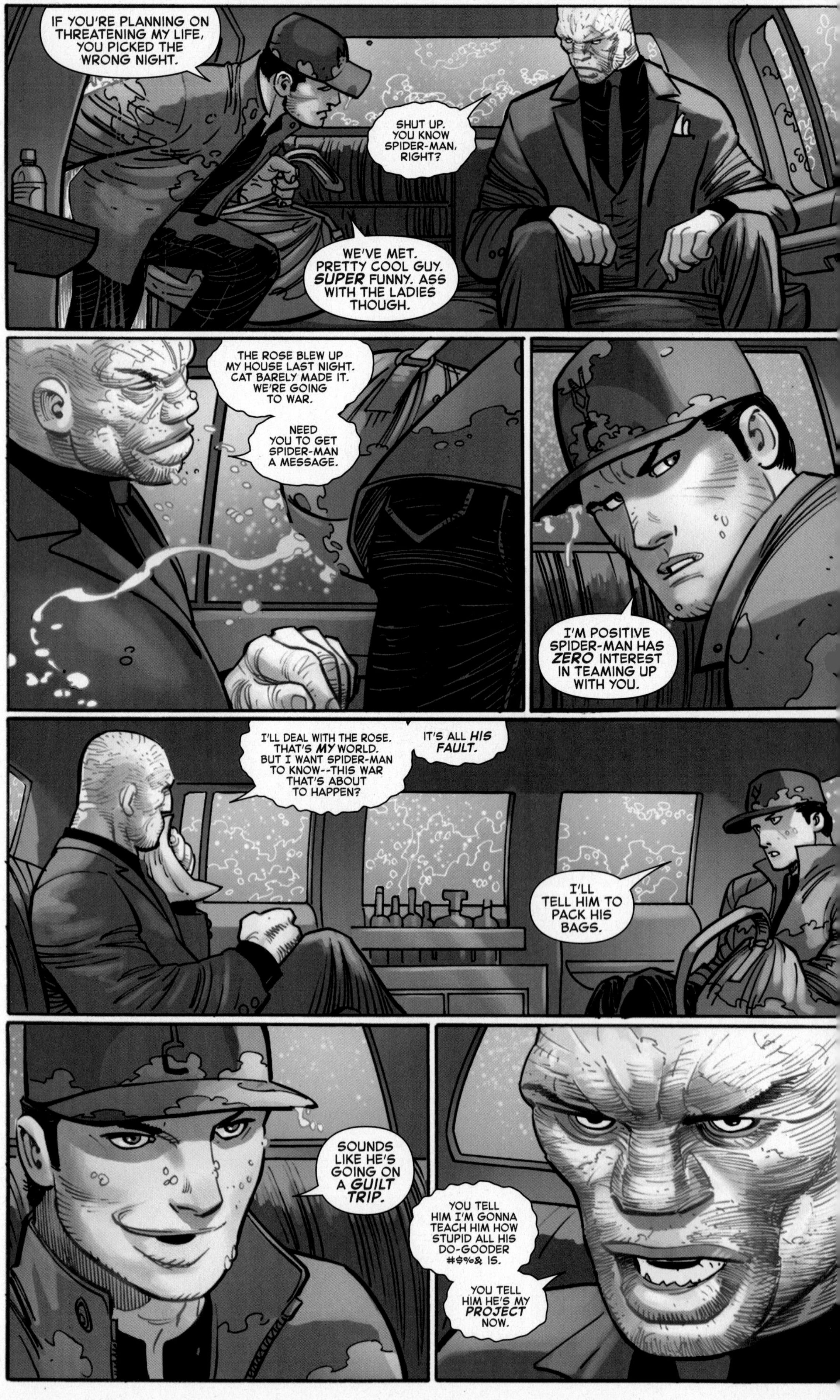

IF YOU'RE PLANNING ON THREATENING MY LIFE, YOU PICKED THE WRONG NIGHT.
SHUT UP. YOU KNOW SPIDER-MAN, RIGHT?
WE'VE MET. PRETTY COOL GUY. SUPER FUNNY. ASS WITH THE LADIES THOUGH.
THE ROSE BLEW UP MY HOUSE LAST NIGHT. CAT BARELY MADE IT. WE'RE GOING TO WAR.
NEED YOU TO GET SPIDER-MAN A MESSAGE.
I'M POSITIVE SPIDER-MAN HAS ZERO INTEREST IN TEAMING UP WITH YOU.
I'LL DEAL WITH THE ROSE. THAT'S MY WORLD. BUT I WANT SPIDER-MAN TO KNOW--THIS WAR THAT'S ABOUT TO HAPPEN?
IT'S ALL HIS FAULT.
I'LL TELL HIM TO PACK HIS BAGS.
SOUNDS LIKE HE'S GOING ON A GUILT TRIP.
YOU TELL HIM I'M GONNA TEACH HIM HOW STUPID ALL HIS DO-GOODER #$%& IS.
YOU TELL HIM HE'S MY PROJECT NOW.

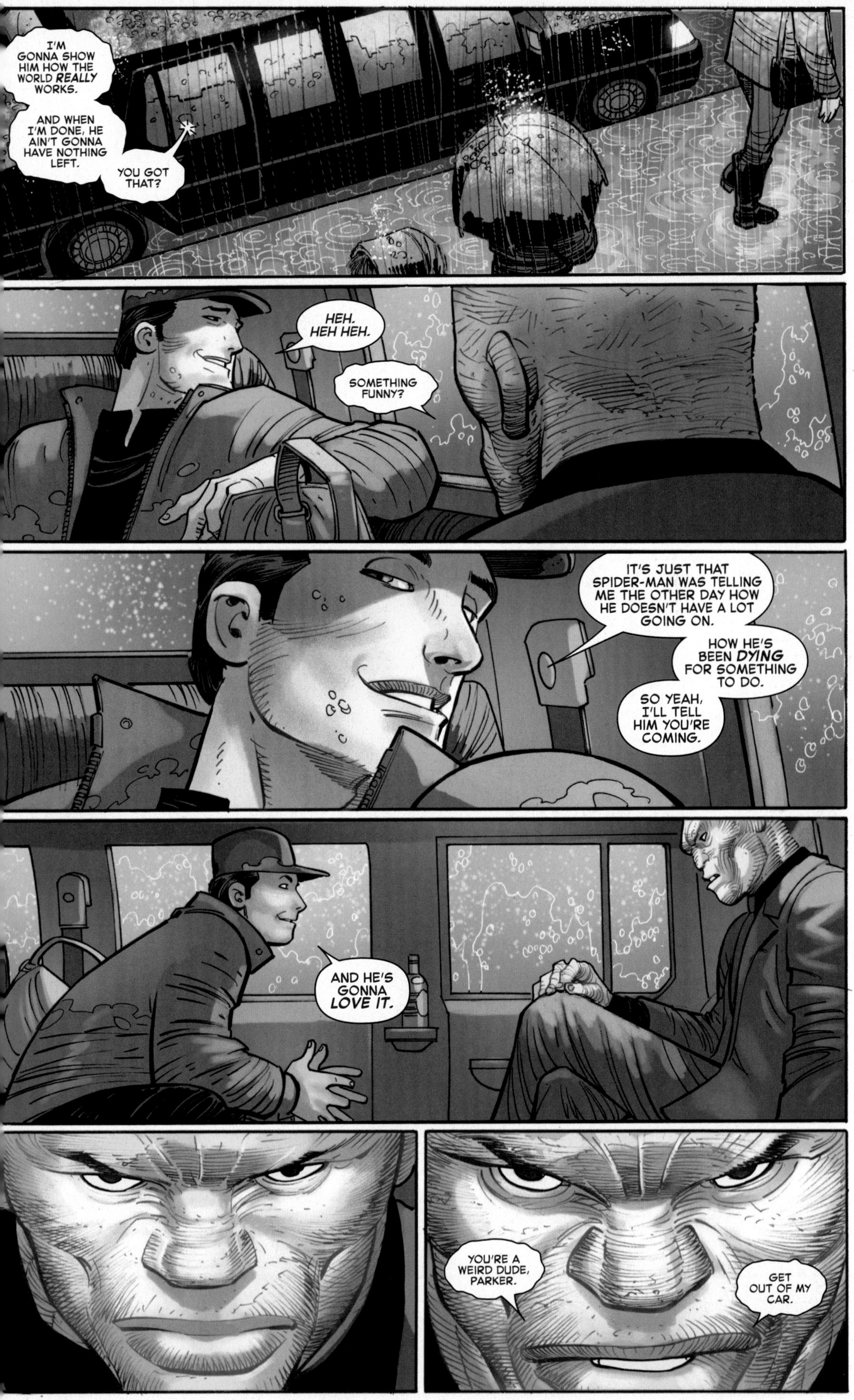
I'M GONNA SHOW HIM HOW THE WORLD *REALLY* WORKS.
AND WHEN I'M DONE, HE AIN'T GONNA HAVE NOTHING LEFT.
YOU GOT THAT?
HEH. HEH HEH.
SOMETHING FUNNY?
IT'S JUST THAT SPIDER-MAN WAS TELLING ME THE OTHER DAY HOW HE DOESN'T HAVE A LOT GOING ON.
HOW HE'S BEEN *DYING* FOR SOMETHING TO DO.
SO YEAH, I'LL TELL HIM YOU'RE COMING.
AND HE'S GONNA *LOVE IT.*
YOU'RE A WEIRD DUDE, PARKER.
GET OUT OF MY CAR.

SEE YOU AROUND.

6:00 P.M.

LOOK AT THAT.

I GOT A JOB AFTER ALL.

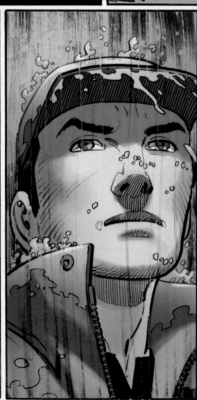

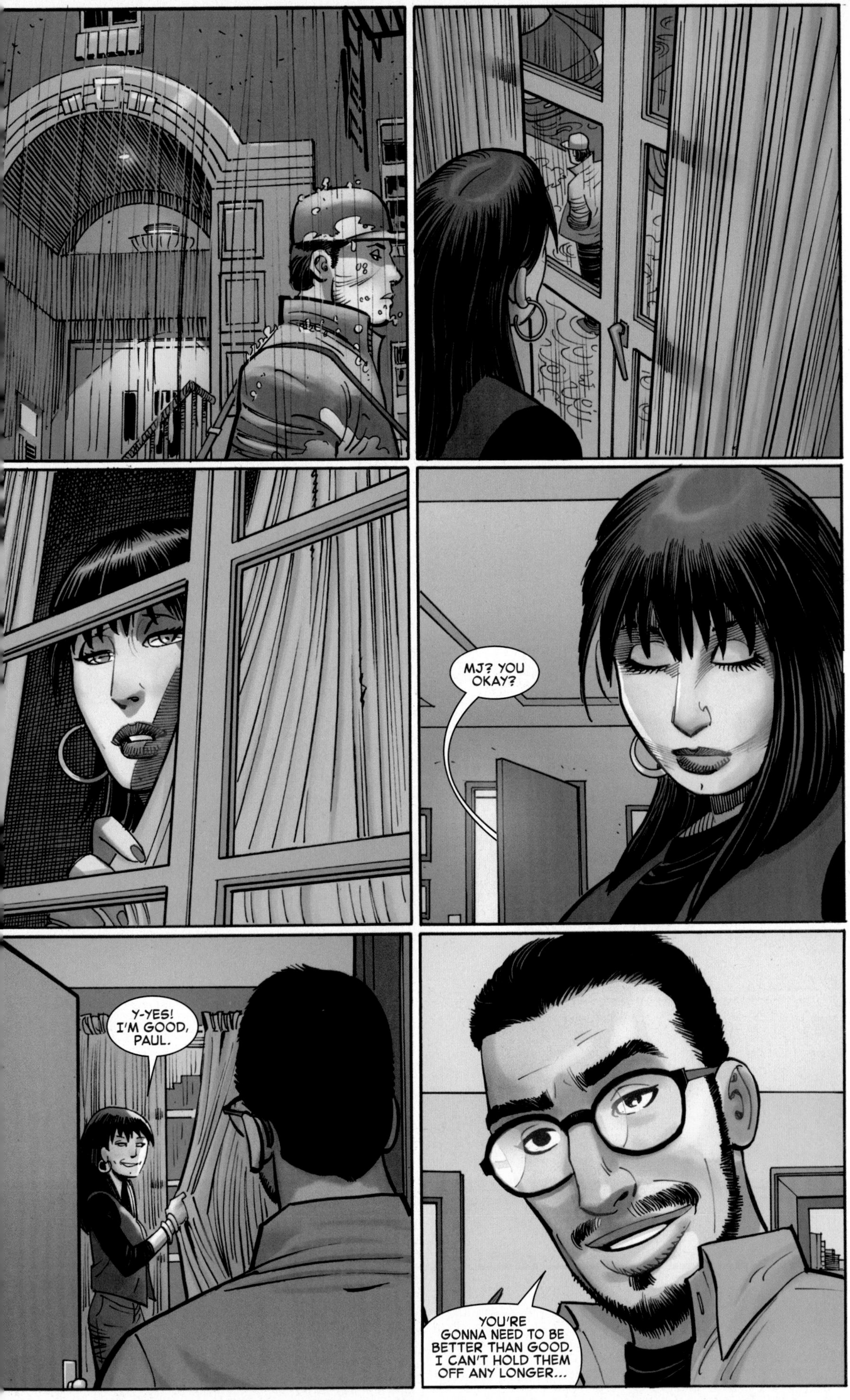
MJ? YOU OKAY?
Y-YES! I'M GOOD, PAUL.
YOU'RE GONNA NEED TO BE BETTER THAN GOOD. I CAN'T HOLD THEM OFF ANY LONGER...

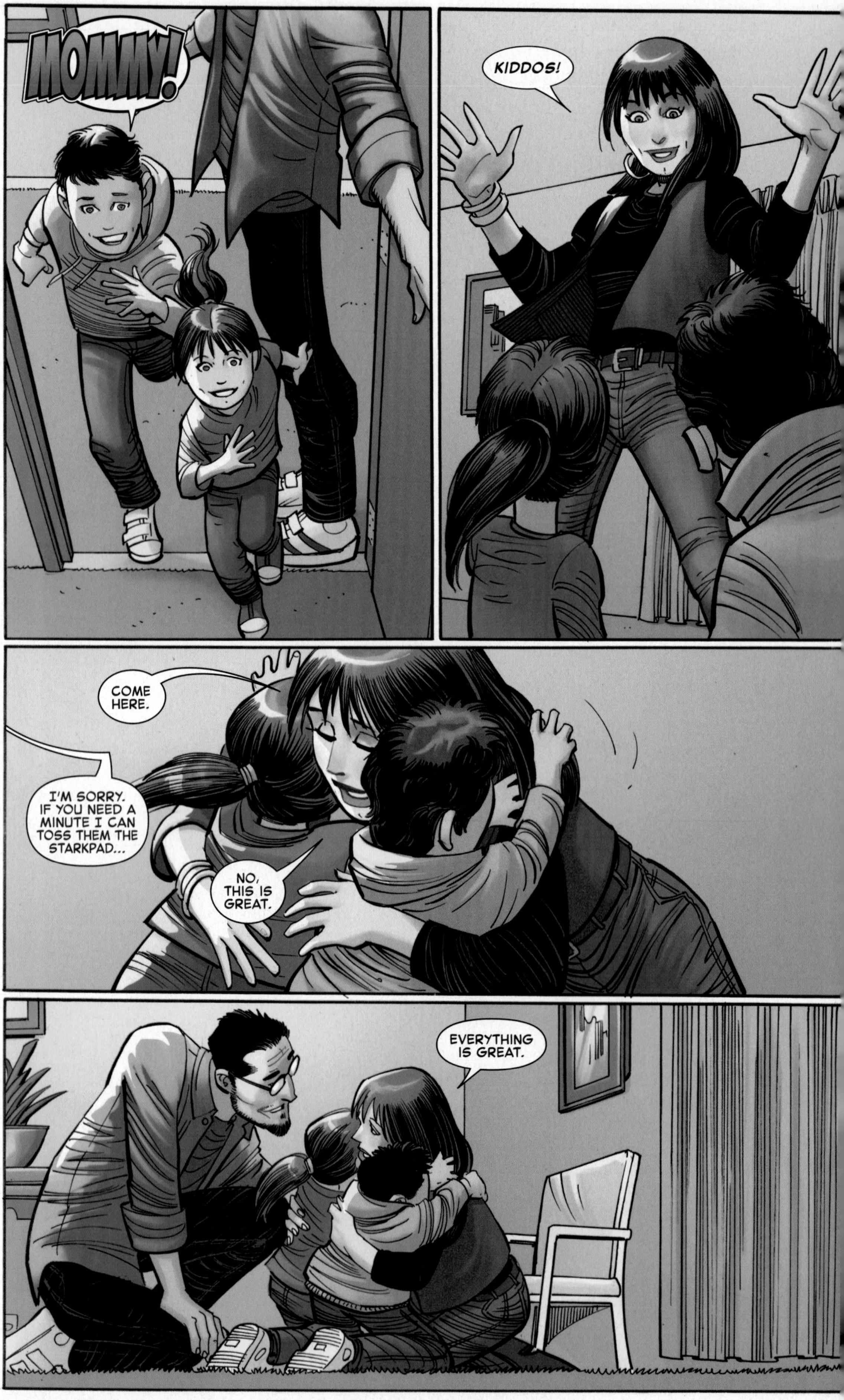
MOMMY!
KIDDOS!
COME HERE.
I'M SORRY. IF YOU NEED A MINUTE I CAN TOSS THEM THE STARKPAD...
NO, THIS IS GREAT.
EVERYTHING IS GREAT.

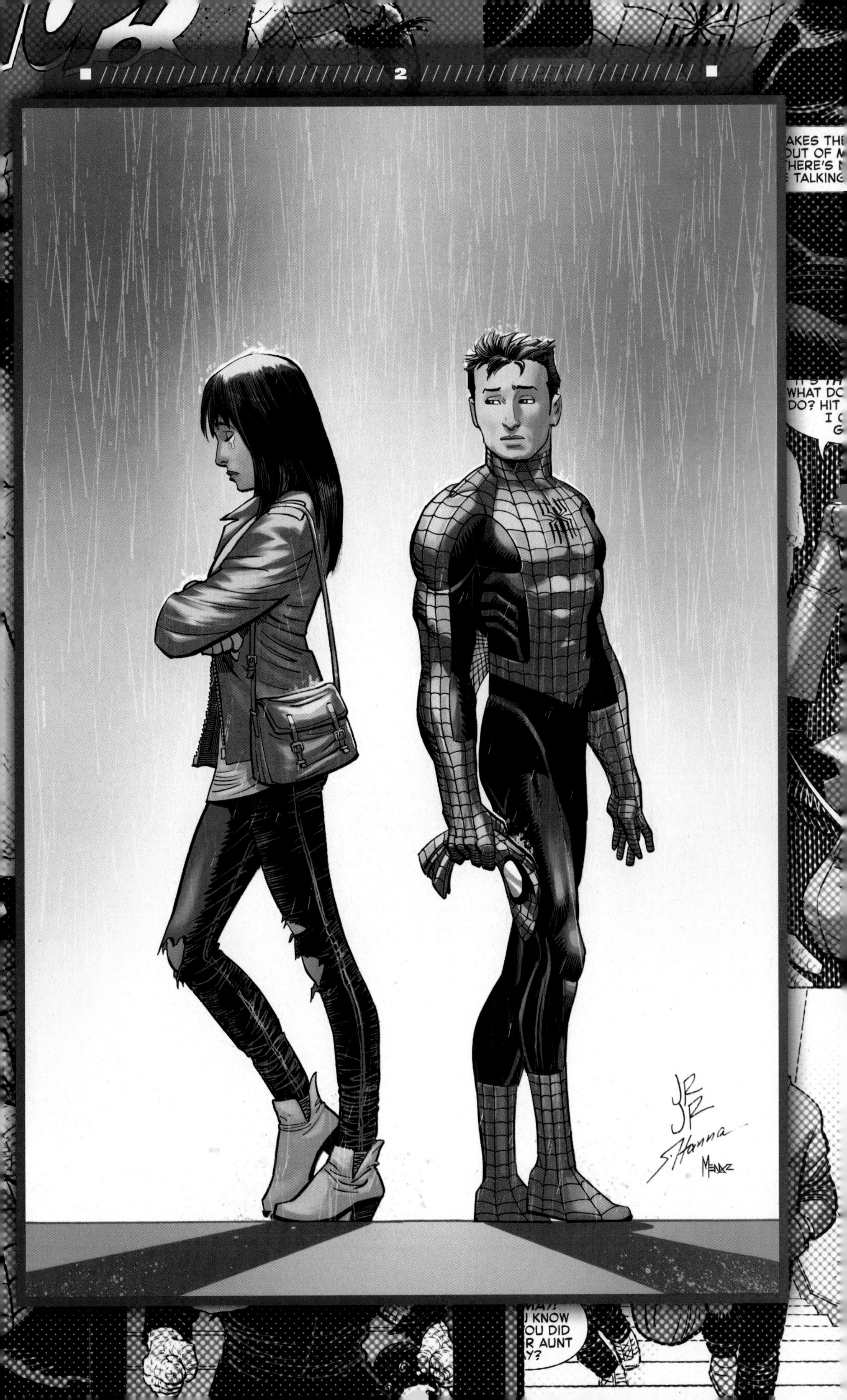

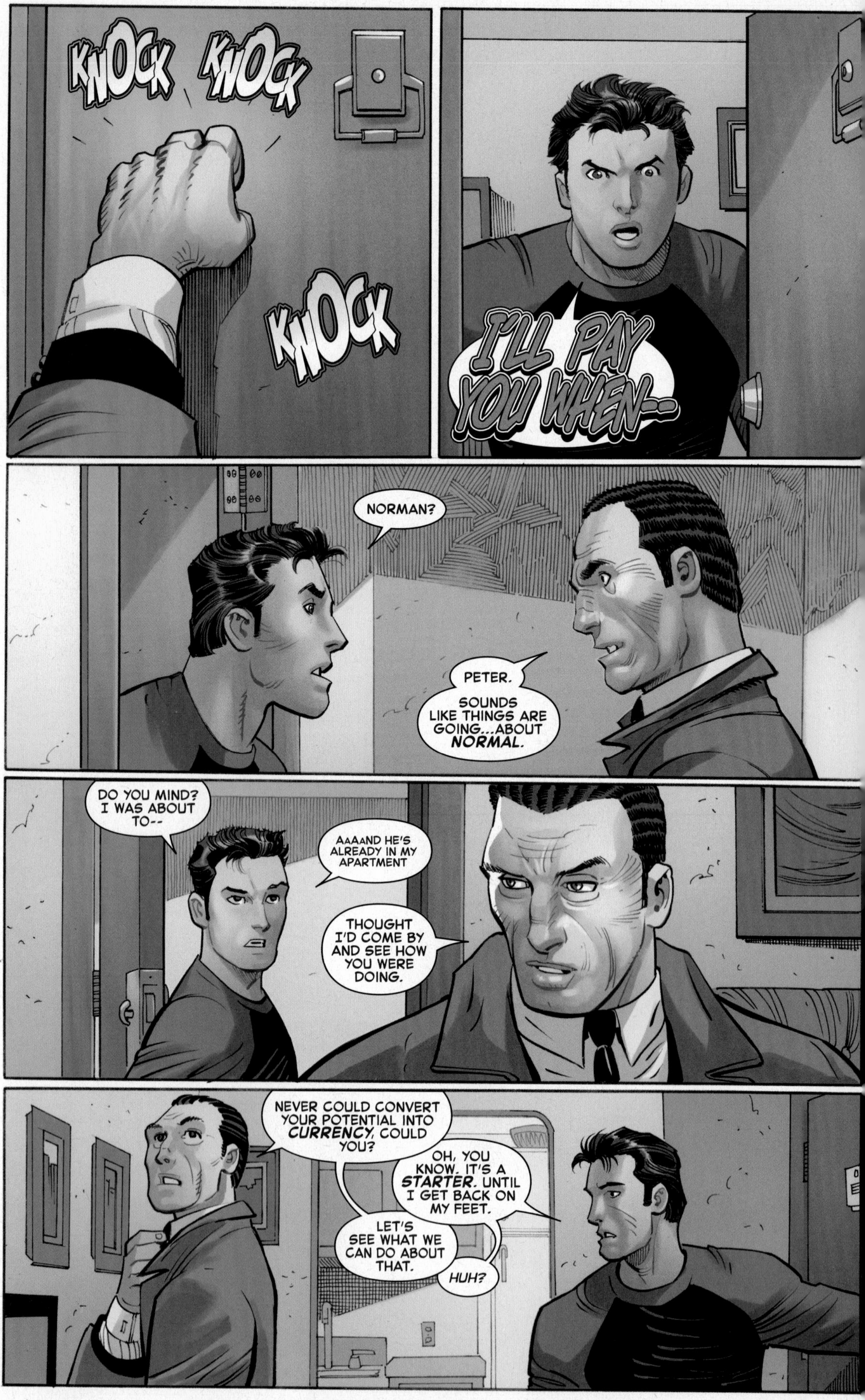
KNOCK KNOCK
KNOCK
I'LL PAY YOU WHEN--
NORMAN?
PETER.
SOUNDS LIKE THINGS ARE GOING...ABOUT NORMAL.
DO YOU MIND? I WAS ABOUT TO--
AAAAND HE'S ALREADY IN MY APARTMENT
THOUGHT I'D COME BY AND SEE HOW YOU WERE DOING.
NEVER COULD CONVERT YOUR POTENTIAL INTO CURRENCY, COULD YOU?
OH, YOU KNOW. IT'S A STARTER. UNTIL I GET BACK ON MY FEET.
LET'S SEE WHAT WE CAN DO ABOUT THAT.
HUH?

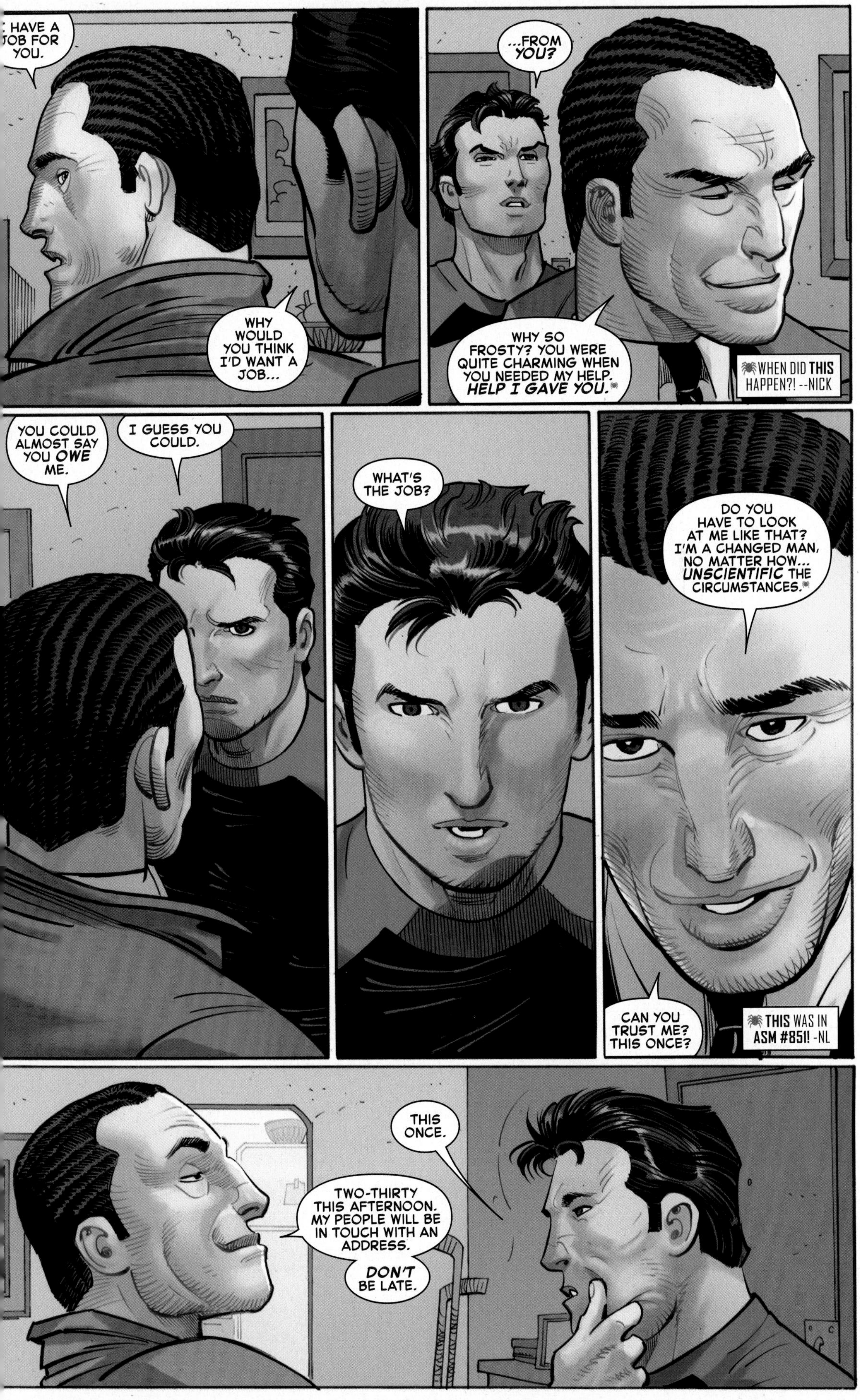

HAVE A JOB FOR YOU.
WHY WOULD YOU THINK I'D WANT A JOB...
...FROM YOU?
WHY SO FROSTY? YOU WERE QUITE CHARMING WHEN YOU NEEDED MY HELP. HELP I GAVE YOU.
WHEN DID THIS HAPPEN?! --NICK
YOU COULD ALMOST SAY YOU OWE ME.
I GUESS YOU COULD.
WHAT'S THE JOB?
DO YOU HAVE TO LOOK AT ME LIKE THAT? I'M A CHANGED MAN, NO MATTER HOW... UNSCIENTIFIC THE CIRCUMSTANCES.
CAN YOU TRUST ME? THIS ONCE?
THIS WAS IN ASM #851! -NL
THIS ONCE.
TWO-THIRTY THIS AFTERNOON. MY PEOPLE WILL BE IN TOUCH WITH AN ADDRESS.
DON'T BE LATE.

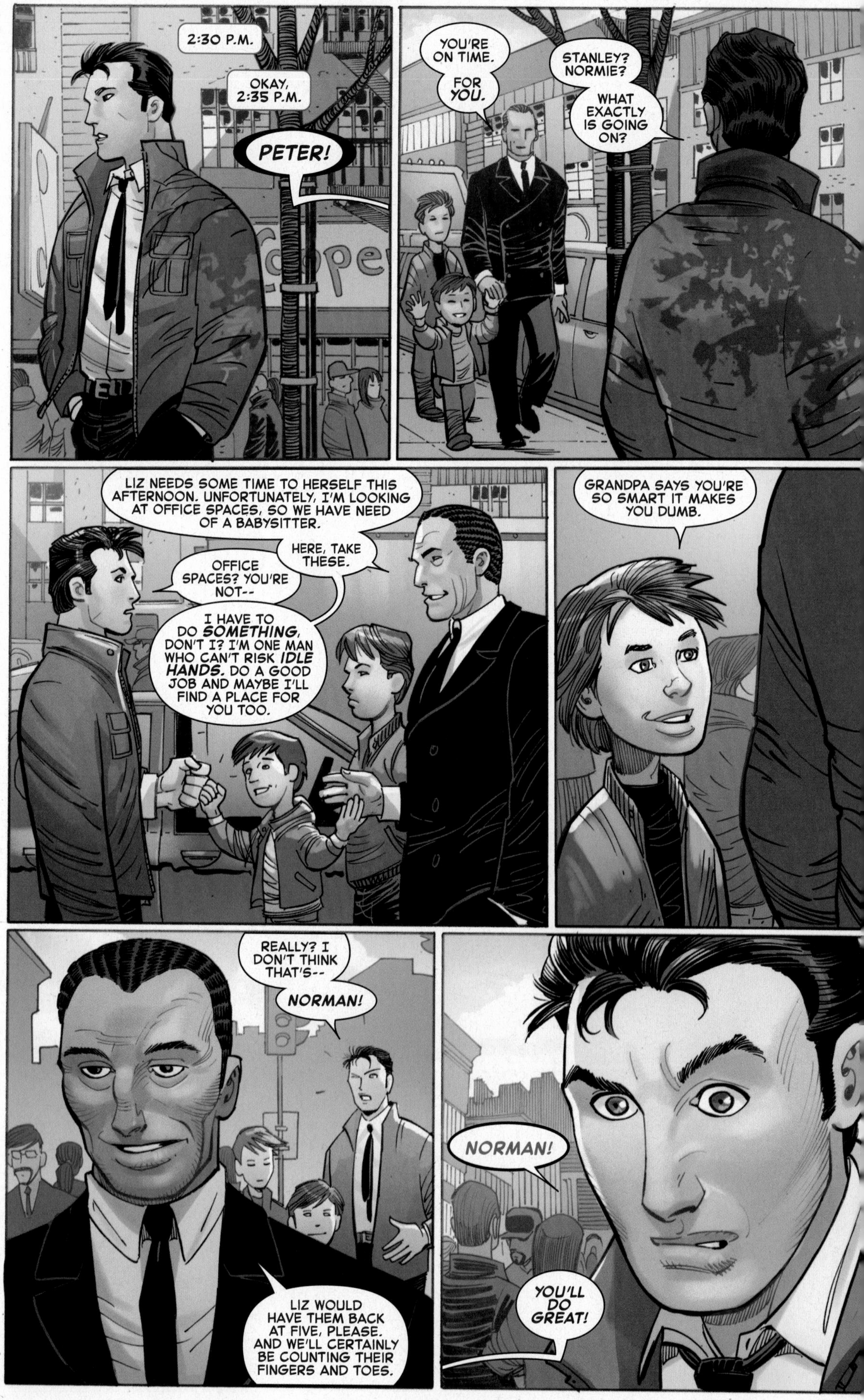

2:30 P.M.
OKAY, 2:35 P.M.
PETER!
YOU'RE ON TIME.
FOR *YOU.*
STANLEY? NORMIE?
WHAT EXACTLY IS GOING ON?
LIZ NEEDS SOME TIME TO HERSELF THIS AFTERNOON. UNFORTUNATELY, I'M LOOKING AT OFFICE SPACES, SO WE HAVE NEED OF A BABYSITTER.
HERE, TAKE THESE.
OFFICE SPACES? YOU'RE NOT--
I HAVE TO DO **SOMETHING**, DON'T I? I'M ONE MAN WHO CAN'T RISK **IDLE HANDS.** DO A GOOD JOB AND MAYBE I'LL FIND A PLACE FOR YOU TOO.
GRANDPA SAYS YOU'RE SO SMART IT MAKES YOU DUMB.
REALLY? I DON'T THINK THAT'S--
NORMAN!
LIZ WOULD HAVE THEM BACK AT FIVE, PLEASE. AND WE'LL CERTAINLY BE COUNTING THEIR FINGERS AND TOES.
NORMAN!
YOU'LL DO GREAT!

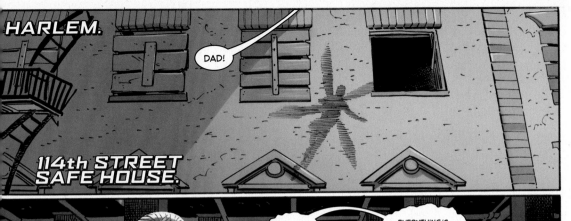

DAD!

114th STREET SAFE HOUSE.

HEY, JANICE.

ARE YOU OKAY? WHAT HAPPENED TO THE MANSION?!

EVERYTHING'S FINE. JUST A LITTLE BUSINESS I HAVE TO TAKE CARE OF.

IT'S *THE ROSE*, RIGHT? WHAT DO YOU WANT ME TO DO? HIT HIS OPERATIONS? I CAN GET THE GIRLS AND--

NO. THINGS ARE GONNA GET UGLY. I WANT YOU TO GO SEE THAT BOY OF YOURS. TAKE A VACATION.

LET ME HANDLE THIS.

WHAT DID YOU JUST SAY TO ME?

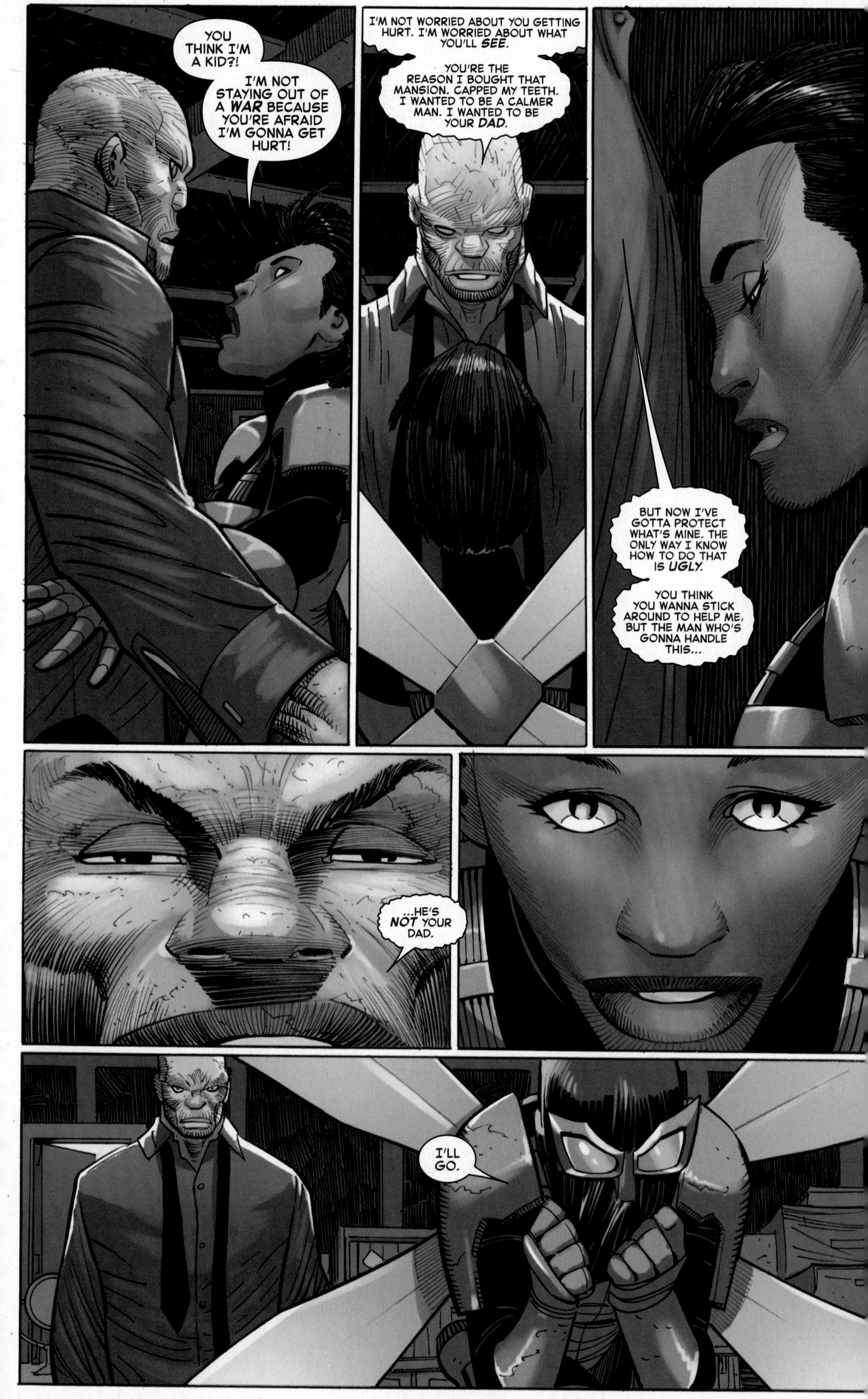

YOU THINK I'M A KID?!
I'M NOT STAYING OUT OF A WAR BECAUSE YOU'RE AFRAID I'M GONNA GET HURT!
I'M NOT WORRIED ABOUT YOU GETTING HURT. I'M WORRIED ABOUT WHAT YOU'LL SEE.
YOU'RE THE REASON I BOUGHT THAT MANSION. CAPPED MY TEETH. I WANTED TO BE A CALMER MAN. I WANTED TO BE YOUR DAD.
BUT NOW I'VE GOTTA PROTECT WHAT'S MINE. THE ONLY WAY I KNOW HOW TO DO THAT IS UGLY.
YOU THINK YOU WANNA STICK AROUND TO HELP ME, BUT THE MAN WHO'S GONNA HANDLE THIS...
...HE'S NOT YOUR DAD.
I'LL GO.

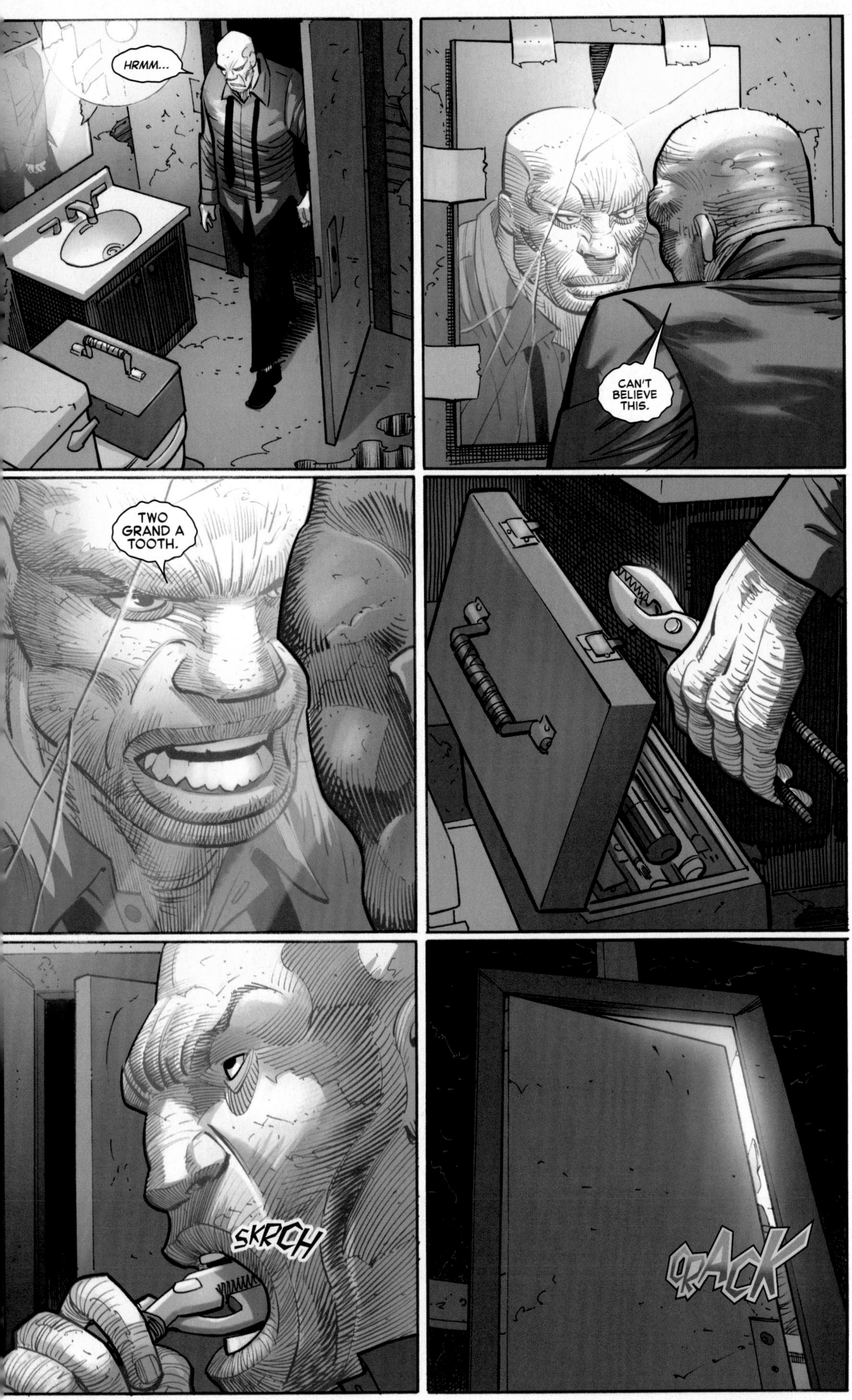
HRMM...
CAN'T BELIEVE THIS.
TWO GRAND A TOOTH.
SKRCH
CRACK

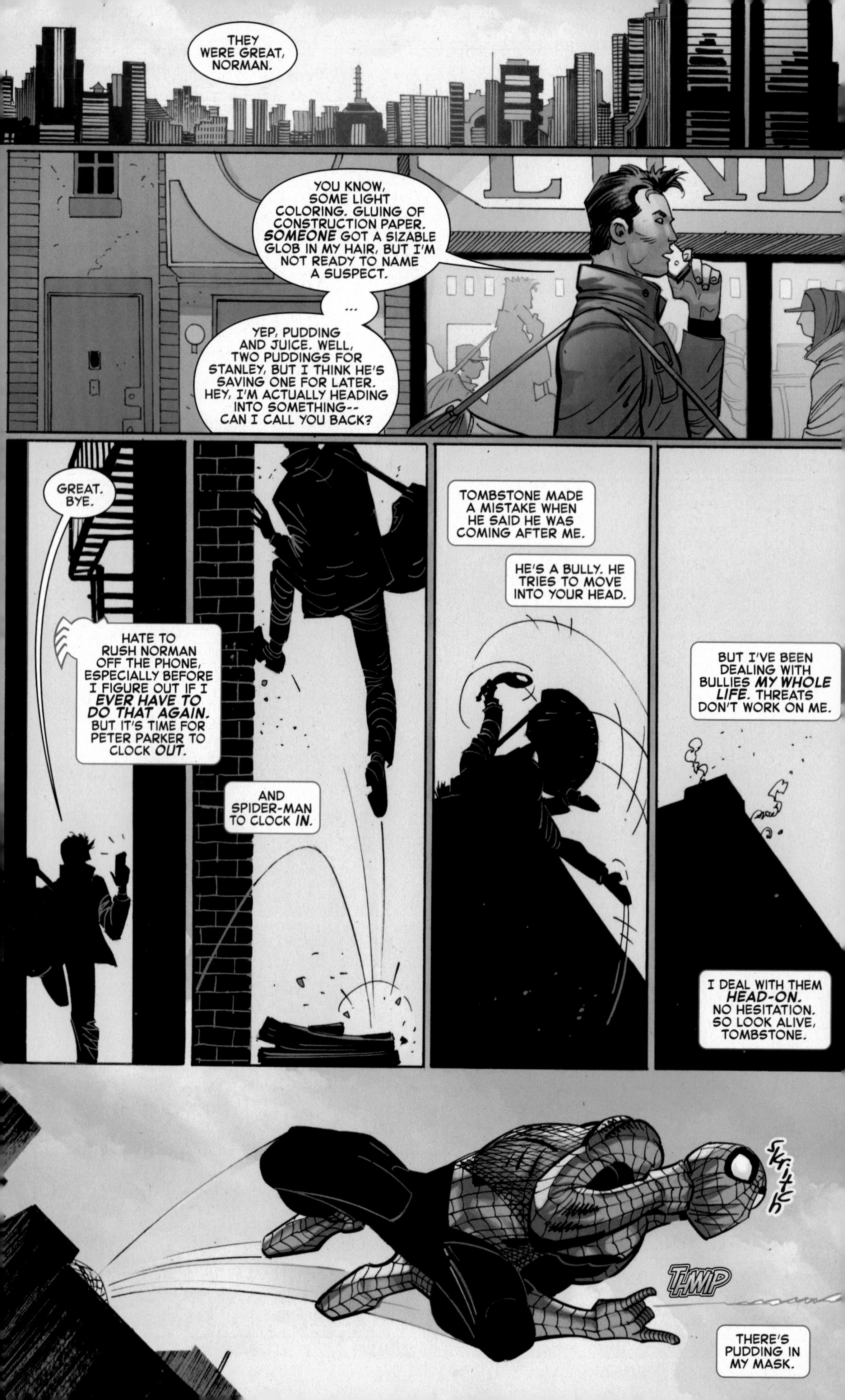
THEY WERE GREAT, NORMAN.
YOU KNOW, SOME LIGHT COLORING. GLUING OF CONSTRUCTION PAPER. SOMEONE GOT A SIZABLE GLOB IN MY HAIR, BUT I'M NOT READY TO NAME A SUSPECT.
...
YEP, PUDDING AND JUICE. WELL, TWO PUDDINGS FOR STANLEY, BUT I THINK HE'S SAVING ONE FOR LATER. HEY, I'M ACTUALLY HEADING INTO SOMETHING-- CAN I CALL YOU BACK?
GREAT. BYE.
HATE TO RUSH NORMAN OFF THE PHONE, ESPECIALLY BEFORE I FIGURE OUT IF I EVER HAVE TO DO THAT AGAIN. BUT IT'S TIME FOR PETER PARKER TO CLOCK OUT.
AND SPIDER-MAN TO CLOCK IN.
TOMBSTONE MADE A MISTAKE WHEN HE SAID HE WAS COMING AFTER ME.
HE'S A BULLY. HE TRIES TO MOVE INTO YOUR HEAD.
BUT I'VE BEEN DEALING WITH BULLIES MY WHOLE LIFE. THREATS DON'T WORK ON ME.
I DEAL WITH THEM HEAD-ON. NO HESITATION. SO LOOK ALIVE, TOMBSTONE.
SKRITCH
THWIP
THERE'S PUDDING IN MY MASK.

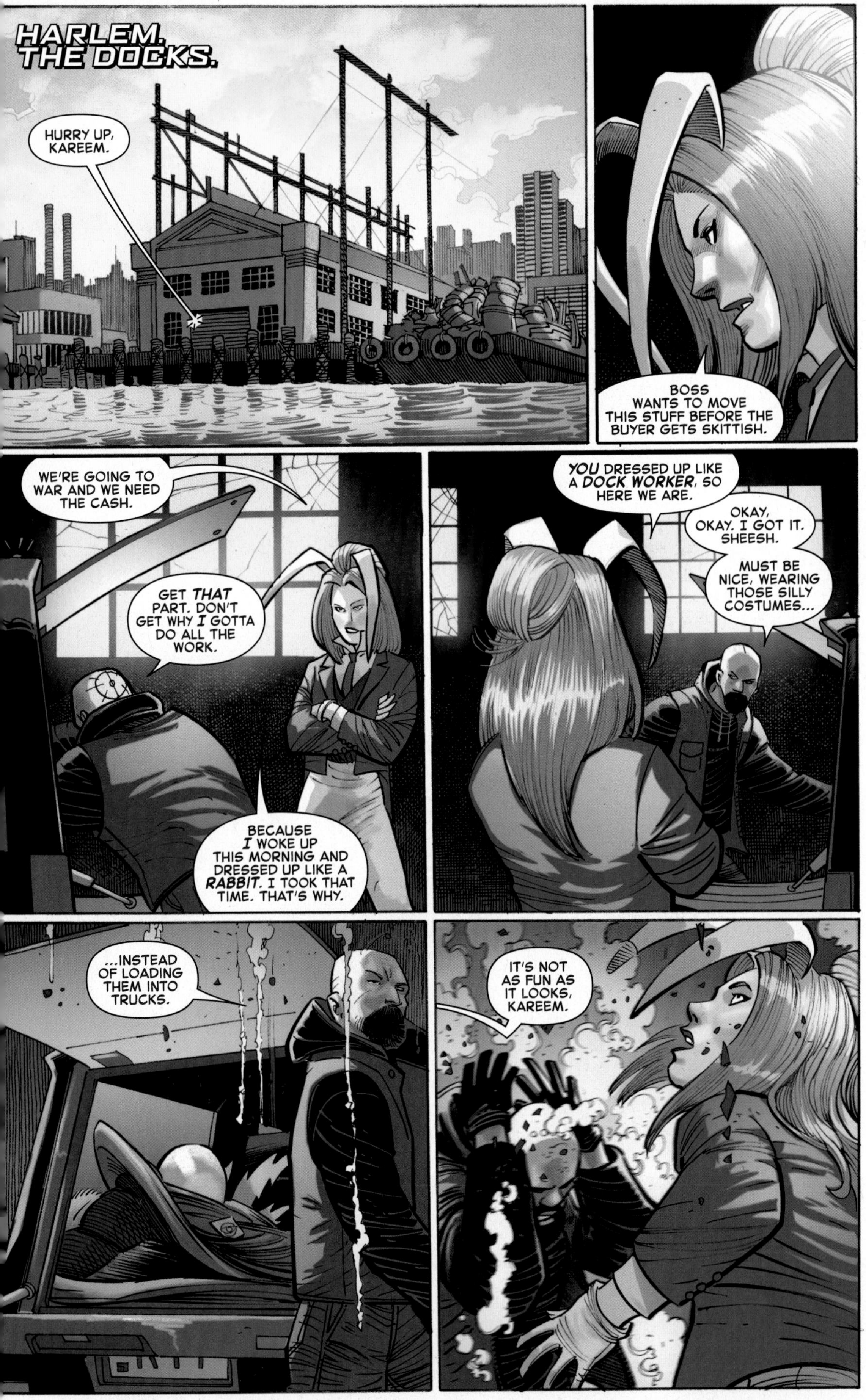
HARLEM. THE DOCKS.
HURRY UP, KAREEM.
BOSS WANTS TO MOVE THIS STUFF BEFORE THE BUYER GETS SKITTISH.
WE'RE GOING TO WAR AND WE NEED THE CASH.
GET THAT PART. DON'T GET WHY I GOTTA DO ALL THE WORK.
BECAUSE I WOKE UP THIS MORNING AND DRESSED UP LIKE A RABBIT. I TOOK THAT TIME. THAT'S WHY.
YOU DRESSED UP LIKE A DOCK WORKER, SO HERE WE ARE.
OKAY, OKAY. I GOT IT. SHEESH.
MUST BE NICE, WEARING THOSE SILLY COSTUMES...
...INSTEAD OF LOADING THEM INTO TRUCKS.
IT'S NOT AS FUN AS IT LOOKS, KAREEM.

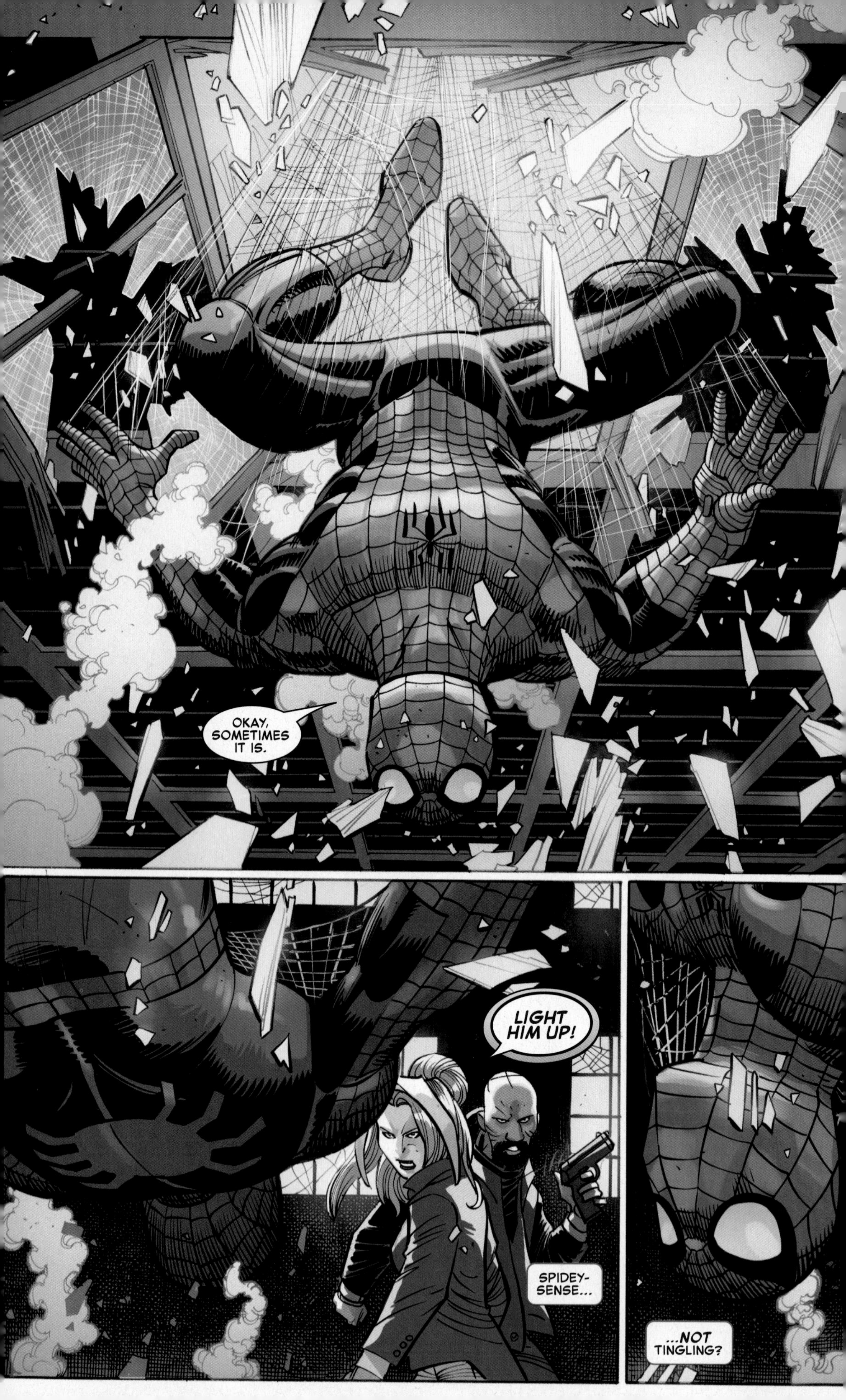

OKAY, SOMETIMES IT IS.
LIGHT HIM UP!
SPIDEY-SENSE...
...NOT TINGLING?

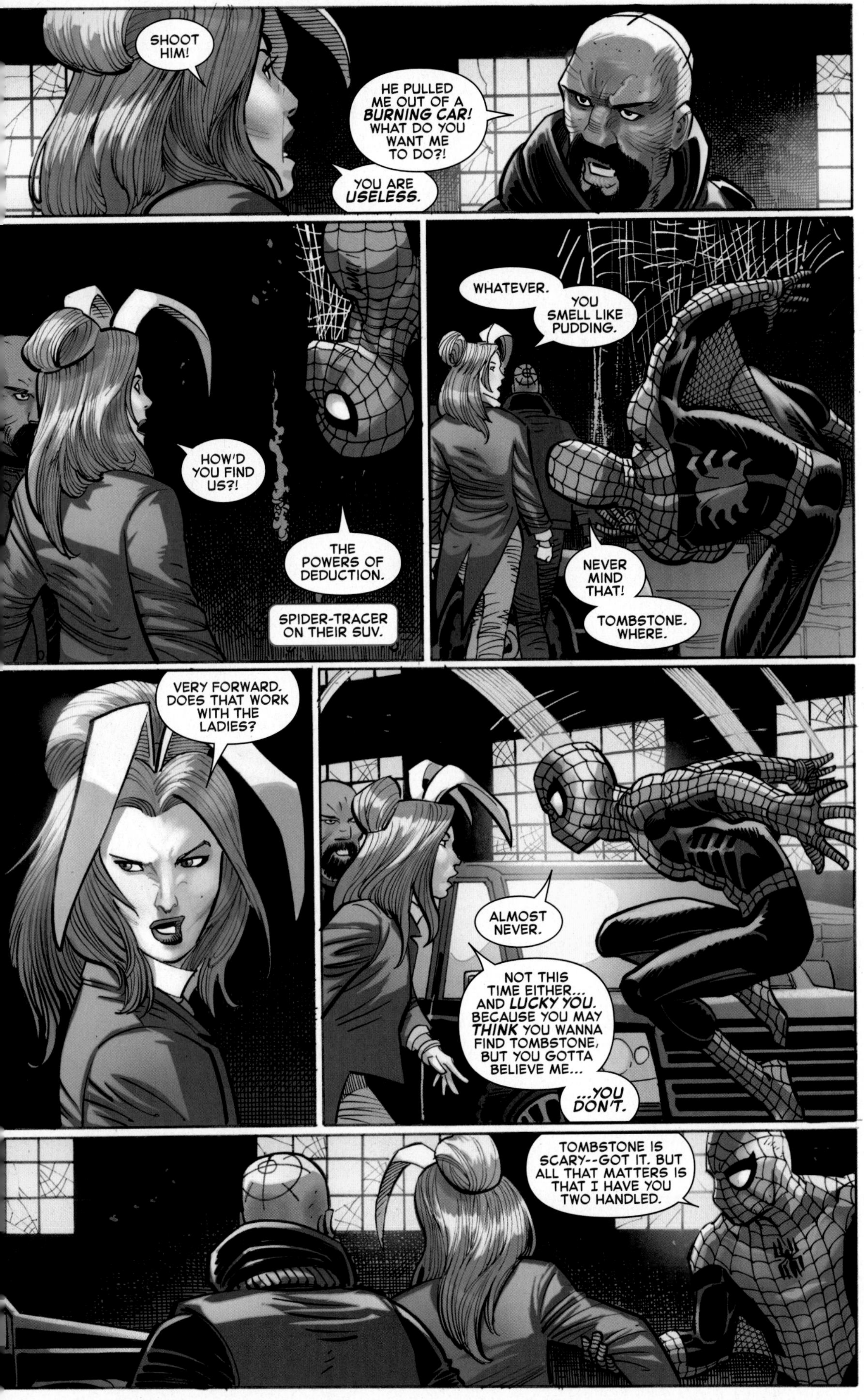
SHOOT HIM!
HE PULLED ME OUT OF A BURNING CAR! WHAT DO YOU WANT ME TO DO?!
YOU ARE USELESS.
HOW'D YOU FIND US?!
THE POWERS OF DEDUCTION.
SPIDER-TRACER ON THEIR SUV.
WHATEVER.
YOU SMELL LIKE PUDDING.
NEVER MIND THAT!
TOMBSTONE. WHERE.
VERY FORWARD. DOES THAT WORK WITH THE LADIES?
ALMOST NEVER.
NOT THIS TIME EITHER... AND LUCKY YOU. BECAUSE YOU MAY THINK YOU WANNA FIND TOMBSTONE, BUT YOU GOTTA BELIEVE ME...
...YOU DON'T.
TOMBSTONE IS SCARY--GOT IT. BUT ALL THAT MATTERS IS THAT I HAVE YOU TWO HANDLED.

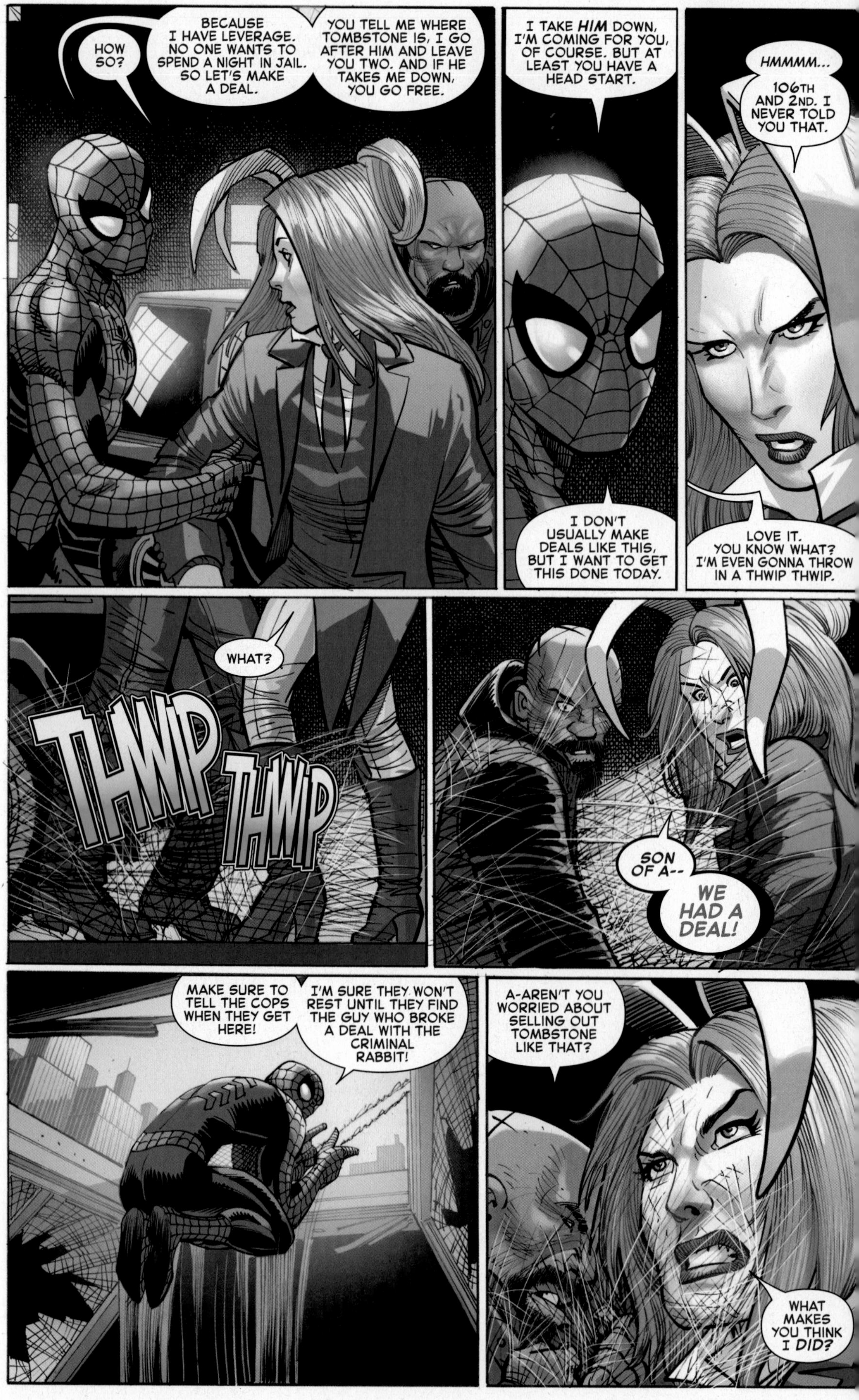

HOW SO?
BECAUSE I HAVE LEVERAGE. NO ONE WANTS TO SPEND A NIGHT IN JAIL. SO LET'S MAKE A DEAL.
YOU TELL ME WHERE TOMBSTONE IS, I GO AFTER HIM AND LEAVE YOU TWO. AND IF HE TAKES ME DOWN, YOU GO FREE.
I TAKE *HIM* DOWN, I'M COMING FOR YOU, OF COURSE. BUT AT LEAST YOU HAVE A HEAD START.
I DON'T USUALLY MAKE DEALS LIKE THIS, BUT I WANT TO GET THIS DONE TODAY.
HMMMM...
106TH AND 2ND. I NEVER TOLD YOU THAT.
LOVE IT. YOU KNOW WHAT? I'M EVEN GONNA THROW IN A THWIP THWIP.
WHAT?
THWIP
THWIP
SON OF A--
WE HAD A DEAL!
MAKE SURE TO TELL THE COPS WHEN THEY GET HERE!
I'M SURE THEY WON'T REST UNTIL THEY FIND THE GUY WHO BROKE A DEAL WITH THE CRIMINAL RABBIT!
A-AREN'T YOU WORRIED ABOUT SELLING OUT TOMBSTONE LIKE THAT?
WHAT MAKES YOU THINK I *DID*?

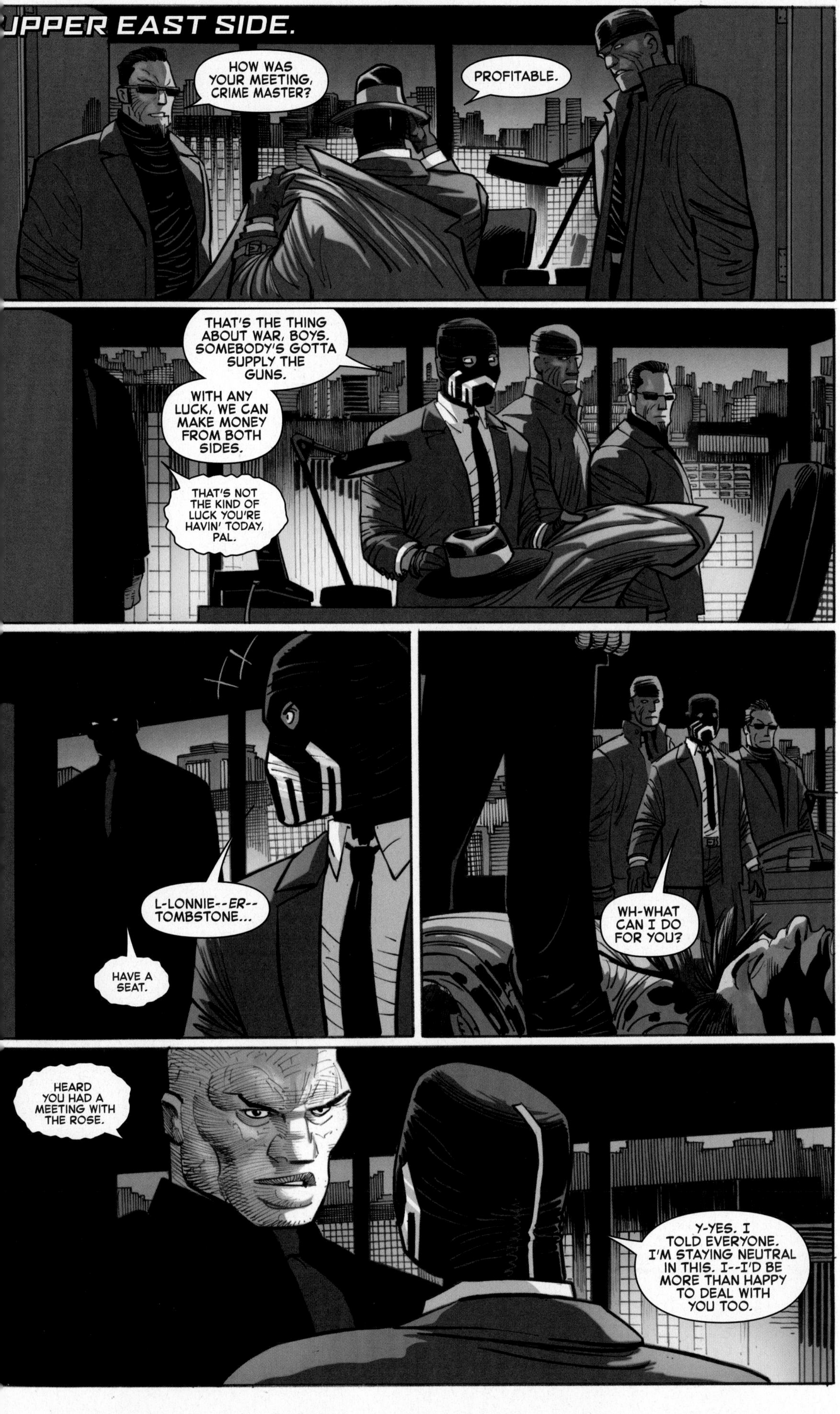
UPPER EAST SIDE.
HOW WAS YOUR MEETING, CRIME MASTER?
PROFITABLE.
THAT'S THE THING ABOUT WAR, BOYS. SOMEBODY'S GOTTA SUPPLY THE GUNS.
WITH ANY LUCK, WE CAN MAKE MONEY FROM BOTH SIDES.
THAT'S NOT THE KIND OF LUCK YOU'RE HAVIN' TODAY, PAL.
L-LONNIE--ER--TOMBSTONE...
HAVE A SEAT.
WH-WHAT CAN I DO FOR YOU?
HEARD YOU HAD A MEETING WITH THE ROSE.
Y-YES. I TOLD EVERYONE. I'M STAYING NEUTRAL IN THIS. I--I'D BE MORE THAN HAPPY TO DEAL WITH YOU TOO.

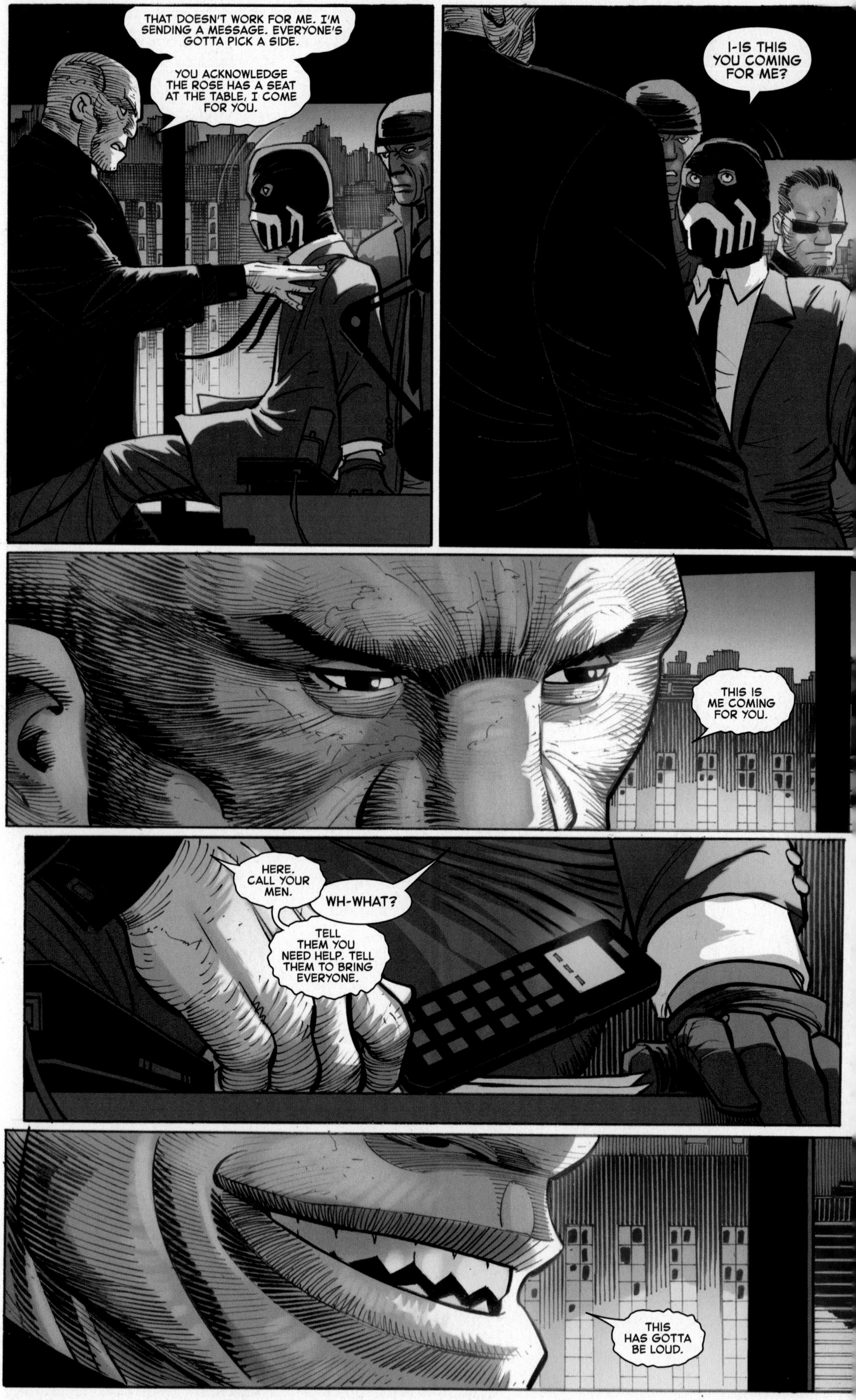
THAT DOESN'T WORK FOR ME. I'M SENDING A MESSAGE. EVERYONE'S GOTTA PICK A SIDE.
YOU ACKNOWLEDGE THE ROSE HAS A SEAT AT THE TABLE, I COME FOR YOU.
I-IS THIS YOU COMING FOR ME?
THIS IS ME COMING FOR YOU.
HERE. CALL YOUR MEN.
WH-WHAT?
TELL THEM YOU NEED HELP. TELL THEM TO BRING EVERYONE.
THIS HAS GOTTA BE LOUD.

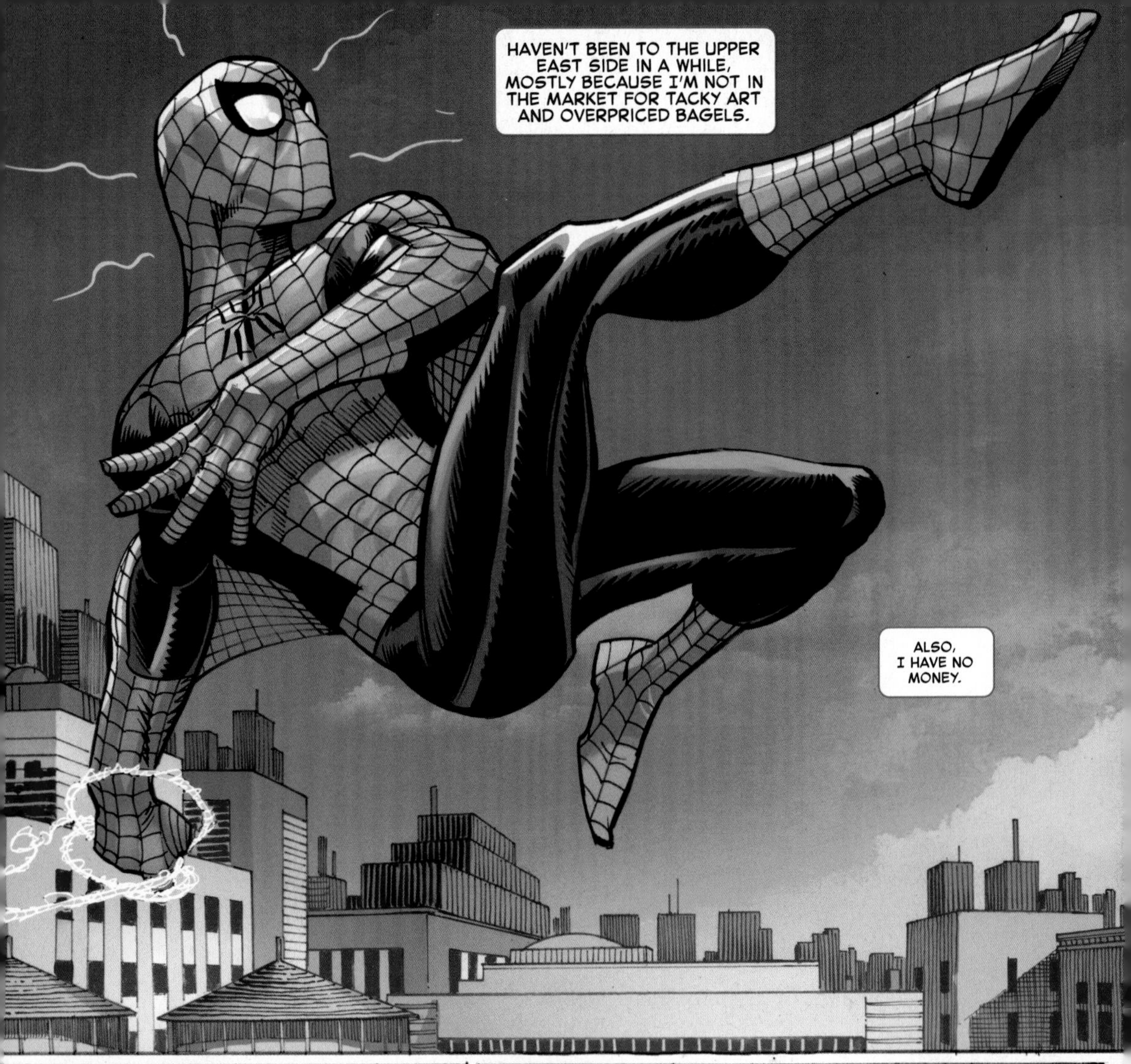
HAVEN'T BEEN TO THE UPPER EAST SIDE IN A WHILE, MOSTLY BECAUSE I'M NOT IN THE MARKET FOR TACKY ART AND OVERPRICED BAGELS.
ALSO, I HAVE NO MONEY.

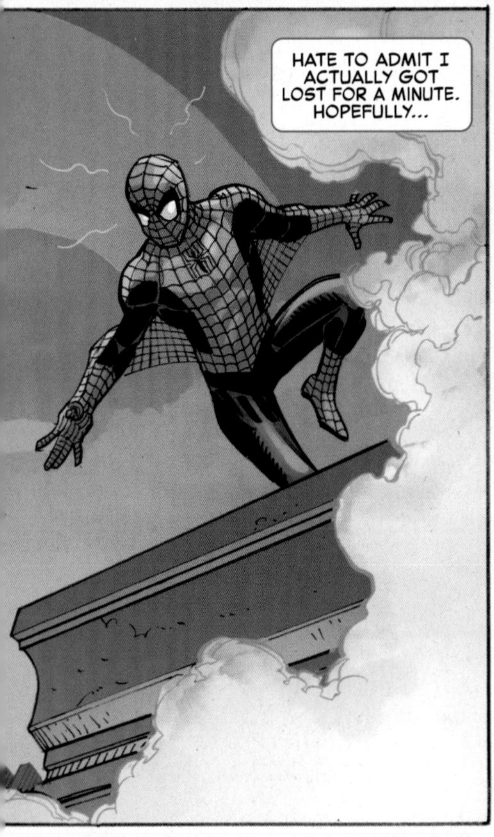
HATE TO ADMIT I ACTUALLY GOT LOST FOR A MINUTE. HOPEFULLY...

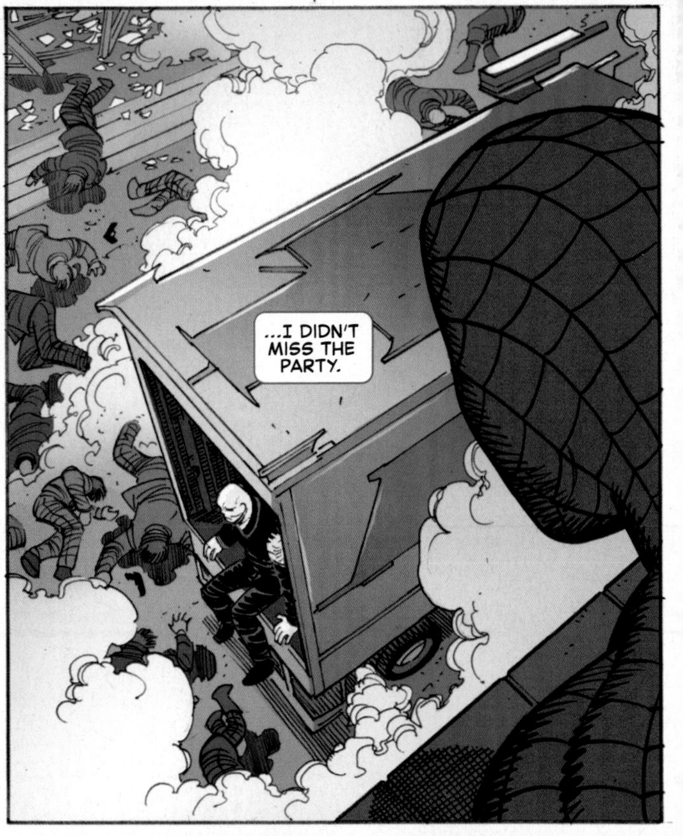
...I DIDN'T MISS THE PARTY.

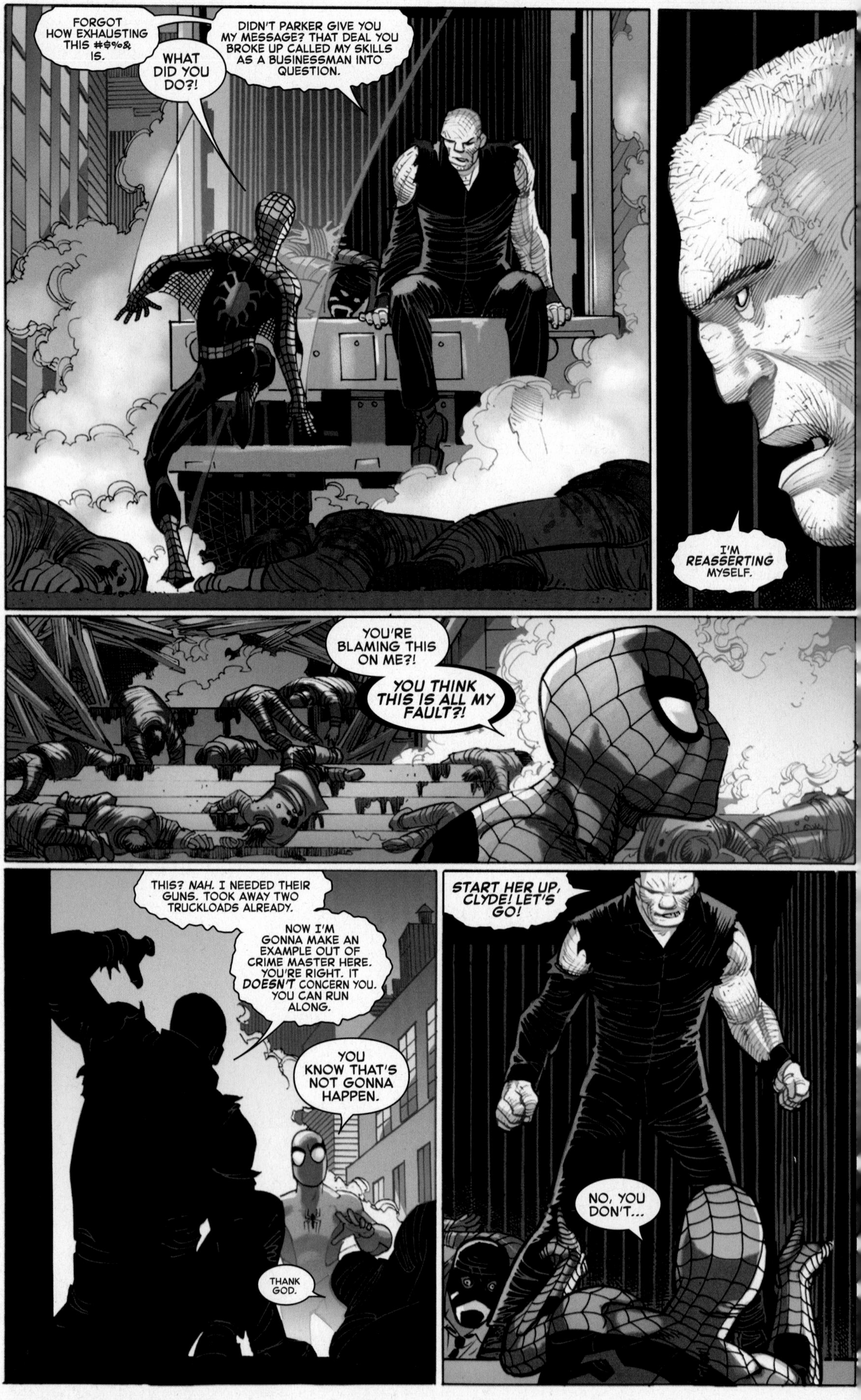
FORGOT HOW EXHAUSTING THIS #$%& IS.
WHAT DID YOU DO?!
DIDN'T PARKER GIVE YOU MY MESSAGE? THAT DEAL YOU BROKE UP CALLED MY SKILLS AS A BUSINESSMAN INTO QUESTION.
I'M *REASSERTING* MYSELF.
YOU'RE BLAMING THIS ON ME?!
YOU THINK THIS IS ALL MY FAULT?!
THIS? *NAH.* I NEEDED THEIR GUNS. TOOK AWAY TWO TRUCKLOADS ALREADY.
NOW I'M GONNA MAKE AN EXAMPLE OUT OF CRIME MASTER HERE. YOU'RE RIGHT. IT *DOESN'T* CONCERN YOU. YOU CAN RUN ALONG.
YOU KNOW THAT'S NOT GONNA HAPPEN.
THANK GOD.
START HER UP, CLYDE! LET'S GO!
NO, YOU DON'T...

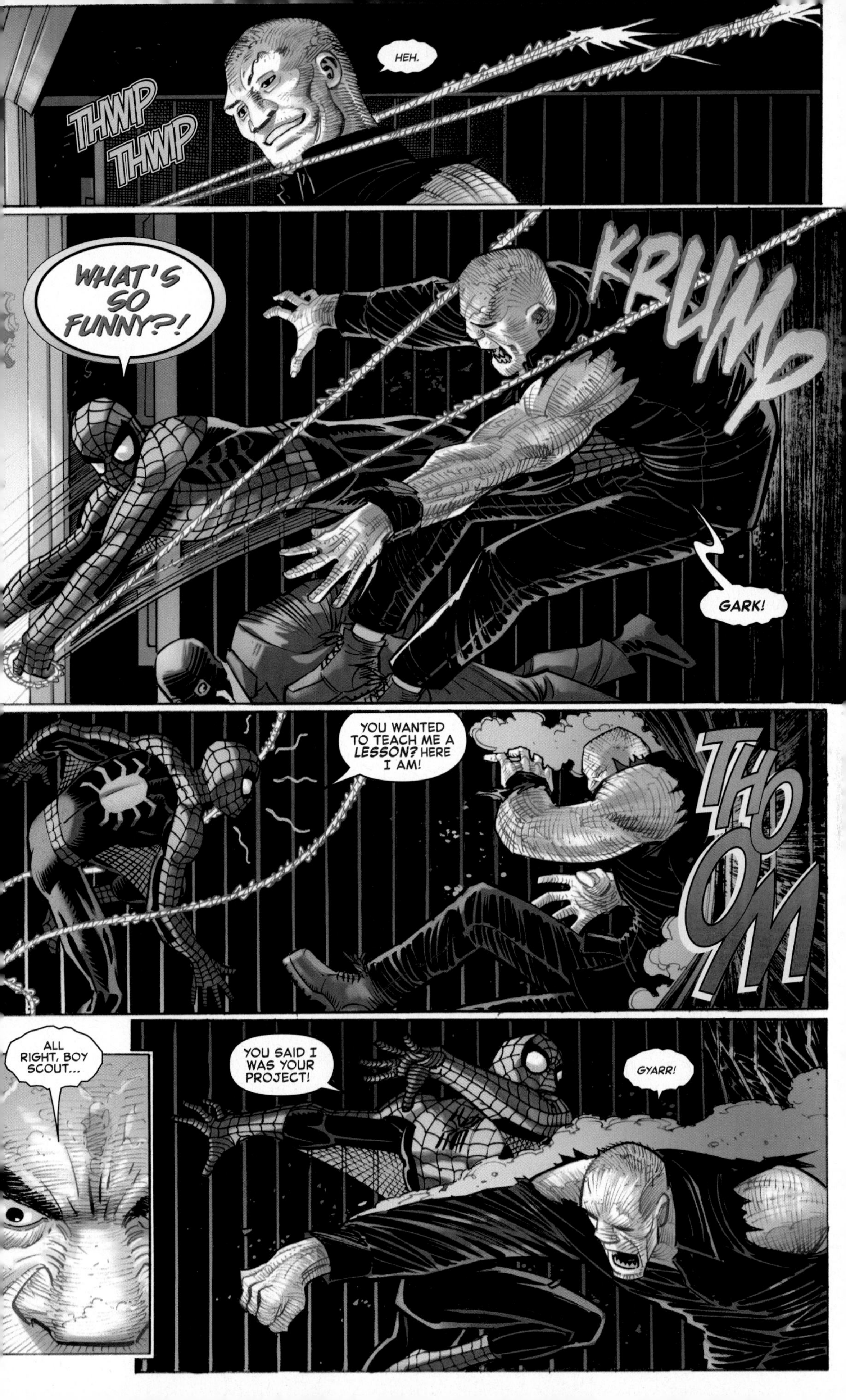
THWIP
THWIP
HEH.
WHAT'S SO FUNNY?!
KRUMP
GARK!
YOU WANTED TO TEACH ME A LESSON? HERE I AM!
THOOM
ALL RIGHT, BOY SCOUT...
YOU SAID I WAS YOUR PROJECT!
GYARR!

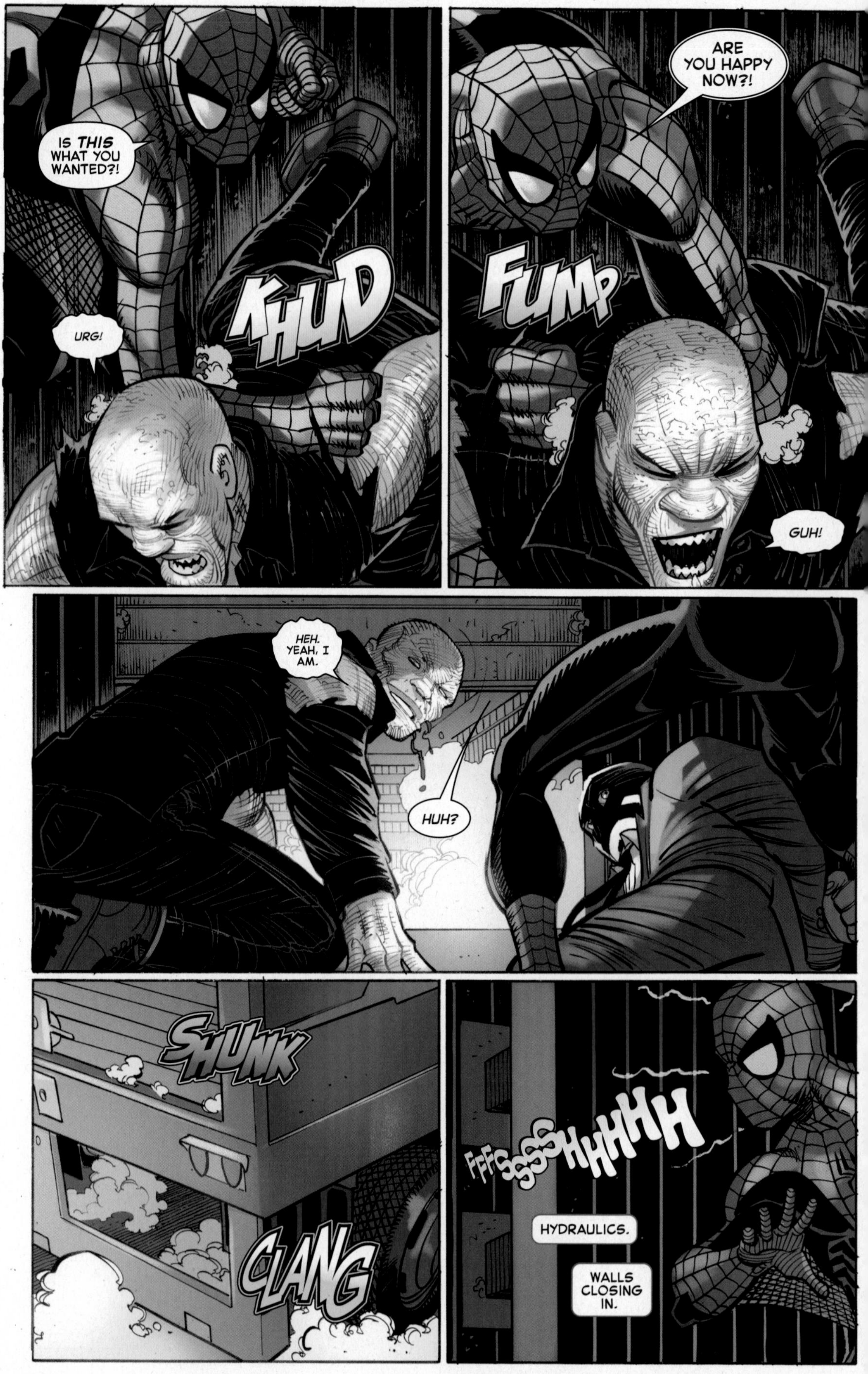
IS THIS WHAT YOU WANTED?!
KHUD
URG!
ARE YOU HAPPY NOW?!
FUMP
GUH!
HEH. YEAH, I AM.
HUH?
SHUNK
CLANG
FFFSSSSHHHHHH
HYDRAULICS.
WALLS CLOSING IN.

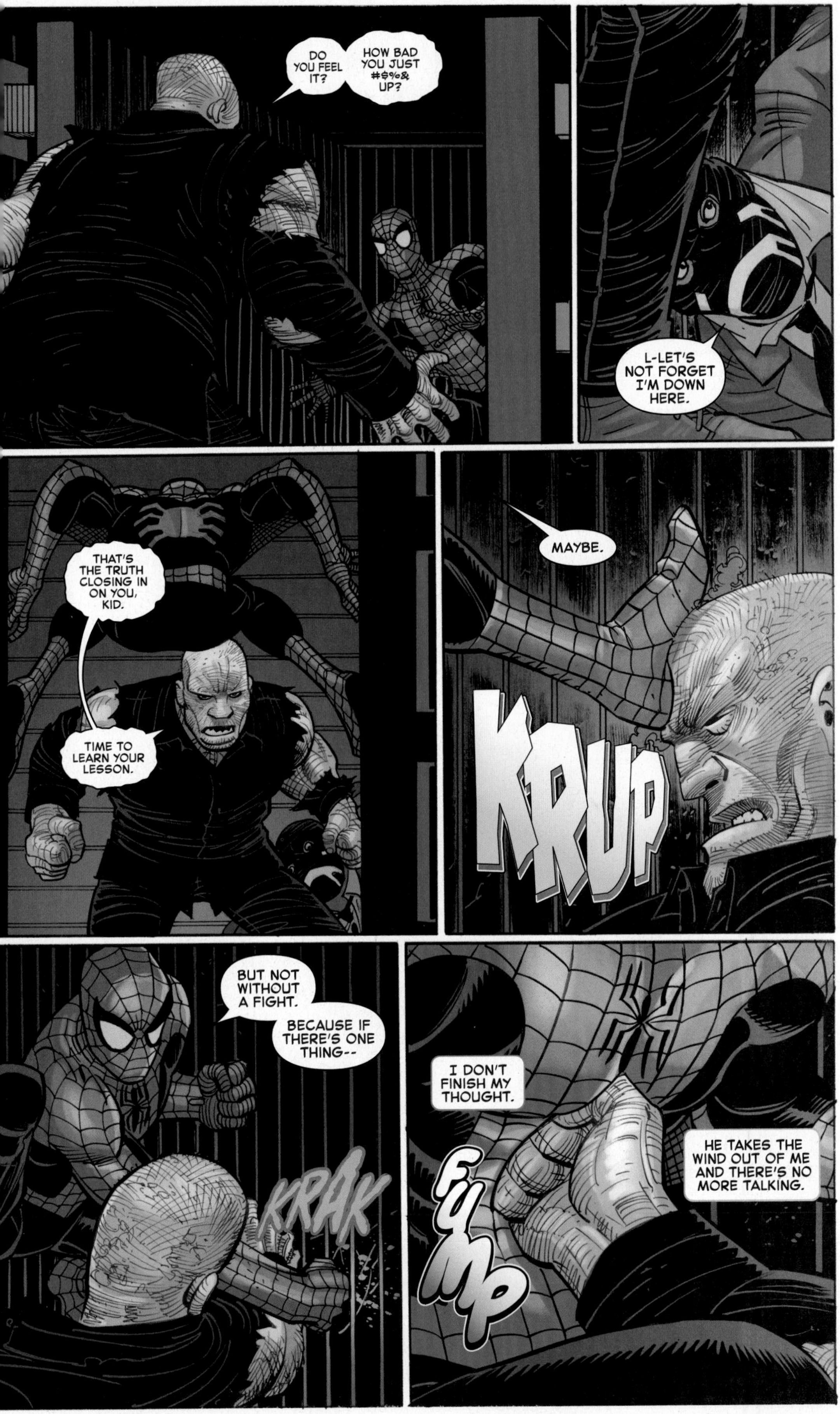
DO YOU FEEL IT?
HOW BAD YOU JUST #$%& UP?
L-LET'S NOT FORGET I'M DOWN HERE.
THAT'S THE TRUTH CLOSING IN ON YOU, KID.
TIME TO LEARN YOUR LESSON.
MAYBE.
KRUP
BUT NOT WITHOUT A FIGHT.
BECAUSE IF THERE'S ONE THING--
KRAK
I DON'T FINISH MY THOUGHT.
FUMP
HE TAKES THE WIND OUT OF ME AND THERE'S NO MORE TALKING.

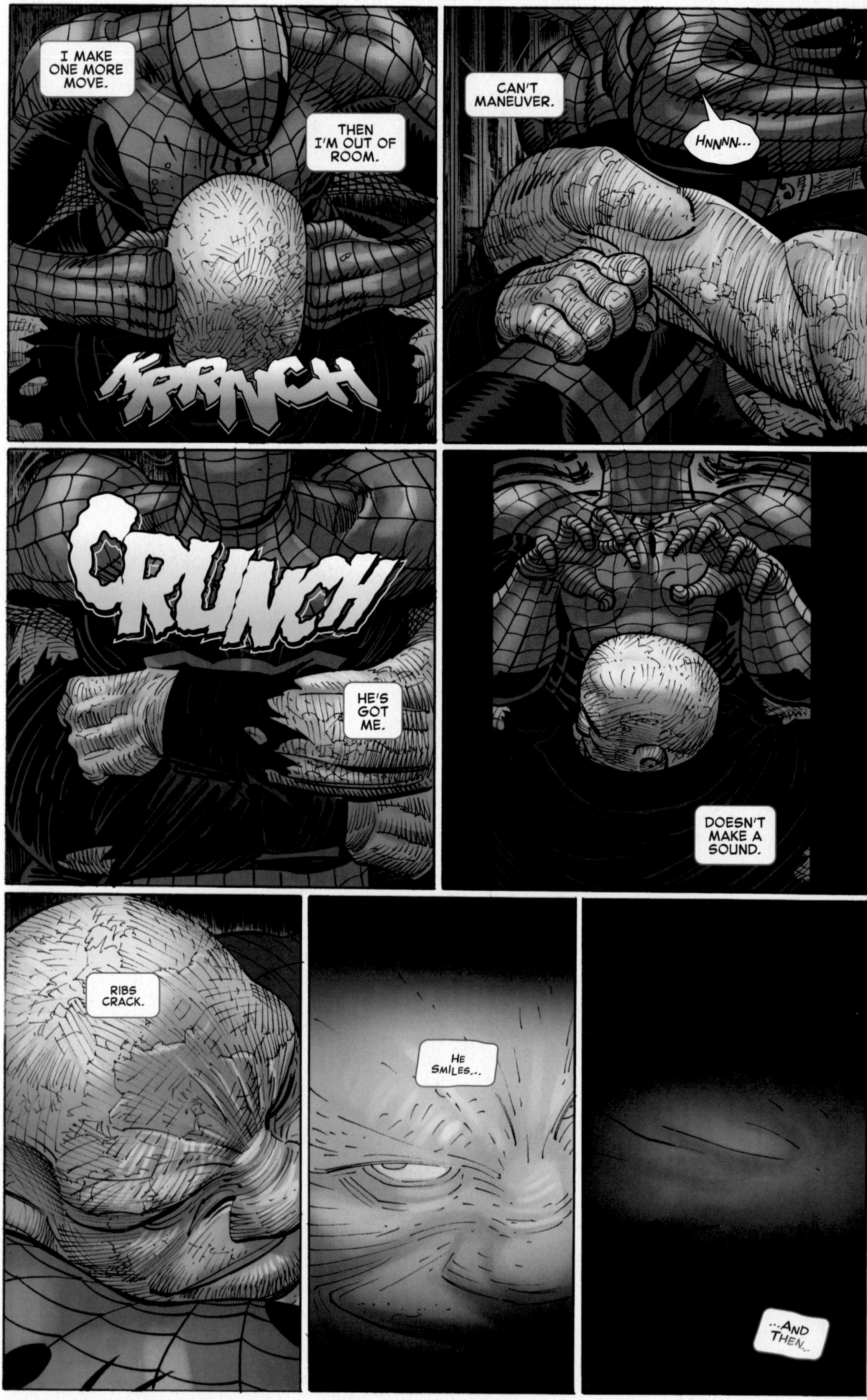
I MAKE ONE MORE MOVE.
THEN I'M OUT OF ROOM.
KRRNCH
CAN'T MANEUVER.
HNNNN...
CRUNCH
HE'S GOT ME.
DOESN'T MAKE A SOUND.
RIBS CRACK.
HE SMILES...
...AND THEN...

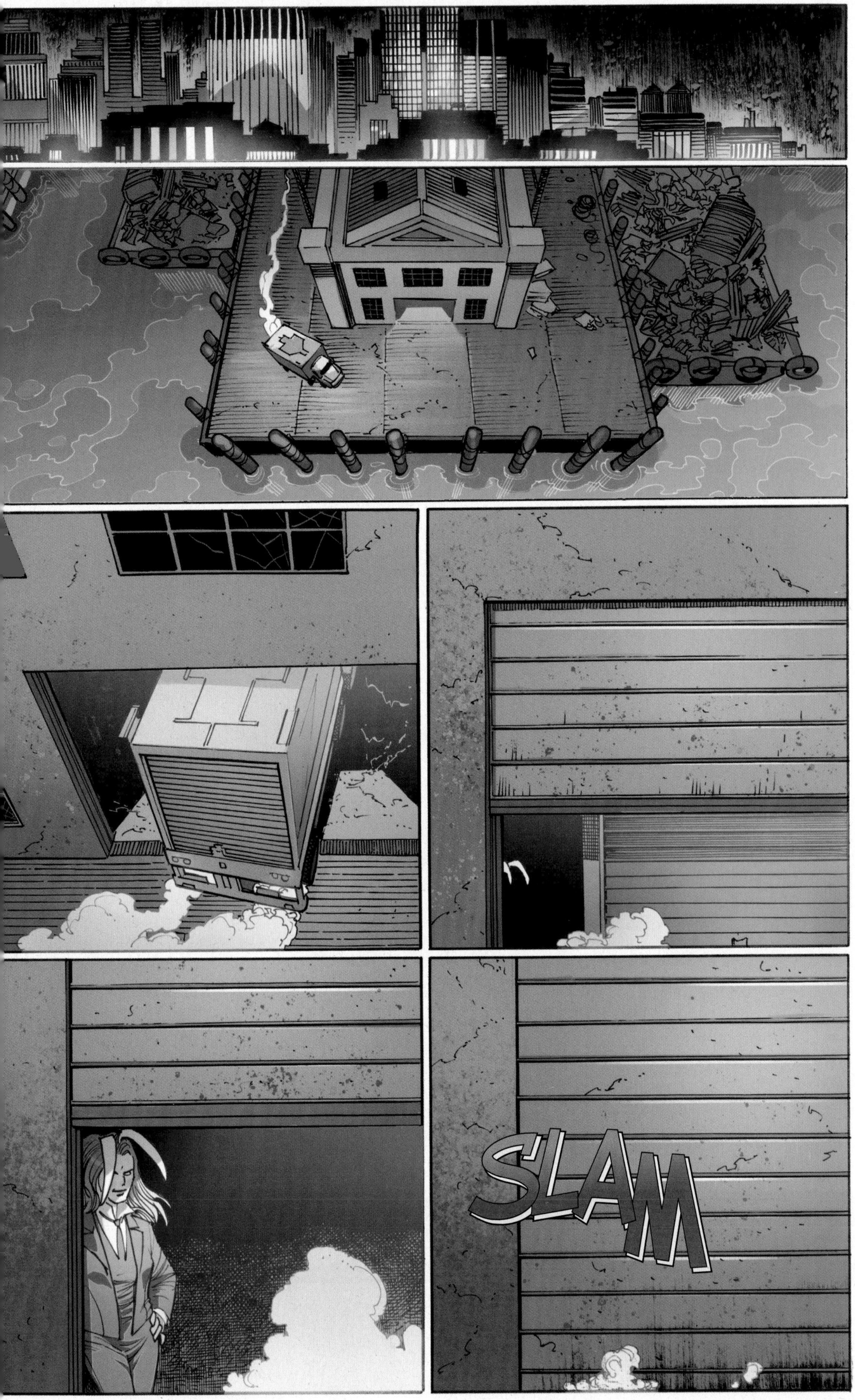
SLAM

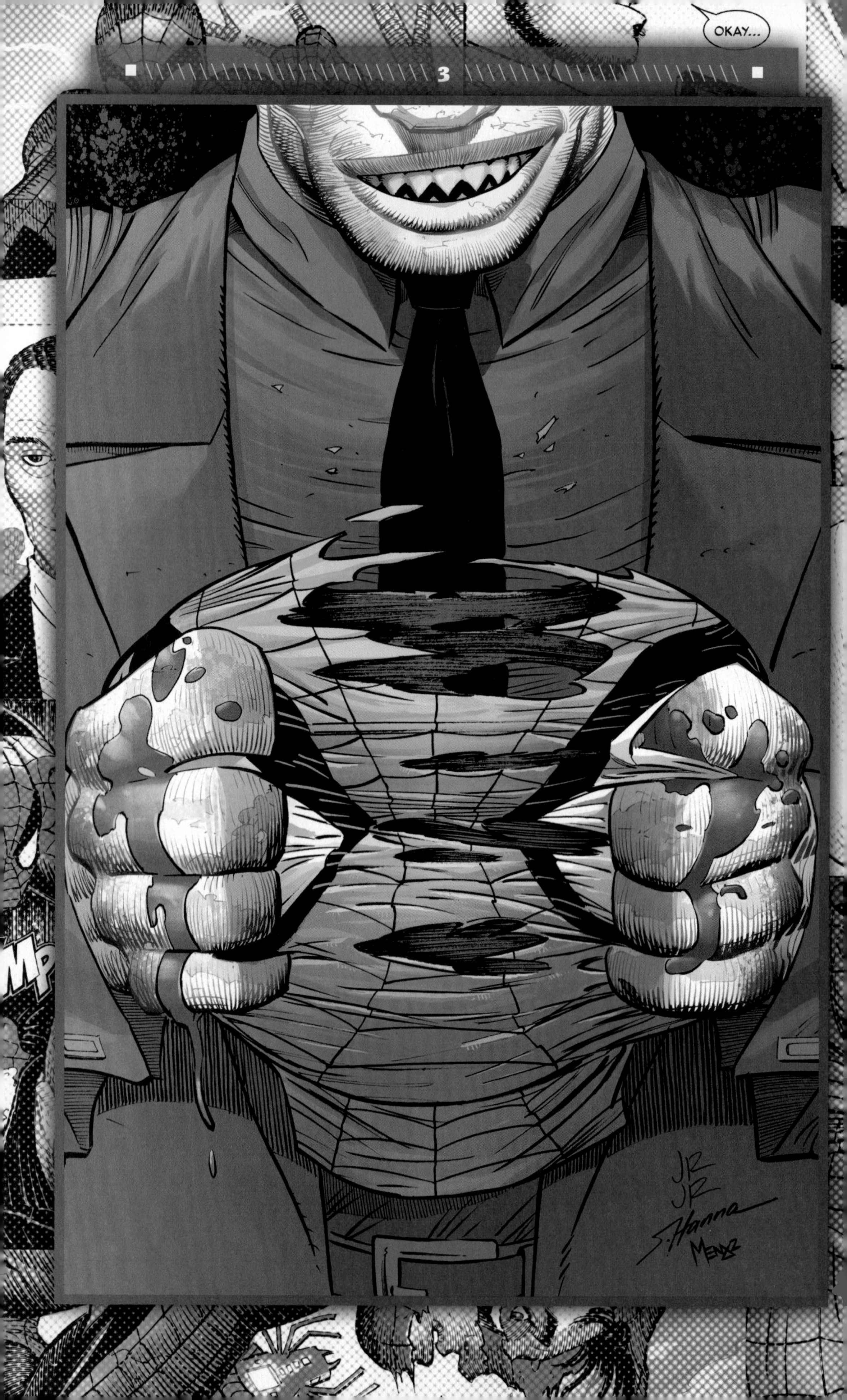
OKAY...
3

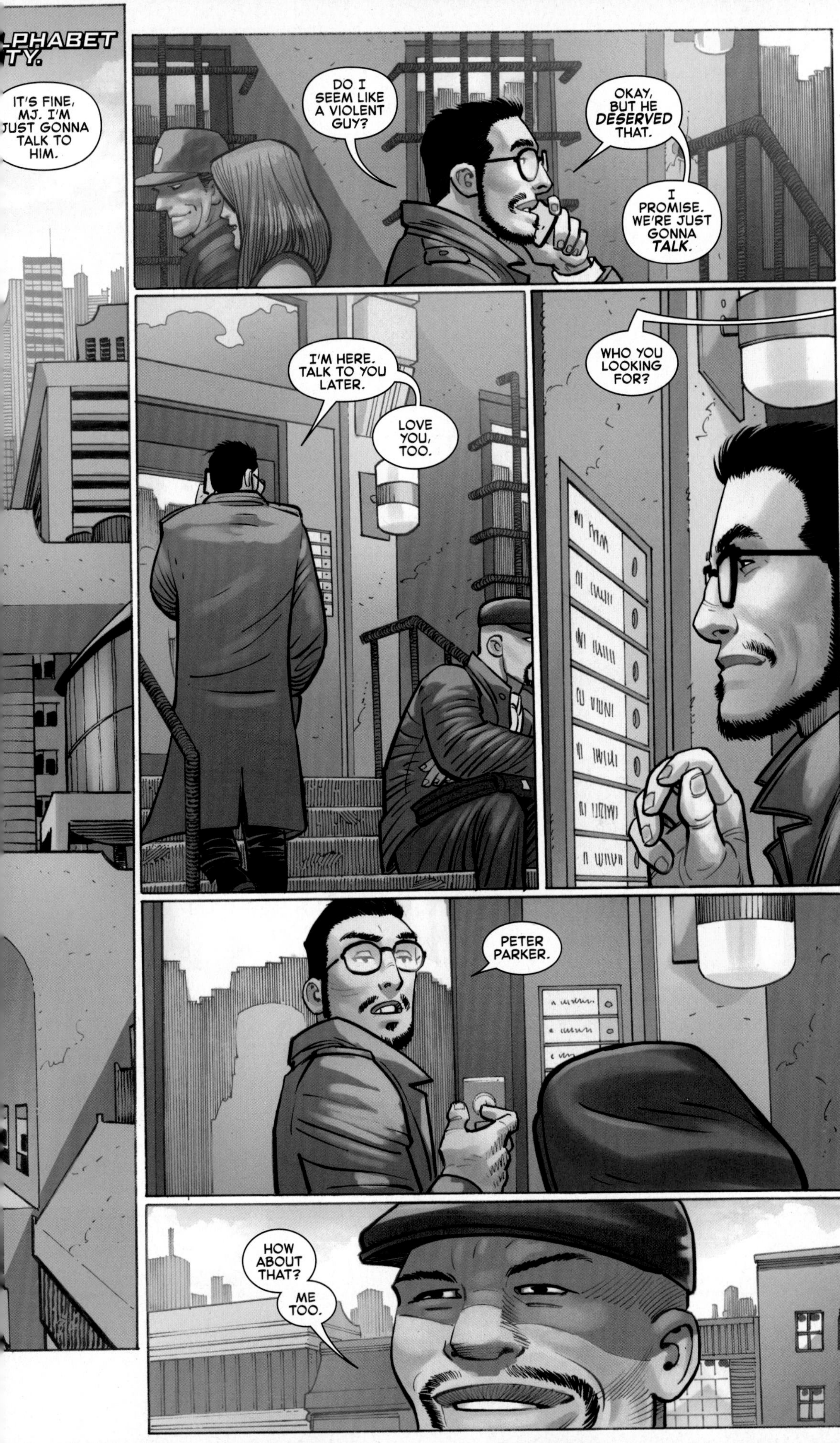
LPHABET
TY.
IT'S FINE, MJ. I'M JUST GONNA TALK TO HIM.
DO I SEEM LIKE A VIOLENT GUY?
OKAY, BUT HE DESERVED THAT.
I PROMISE. WE'RE JUST GONNA TALK.
I'M HERE. TALK TO YOU LATER.
LOVE YOU, TOO.
WHO YOU LOOKING FOR?
PETER PARKER.
HOW ABOUT THAT?
ME TOO.

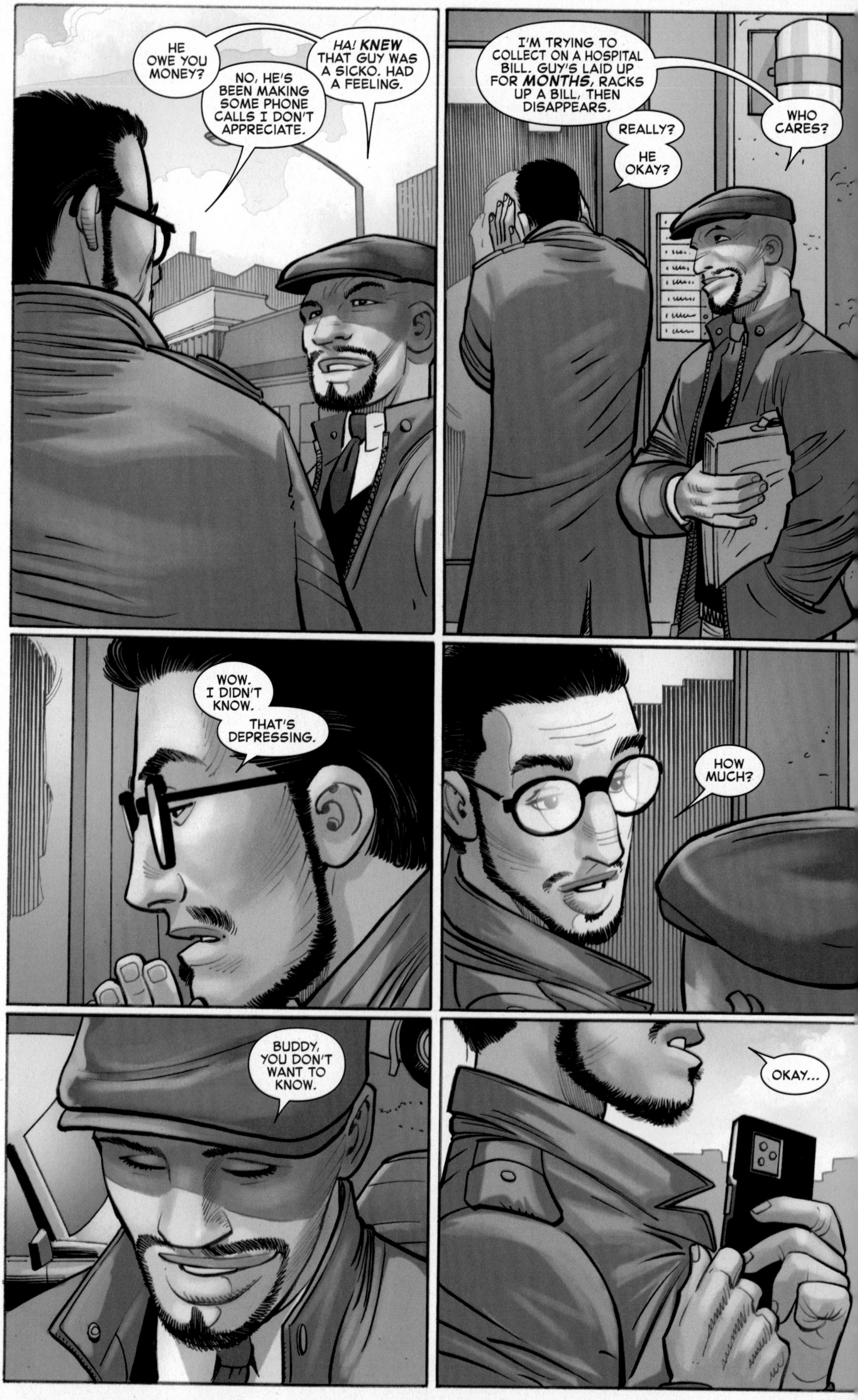
HE OWE YOU MONEY?
NO, HE'S BEEN MAKING SOME PHONE CALLS I DON'T APPRECIATE.
HA! KNEW THAT GUY WAS A SICKO. HAD A FEELING.
I'M TRYING TO COLLECT ON A HOSPITAL BILL. GUY'S LAID UP FOR MONTHS, RACKS UP A BILL, THEN DISAPPEARS.
REALLY?
HE OKAY?
WHO CARES?
WOW. I DIDN'T KNOW.
THAT'S DEPRESSING.
HOW MUCH?
BUDDY, YOU DON'T WANT TO KNOW.
OKAY...

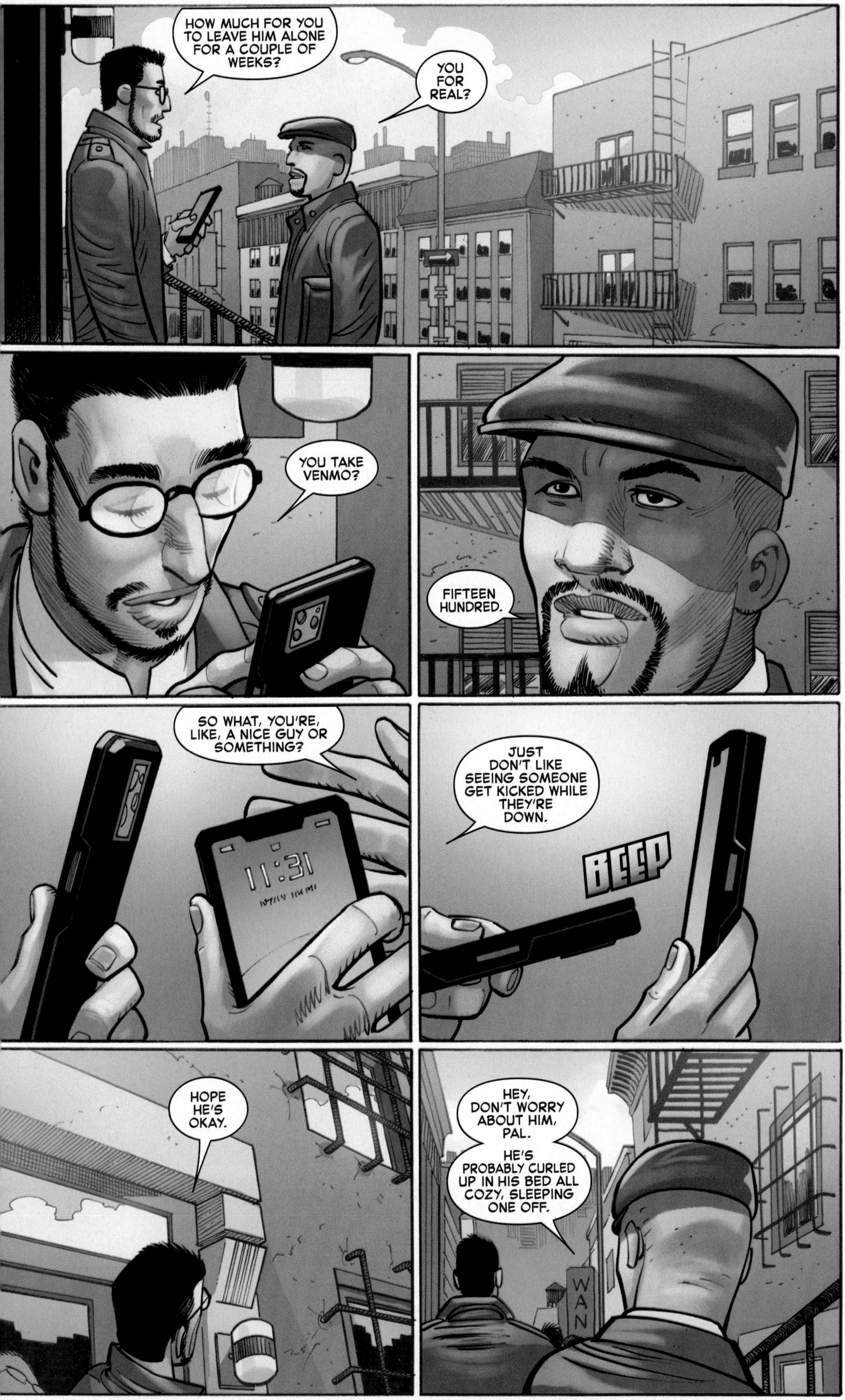
HOW MUCH FOR YOU TO LEAVE HIM ALONE FOR A COUPLE OF WEEKS?
YOU FOR REAL?
YOU TAKE VENMO?
FIFTEEN HUNDRED.
SO WHAT, YOU'RE, LIKE, A NICE GUY OR SOMETHING?
11:31
JUST DON'T LIKE SEEING SOMEONE GET KICKED WHILE THEY'RE DOWN.
BEEP
HOPE HE'S OKAY.
HEY, DON'T WORRY ABOUT HIM, PAL.
HE'S PROBABLY CURLED UP IN HIS BED ALL COZY, SLEEPING ONE OFF.
WAN

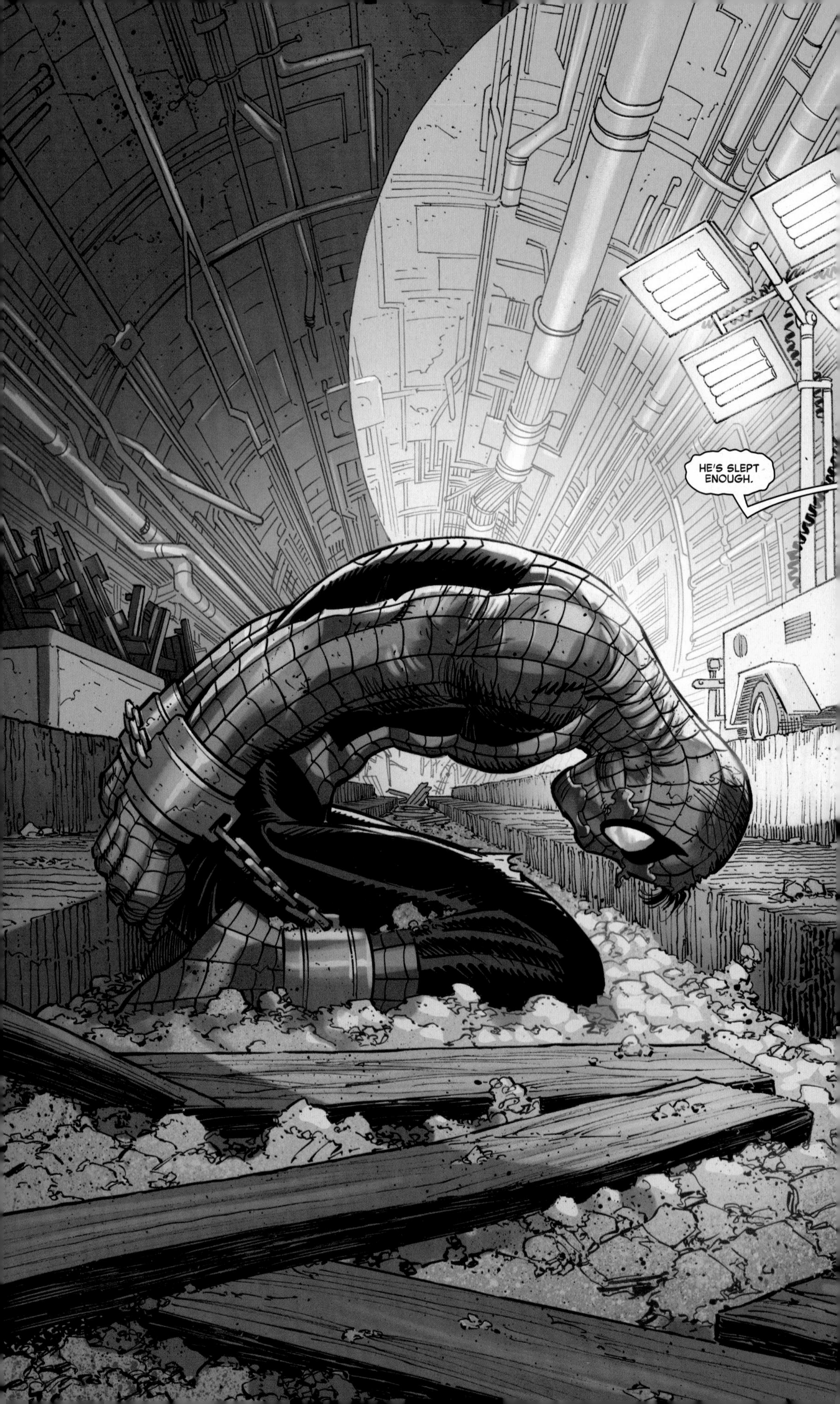
HE'S SLEPT ENOUGH.

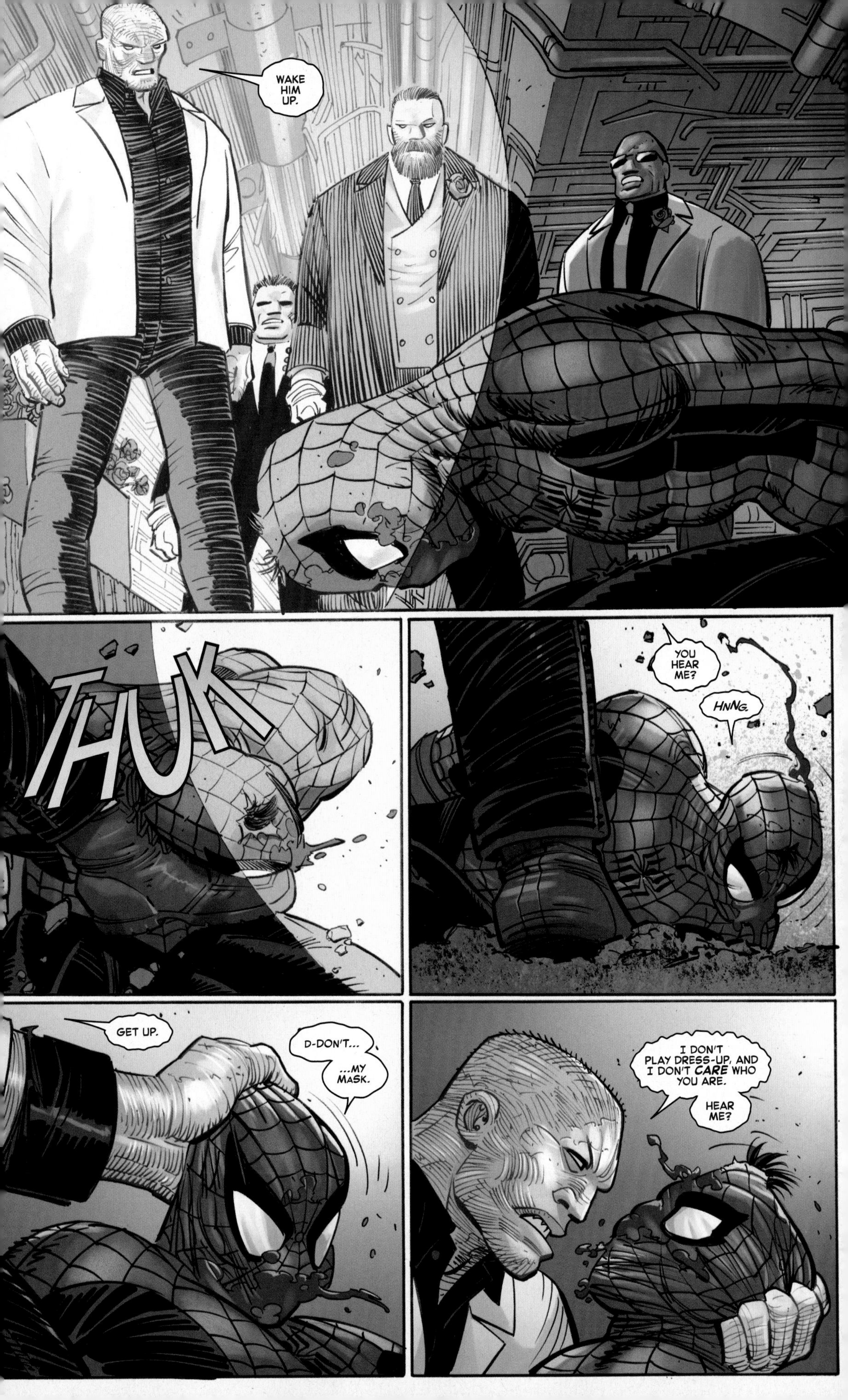
WAKE HIM UP.
THUK
YOU HEAR ME?
HNNG.
GET UP.
D-DON'T...
...MY MASK.
I DON'T PLAY DRESS-UP, AND I DON'T CARE WHO YOU ARE.
HEAR ME?

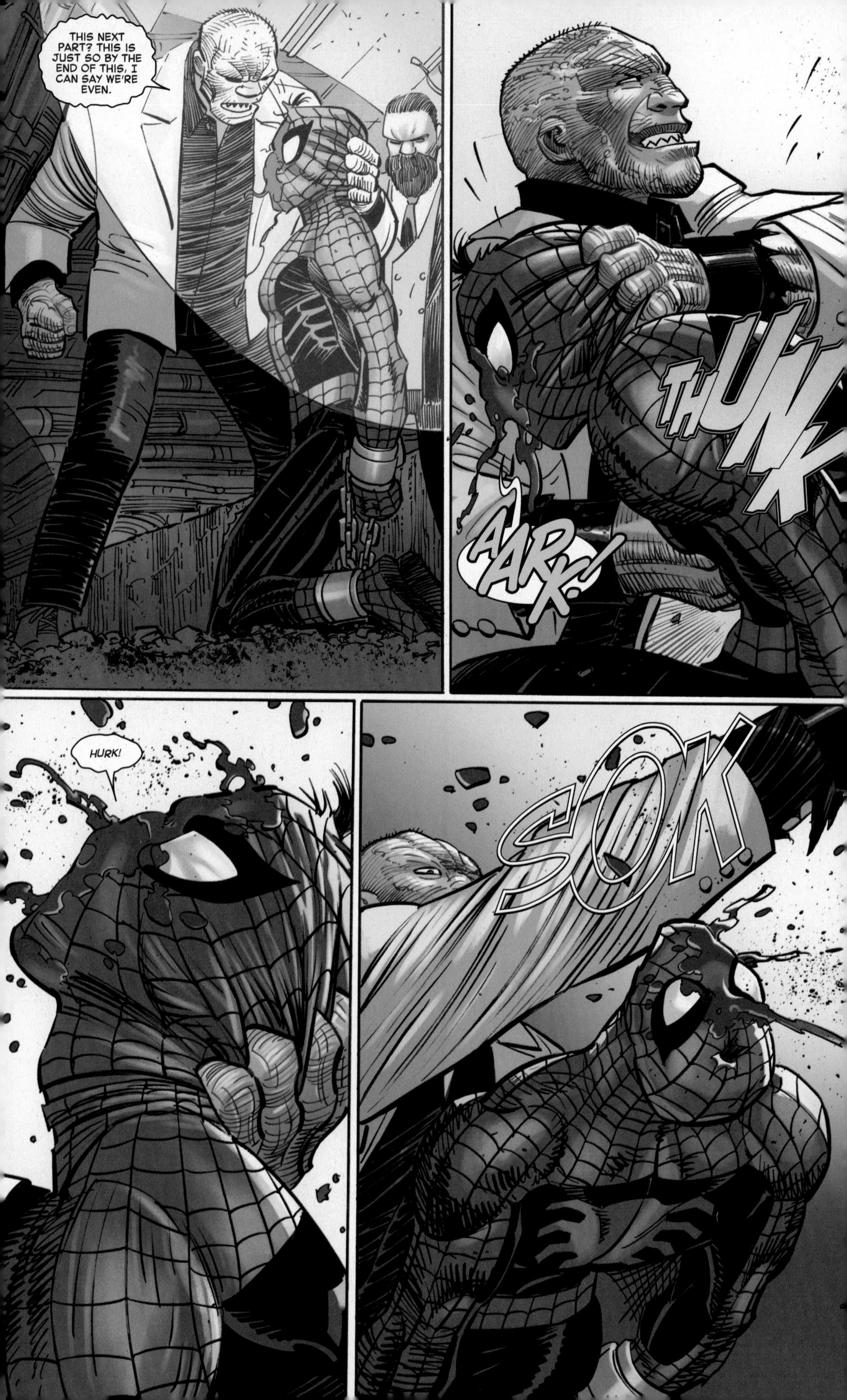
THIS NEXT PART? THIS IS JUST SO BY THE END OF THIS, I CAN SAY WE'RE EVEN.
THUNK
AARK!
HURK!
SOK

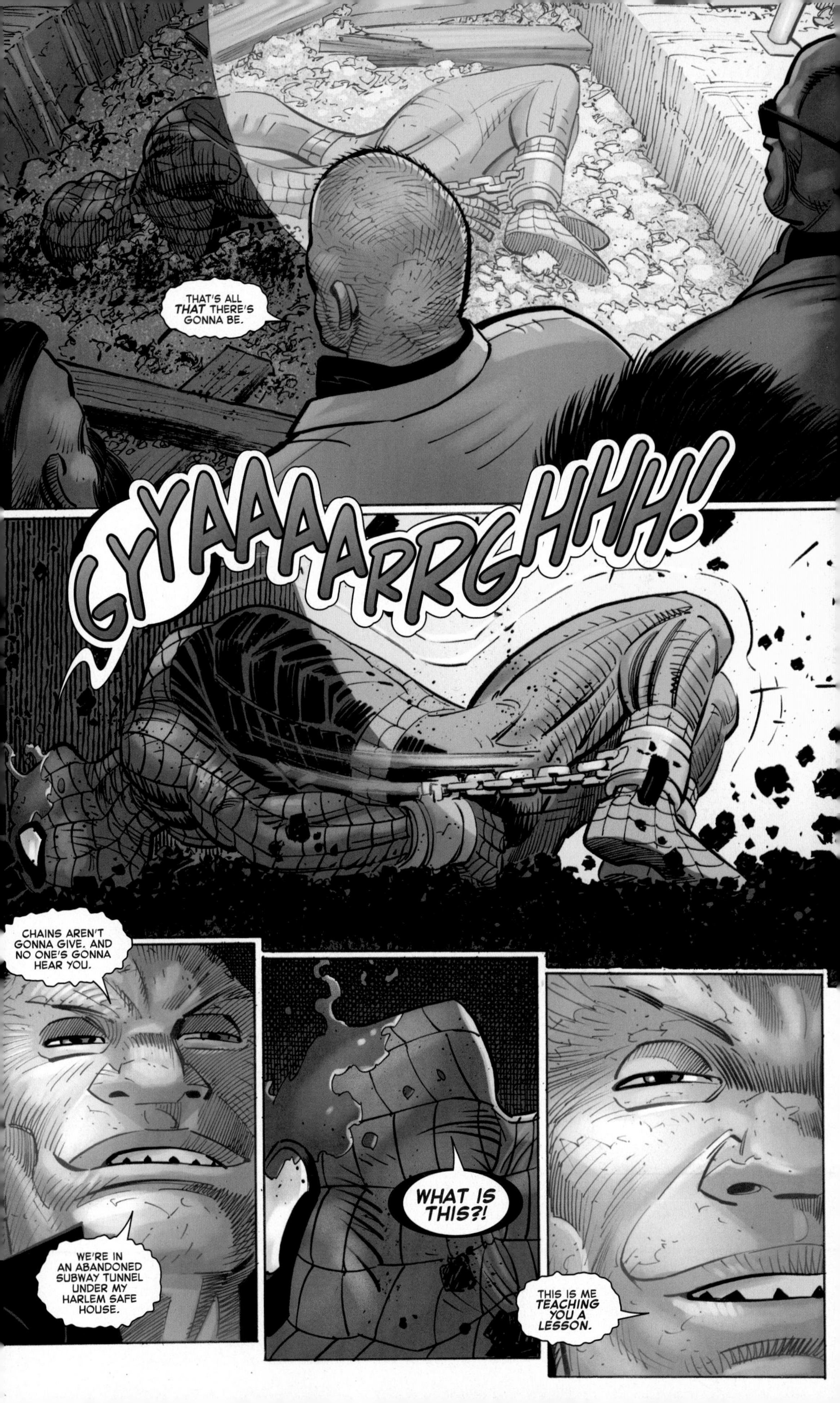
THAT'S ALL THAT THERE'S GONNA BE.
GYAAAARRGHHH!
CHAINS AREN'T GONNA GIVE. AND NO ONE'S GONNA HEAR YOU.
WE'RE IN AN ABANDONED SUBWAY TUNNEL UNDER MY HARLEM SAFE HOUSE.
WHAT IS THIS?!
THIS IS ME TEACHING YOU A LESSON.

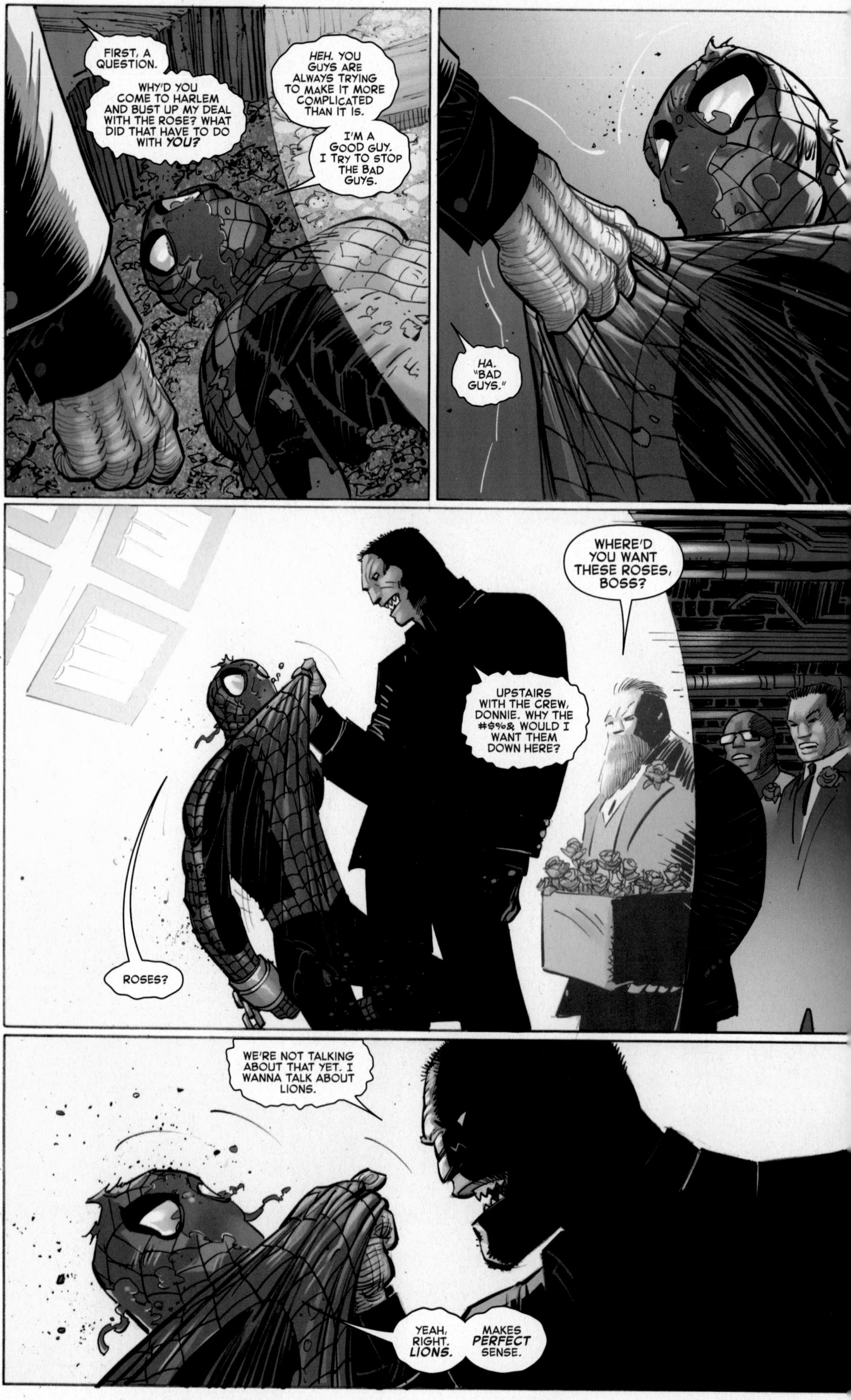

FIRST, A QUESTION.
WHY'D YOU COME TO HARLEM AND BUST UP MY DEAL WITH THE ROSE? WHAT DID THAT HAVE TO DO WITH *YOU?*
HEH. YOU GUYS ARE ALWAYS TRYING TO MAKE IT MORE COMPLICATED THAN IT IS.
I'M A GOOD GUY. I TRY TO STOP THE BAD GUYS.
HA. "BAD GUYS."
WHERE'D YOU WANT THESE ROSES, BOSS?
UPSTAIRS WITH THE CREW, DONNIE. WHY THE #$%& WOULD I WANT THEM DOWN HERE?
ROSES?
WE'RE NOT TALKING ABOUT THAT YET. I WANNA TALK ABOUT LIONS.
YEAH, RIGHT. *LIONS.*
MAKES *PERFECT* SENSE.

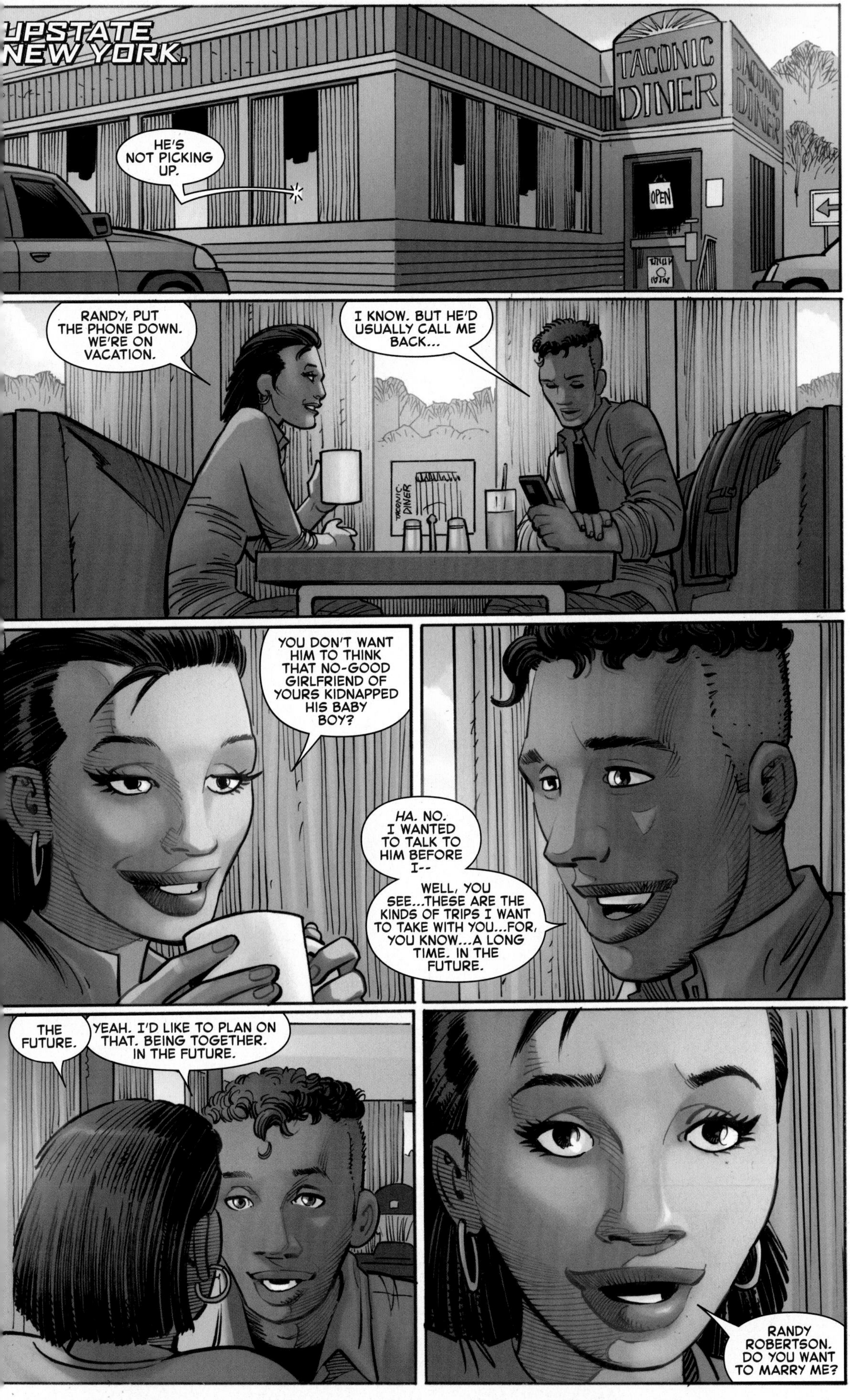
UPSTATE NEW YORK.
TACONIC DINER
HE'S NOT PICKING UP.
OPEN
RANDY, PUT THE PHONE DOWN. WE'RE ON VACATION.
I KNOW. BUT HE'D USUALLY CALL ME BACK...
YOU DON'T WANT HIM TO THINK THAT NO-GOOD GIRLFRIEND OF YOURS KIDNAPPED HIS BABY BOY?
HA. NO. I WANTED TO TALK TO HIM BEFORE I--
WELL, YOU SEE...THESE ARE THE KINDS OF TRIPS I WANT TO TAKE WITH YOU...FOR, YOU KNOW...A LONG TIME. IN THE FUTURE.
THE FUTURE.
YEAH. I'D LIKE TO PLAN ON THAT. BEING TOGETHER. IN THE FUTURE.
RANDY ROBERTSON. DO YOU WANT TO MARRY ME?

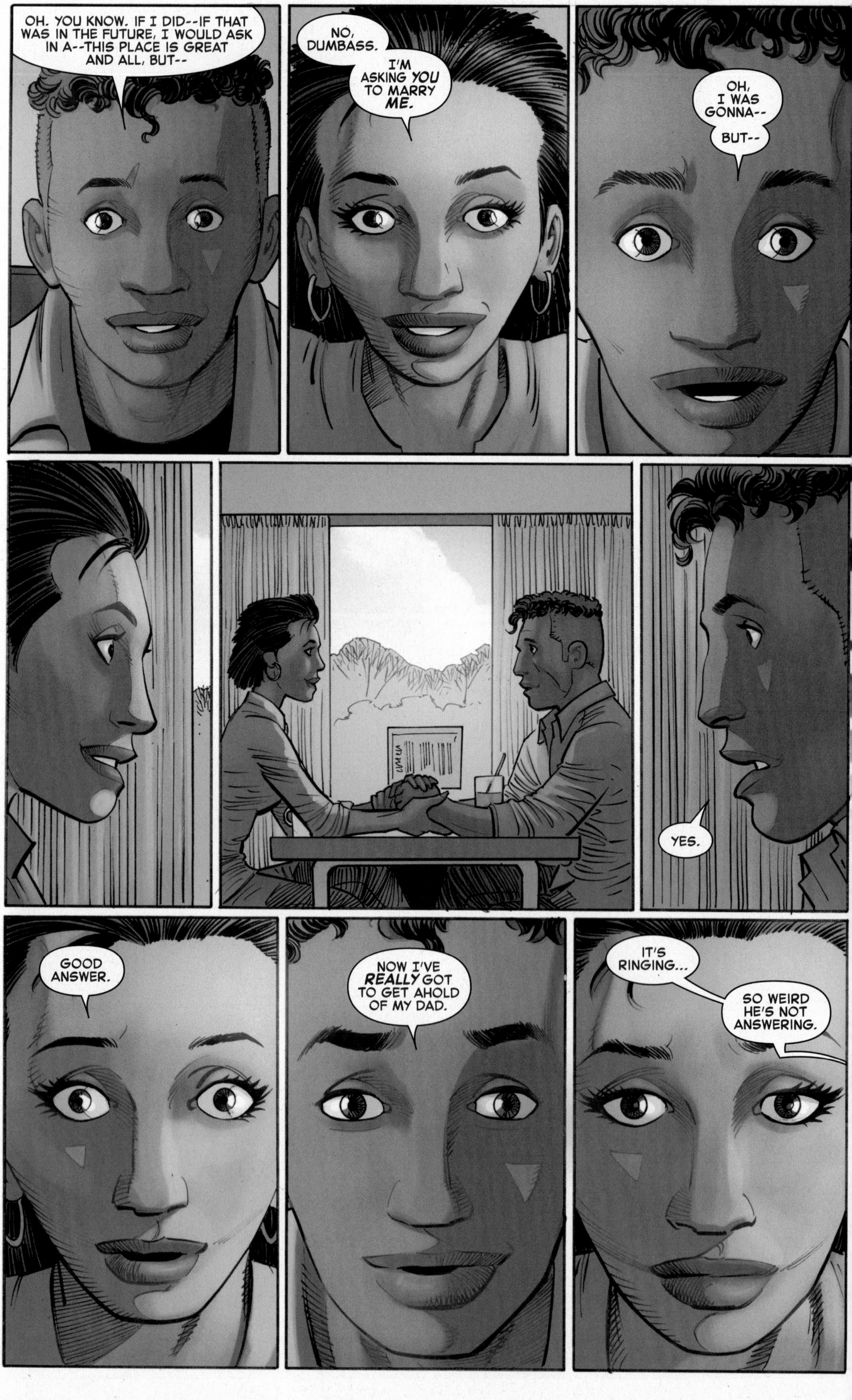
OH. YOU KNOW. IF I DID--IF THAT WAS IN THE FUTURE, I WOULD ASK IN A--THIS PLACE IS GREAT AND ALL, BUT--
NO, DUMBASS.
I'M ASKING *YOU* TO MARRY *ME.*
OH, I WAS GONNA--
BUT--
YES.
GOOD ANSWER.
NOW I'VE ***REALLY*** GOT TO GET AHOLD OF MY DAD.
IT'S RINGING...
SO WEIRD HE'S NOT ANSWERING.

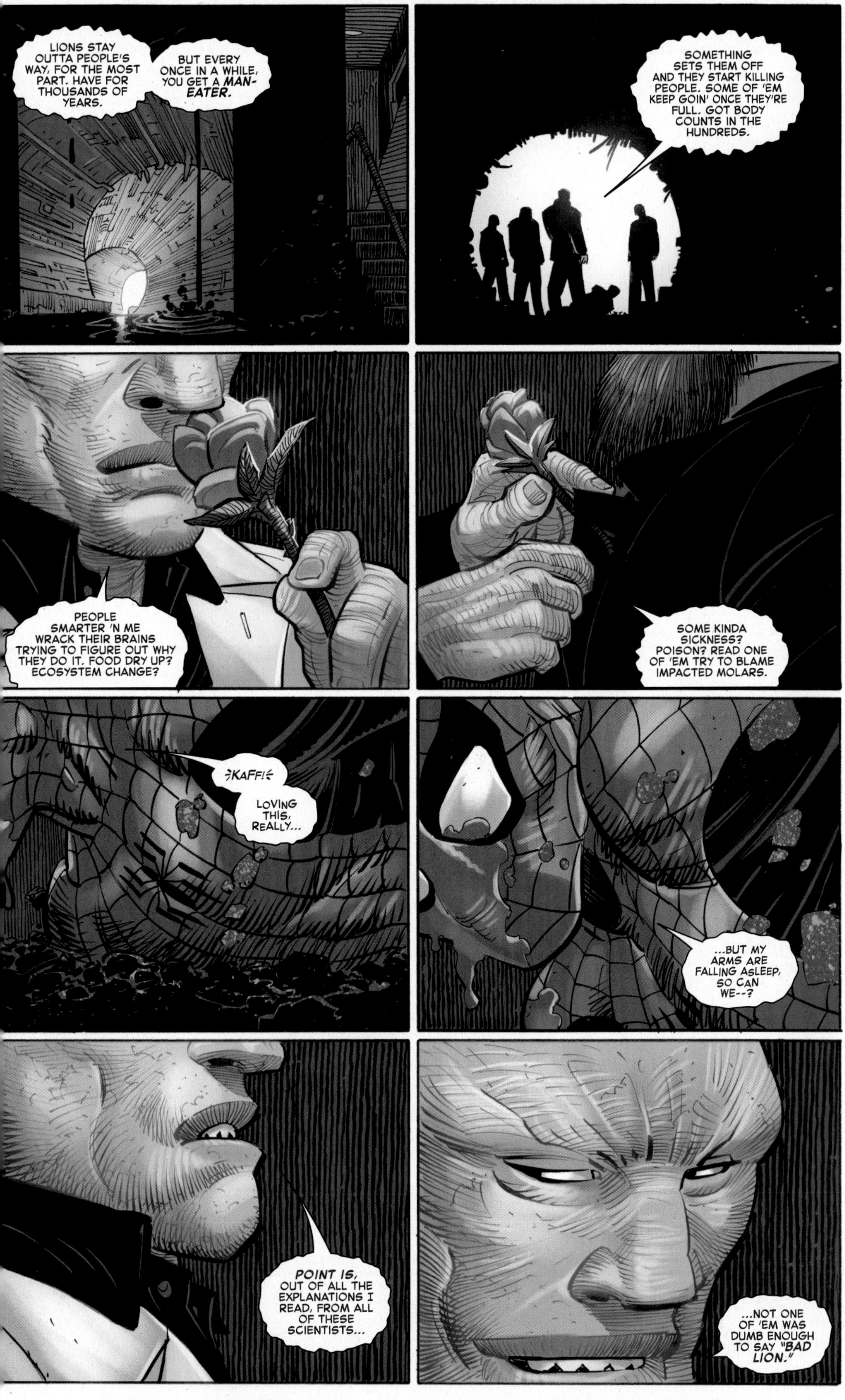
LIONS STAY OUTTA PEOPLE'S WAY, FOR THE MOST PART. HAVE FOR THOUSANDS OF YEARS.
BUT EVERY ONCE IN A WHILE, YOU GET A *MAN-EATER.*
SOMETHING SETS THEM OFF AND THEY START KILLING PEOPLE. SOME OF 'EM KEEP GOIN' ONCE THEY'RE FULL. GOT BODY COUNTS IN THE HUNDREDS.
PEOPLE SMARTER 'N ME WRACK THEIR BRAINS TRYING TO FIGURE OUT WHY THEY DO IT. FOOD DRY UP? ECOSYSTEM CHANGE?
SOME KINDA SICKNESS? POISON? READ ONE OF 'EM TRY TO BLAME IMPACTED MOLARS.
KAFF!
LOVING THIS, REALLY...
...BUT MY ARMS ARE FALLING ASLEEP, SO CAN WE--?
POINT IS, OUT OF ALL THE EXPLANATIONS I READ, FROM ALL OF THESE SCIENTISTS...
...NOT ONE OF 'EM WAS DUMB ENOUGH TO SAY *"BAD LION."*

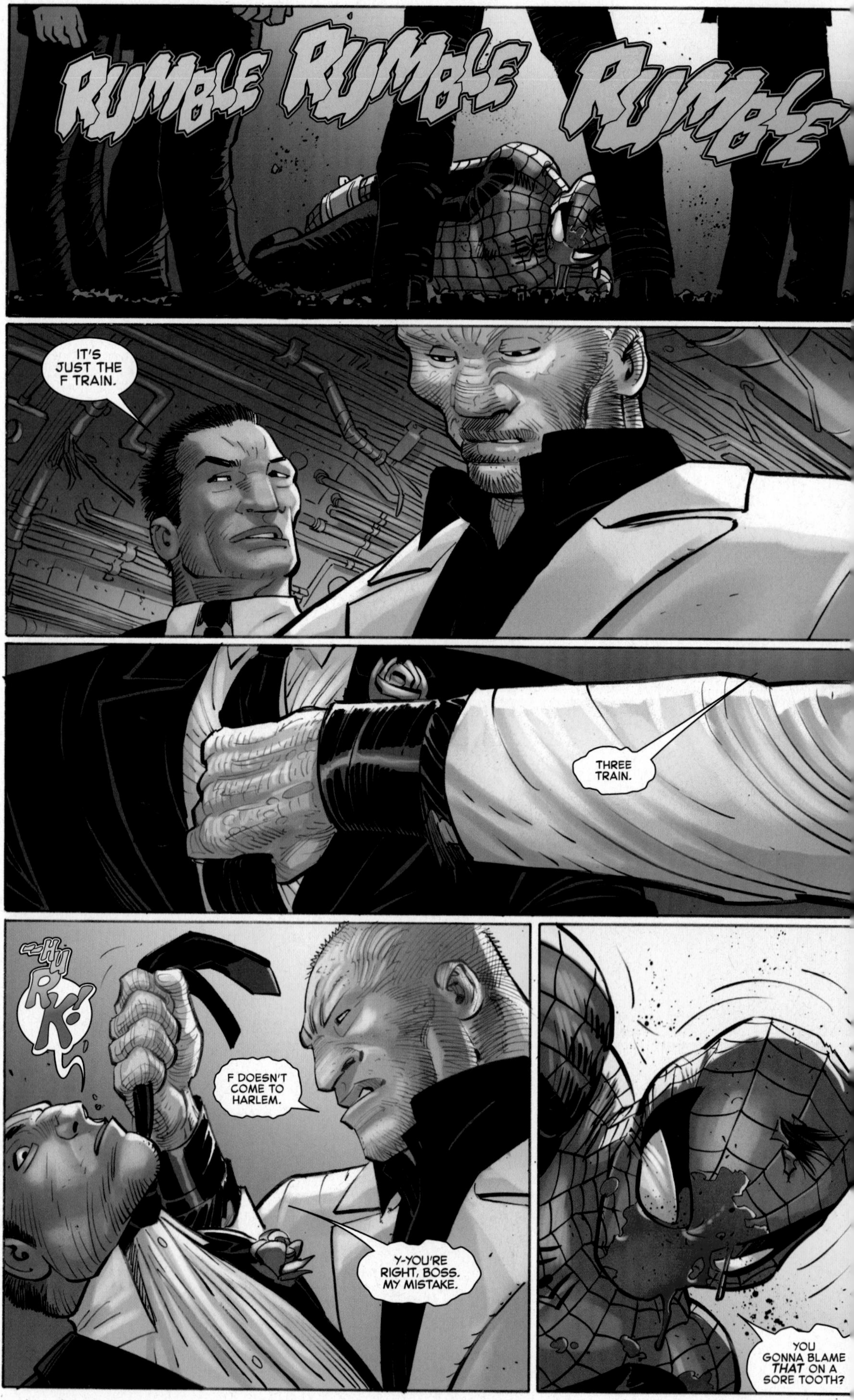
RUMBLE RUMBLE RUMBLE
IT'S JUST THE F TRAIN.
THREE TRAIN.
HURK!
F DOESN'T COME TO HARLEM.
Y-YOU'RE RIGHT, BOSS. MY MISTAKE.
YOU GONNA BLAME *THAT* ON A SORE TOOTH?

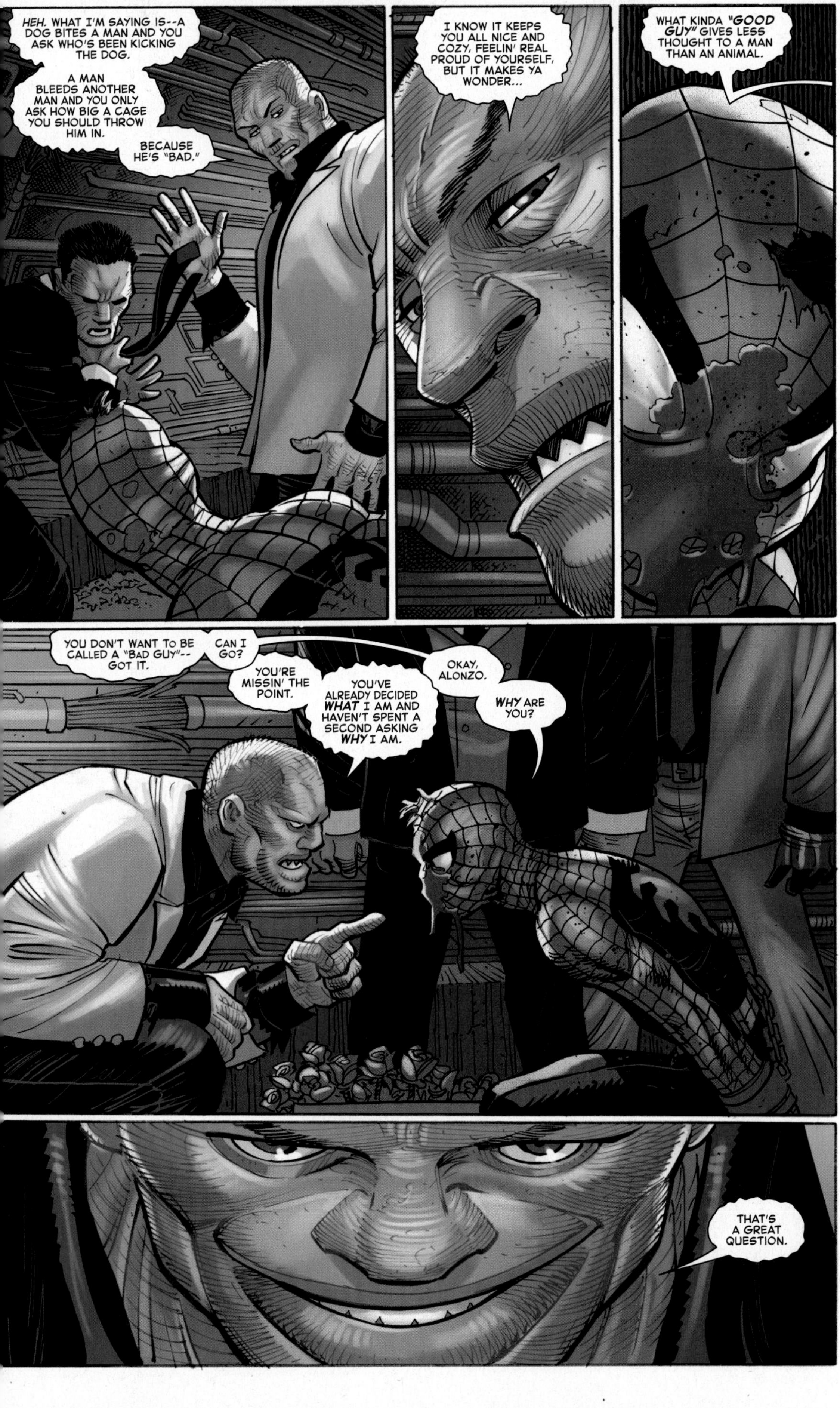
HEH. WHAT I'M SAYING IS--A DOG BITES A MAN AND YOU ASK WHO'S BEEN KICKING THE DOG.
A MAN BLEEDS ANOTHER MAN AND YOU ONLY ASK HOW BIG A CAGE YOU SHOULD THROW HIM IN.
BECAUSE HE'S "BAD."
I KNOW IT KEEPS YOU ALL NICE AND COZY, FEELIN' REAL PROUD OF YOURSELF, BUT IT MAKES YA WONDER...
WHAT KINDA "GOOD GUY" GIVES LESS THOUGHT TO A MAN THAN AN ANIMAL.
YOU DON'T WANT TO BE CALLED A "BAD GUY"--GOT IT.
CAN I GO?
YOU'RE MISSIN' THE POINT.
YOU'VE ALREADY DECIDED WHAT I AM AND HAVEN'T SPENT A SECOND ASKING WHY I AM.
OKAY, ALONZO.
WHY ARE YOU?
THAT'S A GREAT QUESTION.

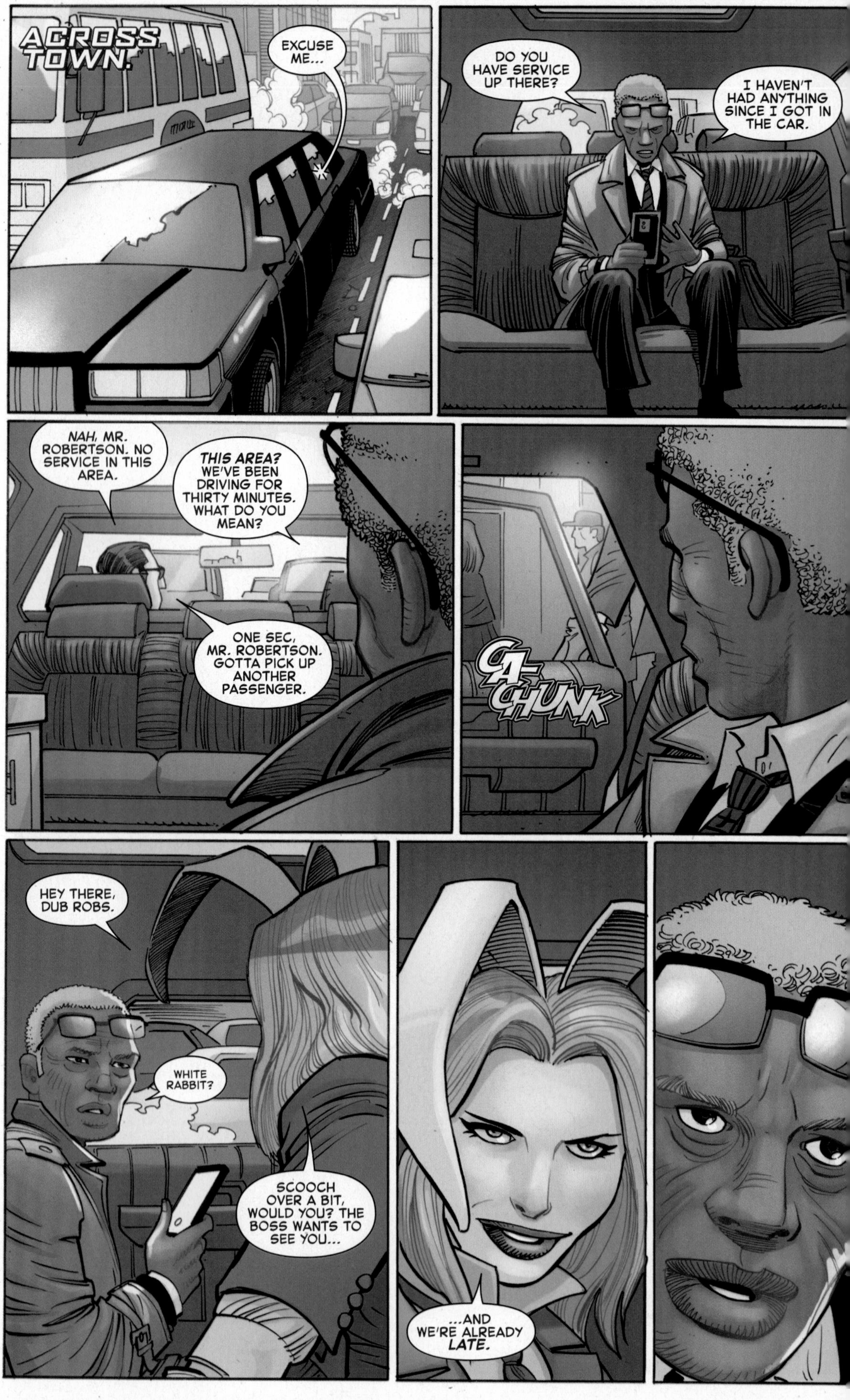
ACROSS TOWN.
EXCUSE ME...
DO YOU HAVE SERVICE UP THERE?
I HAVEN'T HAD ANYTHING SINCE I GOT IN THE CAR.
NAH, MR. ROBERTSON. NO SERVICE IN THIS AREA.
THIS AREA? WE'VE BEEN DRIVING FOR THIRTY MINUTES. WHAT DO YOU MEAN?
ONE SEC, MR. ROBERTSON. GOTTA PICK UP ANOTHER PASSENGER.
CA-CHUNK
HEY THERE, DUB ROBS.
WHITE RABBIT?
SCOOCH OVER A BIT, WOULD YOU? THE BOSS WANTS TO SEE YOU...
...AND WE'RE ALREADY LATE.

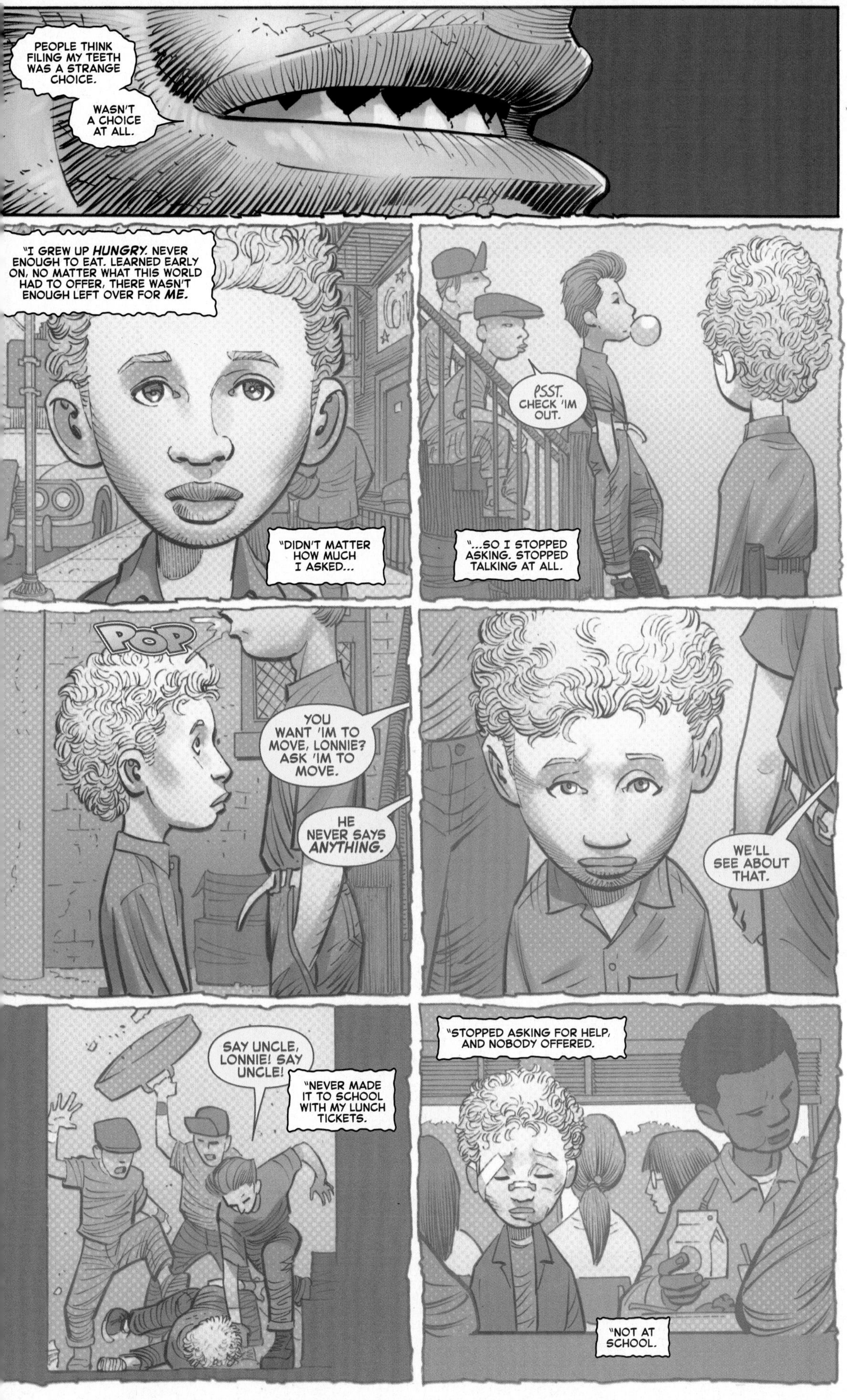
PEOPLE THINK FILING MY TEETH WAS A STRANGE CHOICE.
WASN'T A CHOICE AT ALL.
"I GREW UP HUNGRY. NEVER ENOUGH TO EAT. LEARNED EARLY ON, NO MATTER WHAT THIS WORLD HAD TO OFFER, THERE WASN'T ENOUGH LEFT OVER FOR ME.
"DIDN'T MATTER HOW MUCH I ASKED...
PSST. CHECK 'IM OUT.
"...SO I STOPPED ASKING. STOPPED TALKING AT ALL.
POP
YOU WANT 'IM TO MOVE, LONNIE? ASK 'IM TO MOVE.
HE NEVER SAYS ANYTHING.
WE'LL SEE ABOUT THAT.
SAY UNCLE, LONNIE! SAY UNCLE!
"NEVER MADE IT TO SCHOOL WITH MY LUNCH TICKETS.
"STOPPED ASKING FOR HELP, AND NOBODY OFFERED.
"NOT AT SCHOOL.

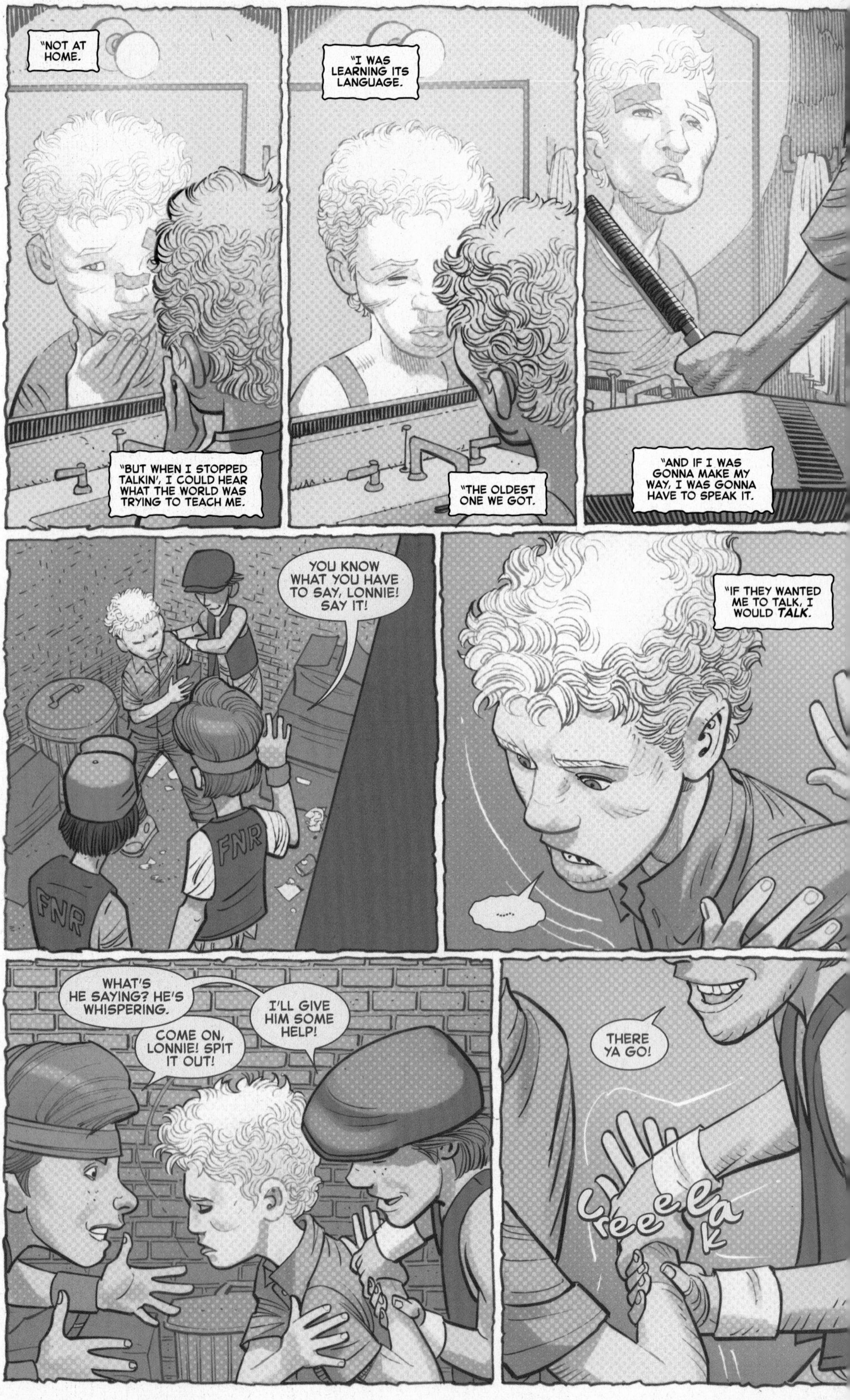
"NOT AT HOME.
"BUT WHEN I STOPPED TALKIN', I COULD HEAR WHAT THE WORLD WAS TRYING TO TEACH ME.
"I WAS LEARNING ITS LANGUAGE.
"THE OLDEST ONE WE GOT.
"AND IF I WAS GONNA MAKE MY WAY, I WAS GONNA HAVE TO SPEAK IT.
YOU KNOW WHAT YOU HAVE TO SAY, LONNIE! SAY IT!
FNR
FNR
"IF THEY WANTED ME TO TALK, I WOULD *TALK*.
WHAT'S HE SAYING? HE'S WHISPERING.
COME ON, LONNIE! SPIT IT OUT!
I'LL GIVE HIM SOME HELP!
THERE YA GO!
Creeelak

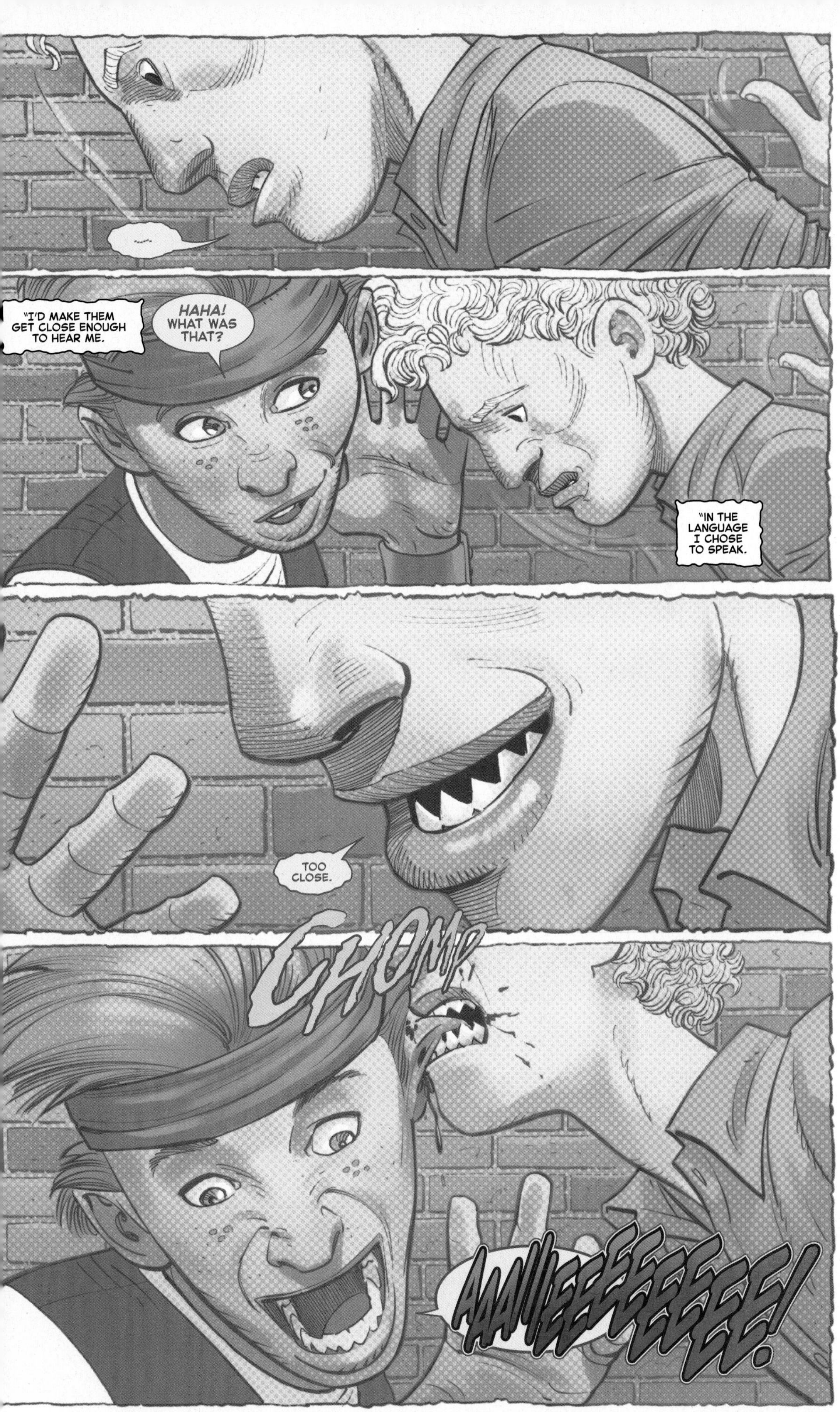
"I'D MAKE THEM GET CLOSE ENOUGH TO HEAR ME.
HAHA! WHAT WAS THAT?
"IN THE LANGUAGE I CHOSE TO SPEAK.
TOO CLOSE.
CHOMP
AAAIIIEEEEEEEEEEE!

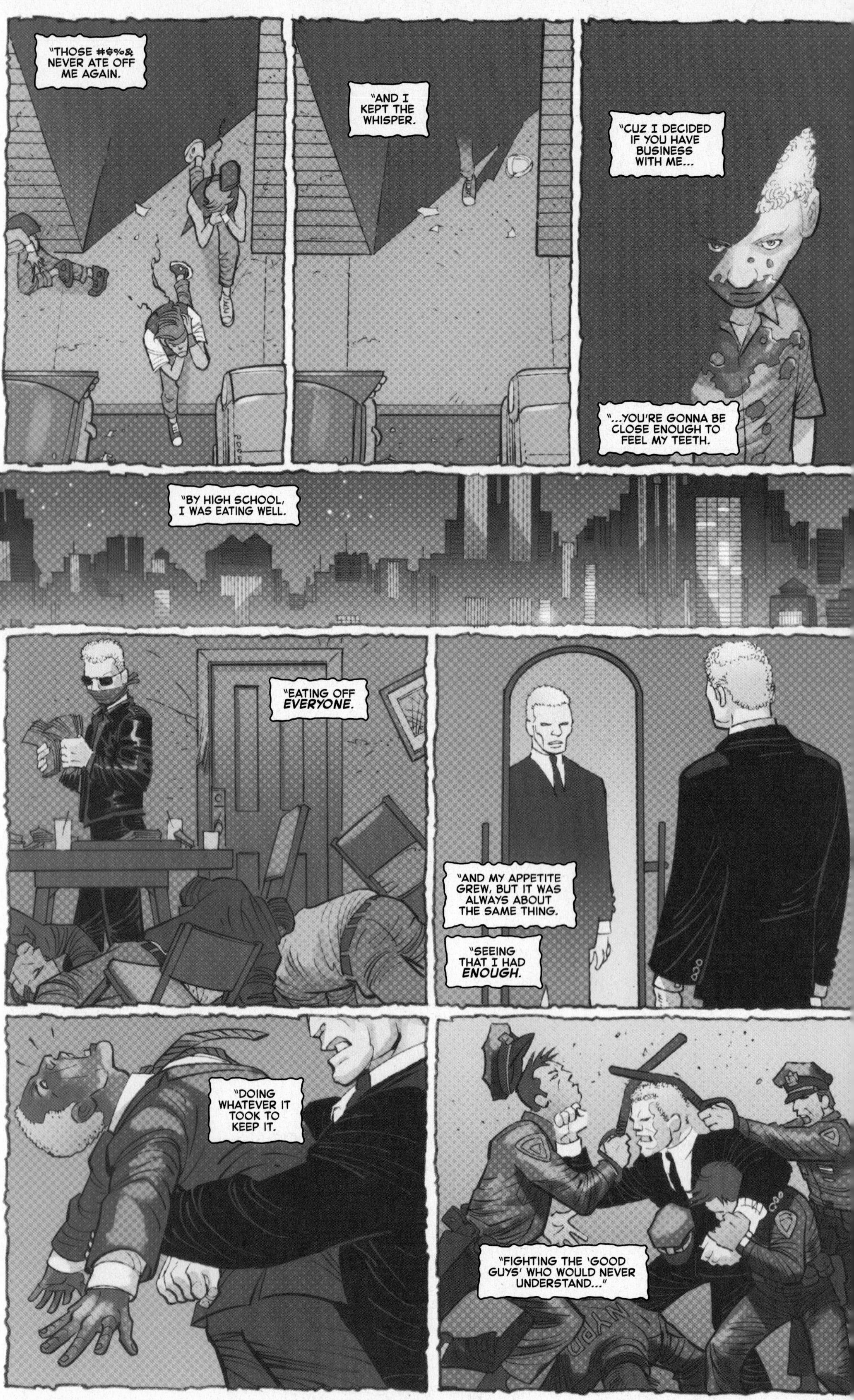
"THOSE #$%& NEVER ATE OFF ME AGAIN.
"AND I KEPT THE WHISPER.
"CUZ I DECIDED IF YOU HAVE BUSINESS WITH ME...
"...YOU'RE GONNA BE CLOSE ENOUGH TO FEEL MY TEETH.
"BY HIGH SCHOOL, I WAS EATING WELL.
"EATING OFF *EVERYONE*.
"AND MY APPETITE GREW, BUT IT WAS ALWAYS ABOUT THE SAME THING.
"SEEING THAT I HAD *ENOUGH*.
"DOING WHATEVER IT TOOK TO KEEP IT.
"FIGHTING THE 'GOOD GUYS' WHO WOULD NEVER UNDERSTAND..."
NYPD

...THAT THERE AIN'T NO SIN A MAN CAN COMMIT IN THE PROCESS OF FEEDING HIMSELF.

WE'RE READY, BOSS.

WHAT'S ALL THIS? THE ROSE'S MEN?

HA. THAT'S JUST WHAT ALL YOUR FRIENDS ARE GONNA THINK.

SEE, A *GOOD GUY* GOT ME INTO THIS MESS, AND THE *GOOD GUYS* ARE GONNA GET ME OUT OF IT.

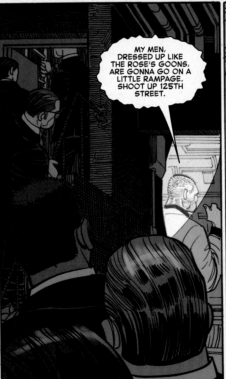

MY MEN, DRESSED UP LIKE THE ROSE'S GOONS, ARE GONNA GO ON A LITTLE RAMPAGE. SHOOT UP 125TH STREET.

AS FAR AS ANYONE WILL KNOW, THE ROSE WILL HAVE ORDERED A MASSACRE.

ONE OF *YOUR FRIENDS* WILL SEE THE CARNAGE AND TAKE CARE OF RICHIE FISK FOR ME. CAPTAIN AMERICA. DAREDEVIL. DON'T CARE.

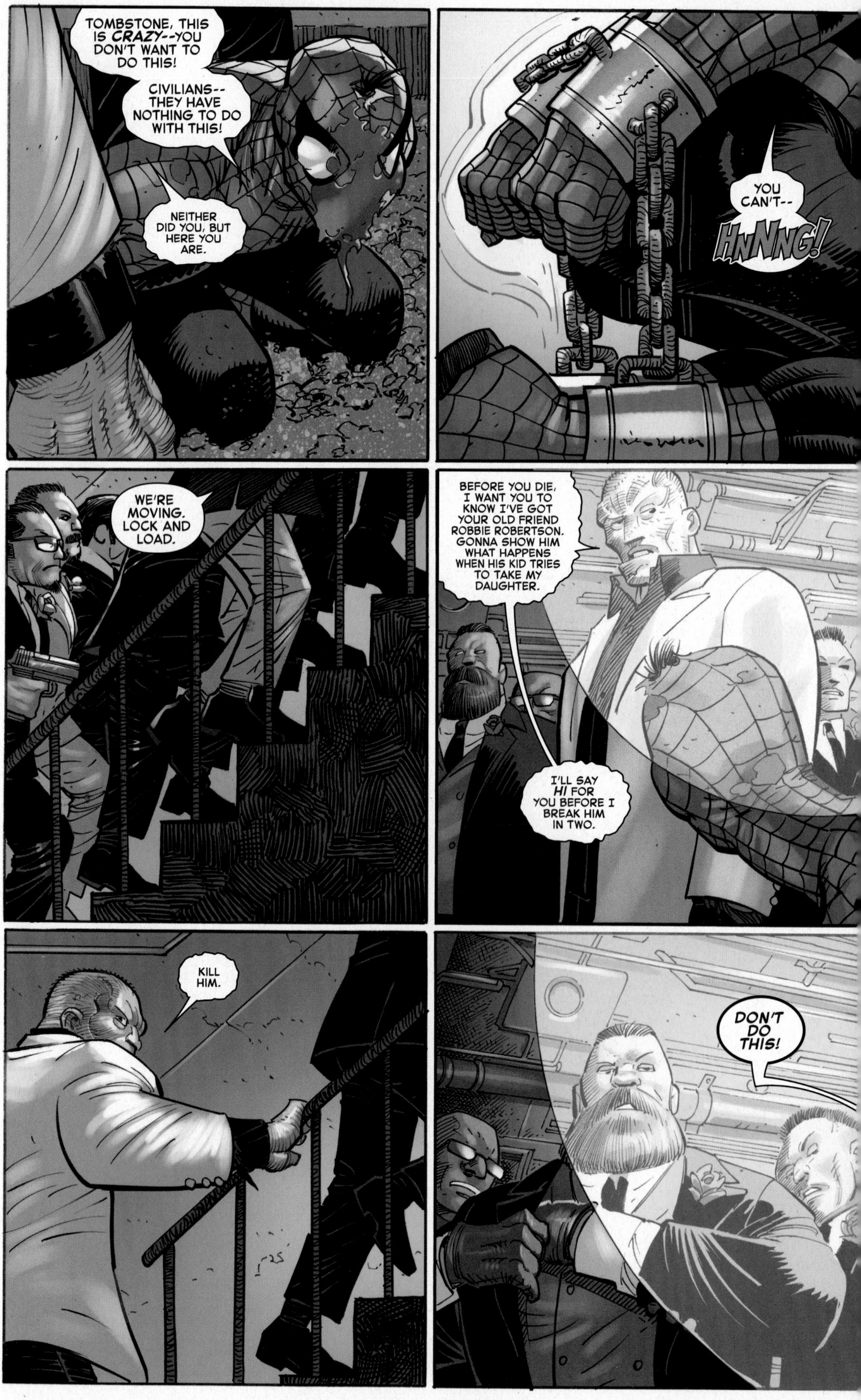
TOMBSTONE, THIS IS CRAZY--YOU DON'T WANT TO DO THIS!
CIVILIANS--THEY HAVE NOTHING TO DO WITH THIS!
NEITHER DID YOU, BUT HERE YOU ARE.
YOU CAN'T--
HNNNG!
WE'RE MOVING. LOCK AND LOAD.
BEFORE YOU DIE, I WANT YOU TO KNOW I'VE GOT YOUR OLD FRIEND ROBBIE ROBERTSON. GONNA SHOW HIM WHAT HAPPENS WHEN HIS KID TRIES TO TAKE MY DAUGHTER.
I'LL SAY HI FOR YOU BEFORE I BREAK HIM IN TWO.
KILL HIM.
DON'T DO THIS!

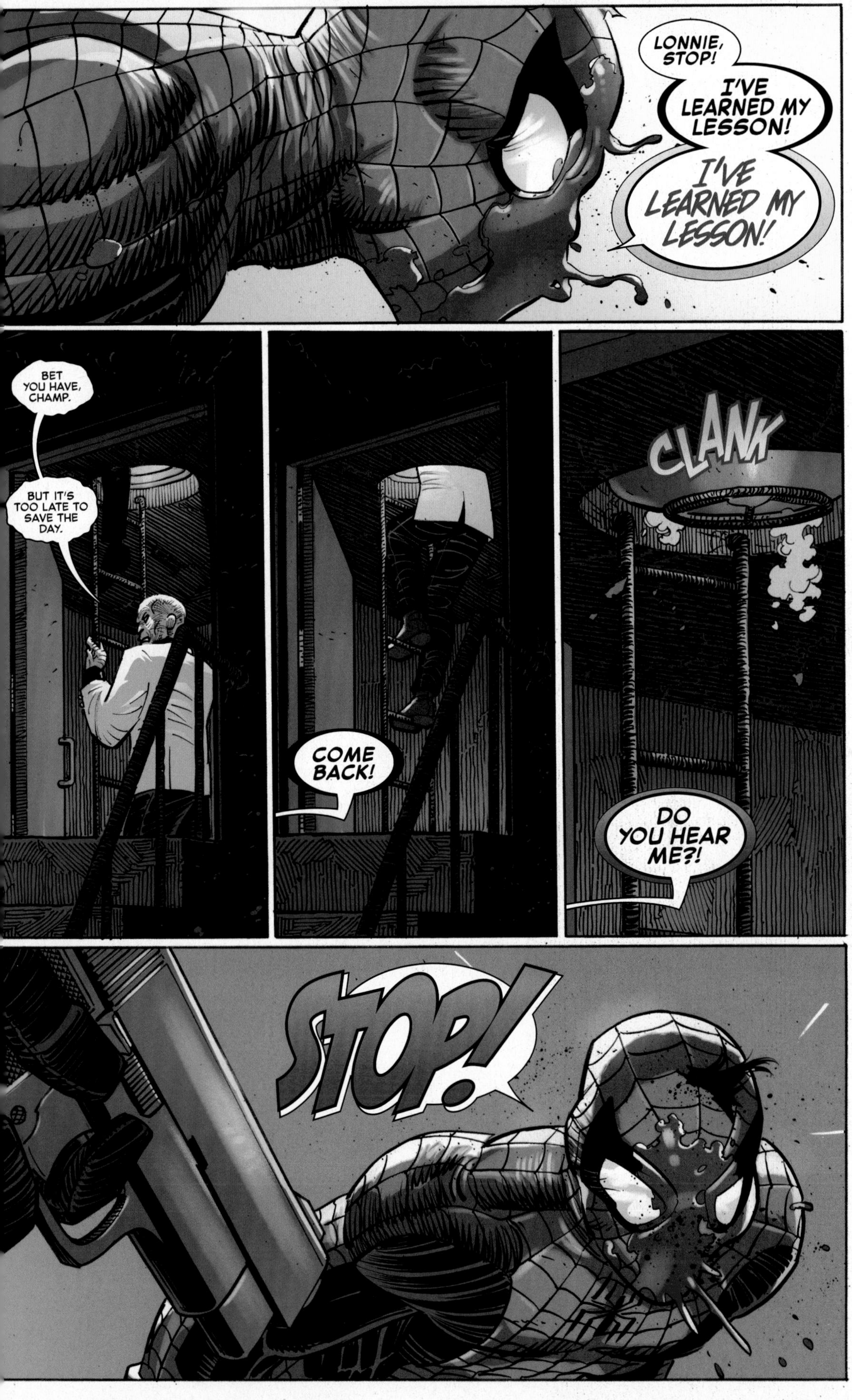
LONNIE, STOP!
I'VE LEARNED MY LESSON!
I'VE LEARNED MY LESSON!
BET YOU HAVE, CHAMP.
BUT IT'S TOO LATE TO SAVE THE DAY.
COME BACK!
CLANK
DO YOU HEAR ME?!
STOP!

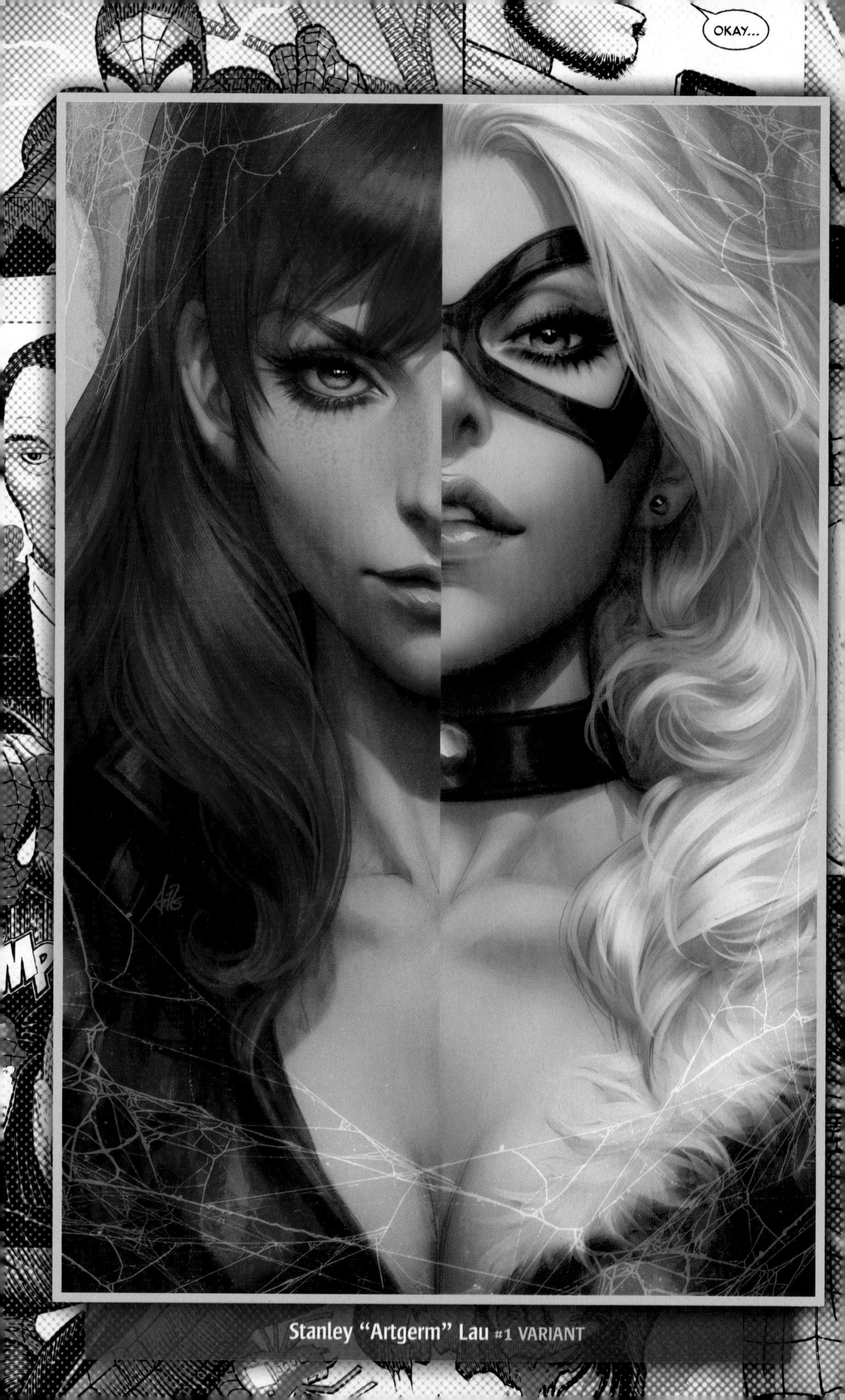
OKAY...

Stanley "Artgerm" Lau #1 VARIANT

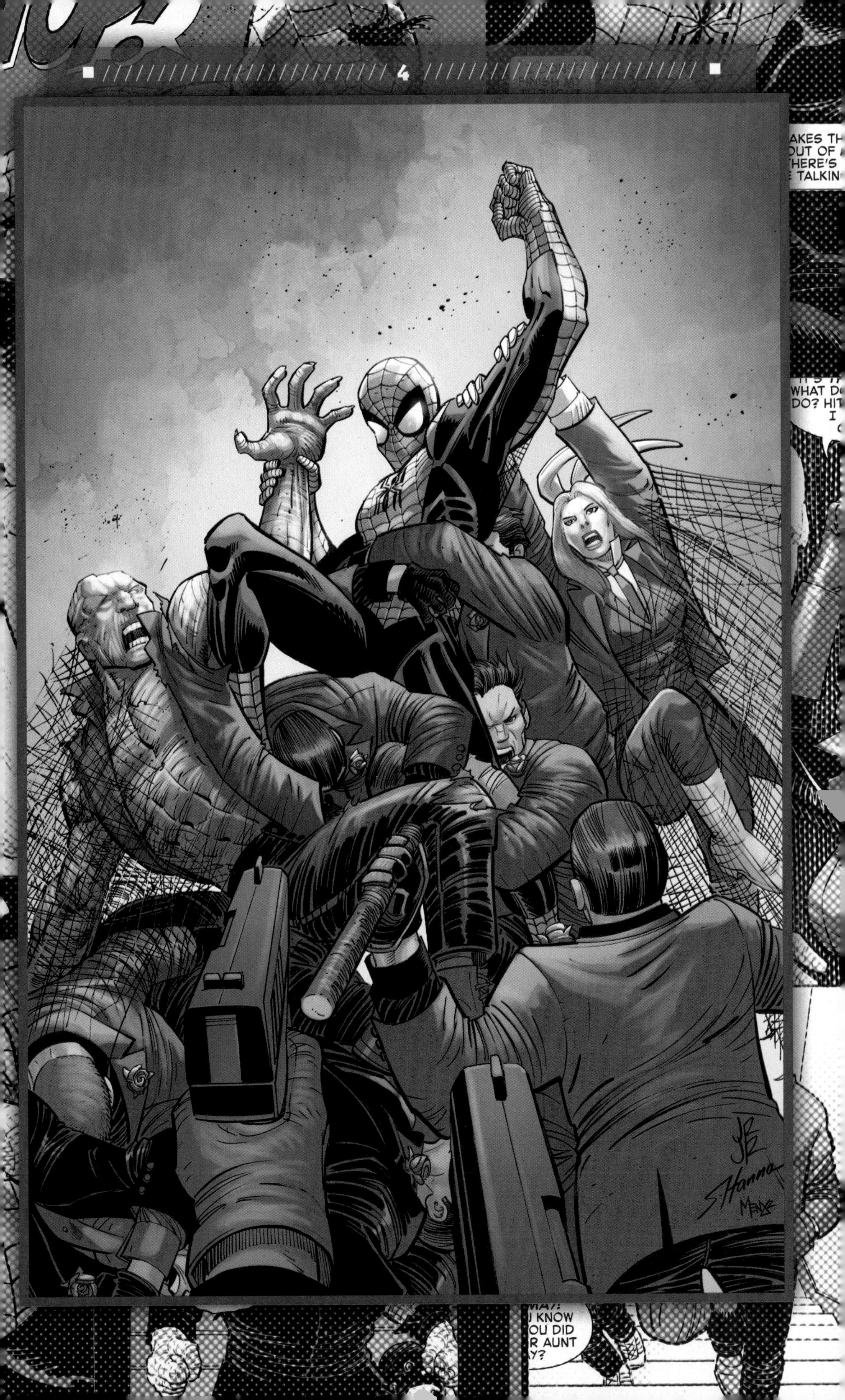
4

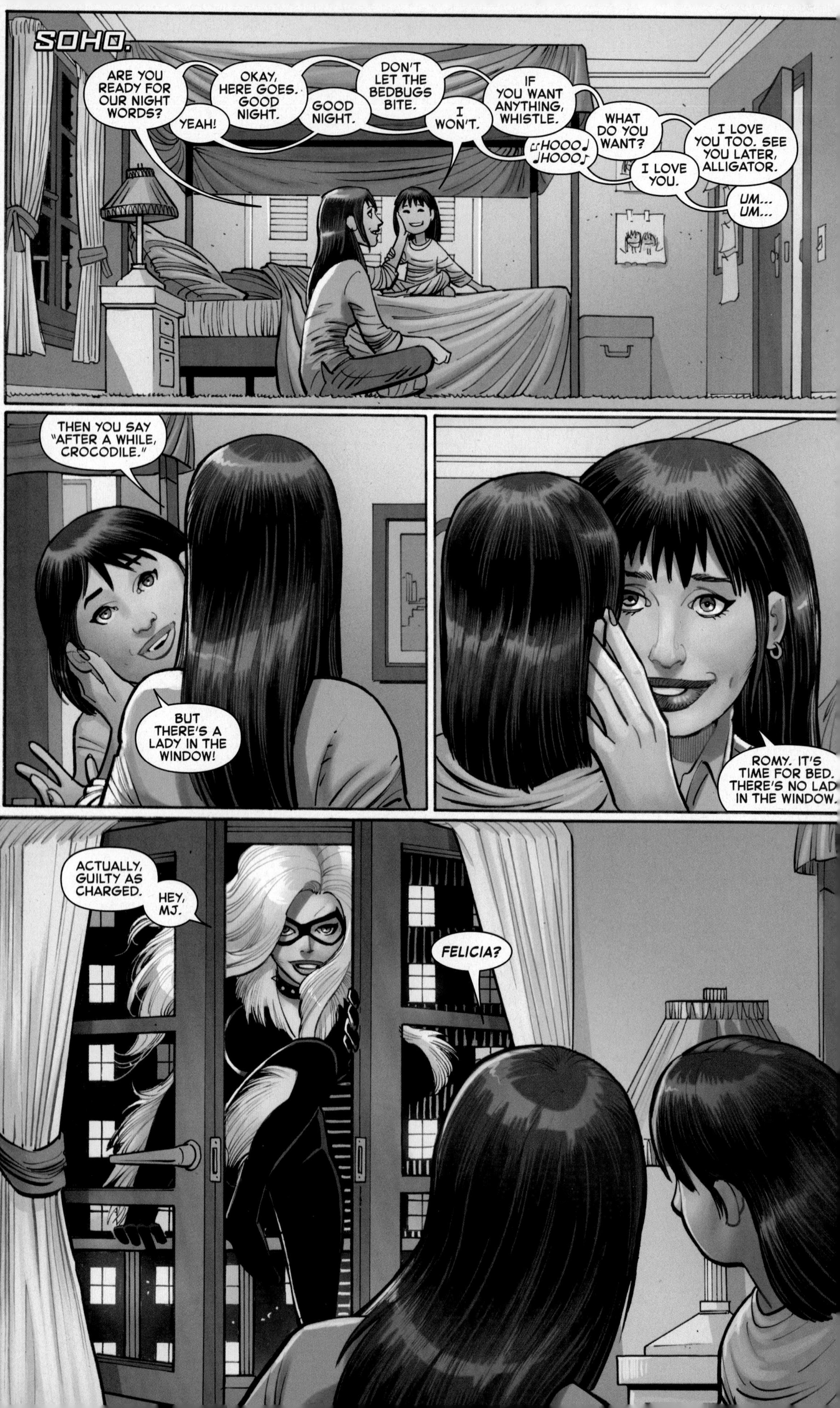
SOHO.
ARE YOU READY FOR OUR NIGHT WORDS?
YEAH!
OKAY, HERE GOES. GOOD NIGHT.
GOOD NIGHT.
DON'T LET THE BEDBUGS BITE.
I WON'T.
IF YOU WANT ANYTHING, WHISTLE.
♫HOOO♩ ♩HOOO♪
WHAT DO YOU WANT?
I LOVE YOU.
I LOVE YOU TOO. SEE YOU LATER, ALLIGATOR.
UM... UM...
THEN YOU SAY "AFTER A WHILE, CROCODILE."
BUT THERE'S A LADY IN THE WINDOW!
ROMY. IT'S TIME FOR BED. THERE'S NO LAD IN THE WINDOW.
ACTUALLY, GUILTY AS CHARGED.
HEY, MJ.
FELICIA?

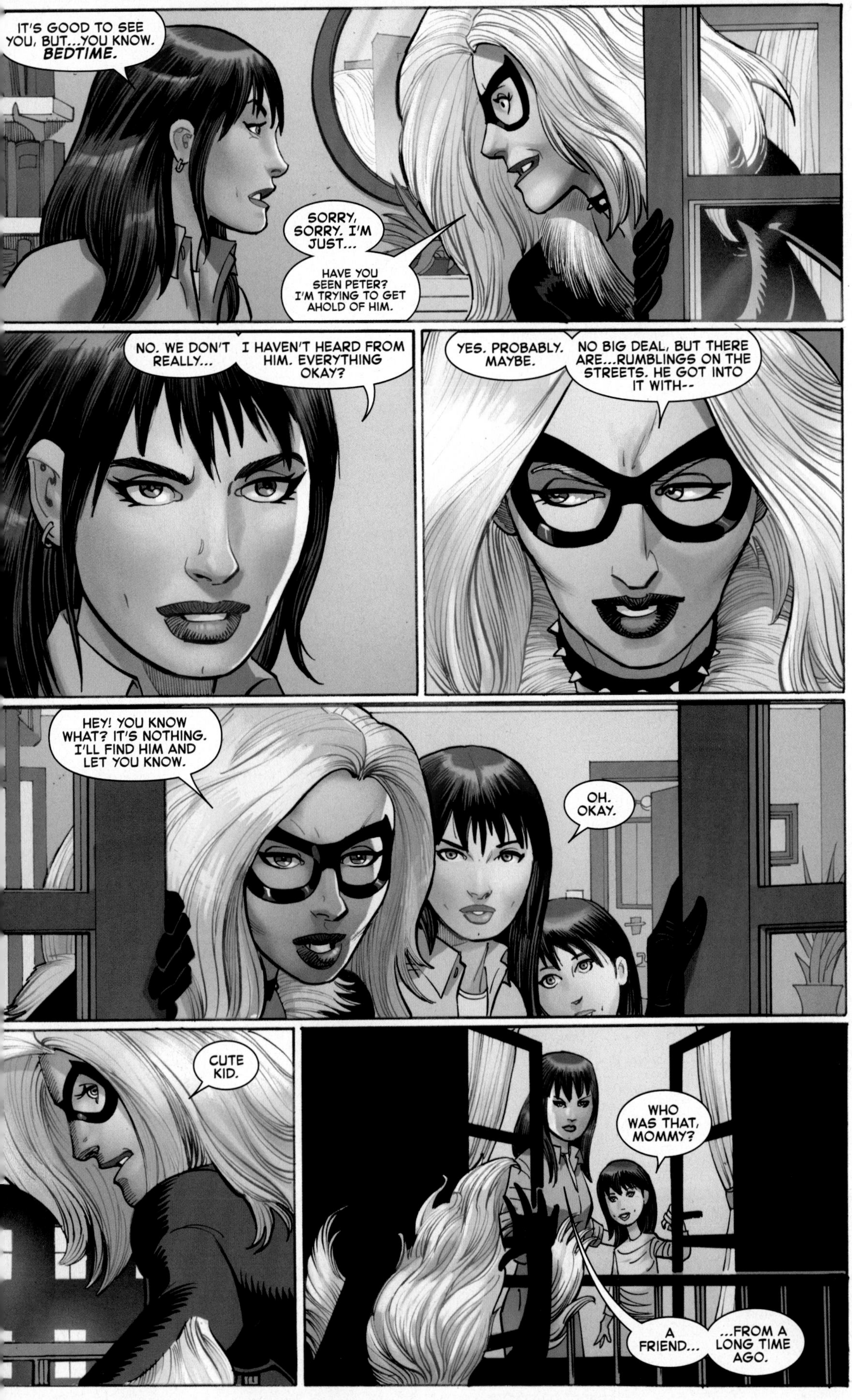
IT'S GOOD TO SEE YOU, BUT...YOU KNOW. BEDTIME.
SORRY, SORRY. I'M JUST...
HAVE YOU SEEN PETER? I'M TRYING TO GET AHOLD OF HIM.
NO. WE DON'T REALLY...
I HAVEN'T HEARD FROM HIM. EVERYTHING OKAY?
YES. PROBABLY. MAYBE.
NO BIG DEAL, BUT THERE ARE...RUMBLINGS ON THE STREETS. HE GOT INTO IT WITH--
HEY! YOU KNOW WHAT? IT'S NOTHING. I'LL FIND HIM AND LET YOU KNOW.
OH. OKAY.
CUTE KID.
WHO WAS THAT, MOMMY?
A FRIEND...
...FROM A LONG TIME AGO.

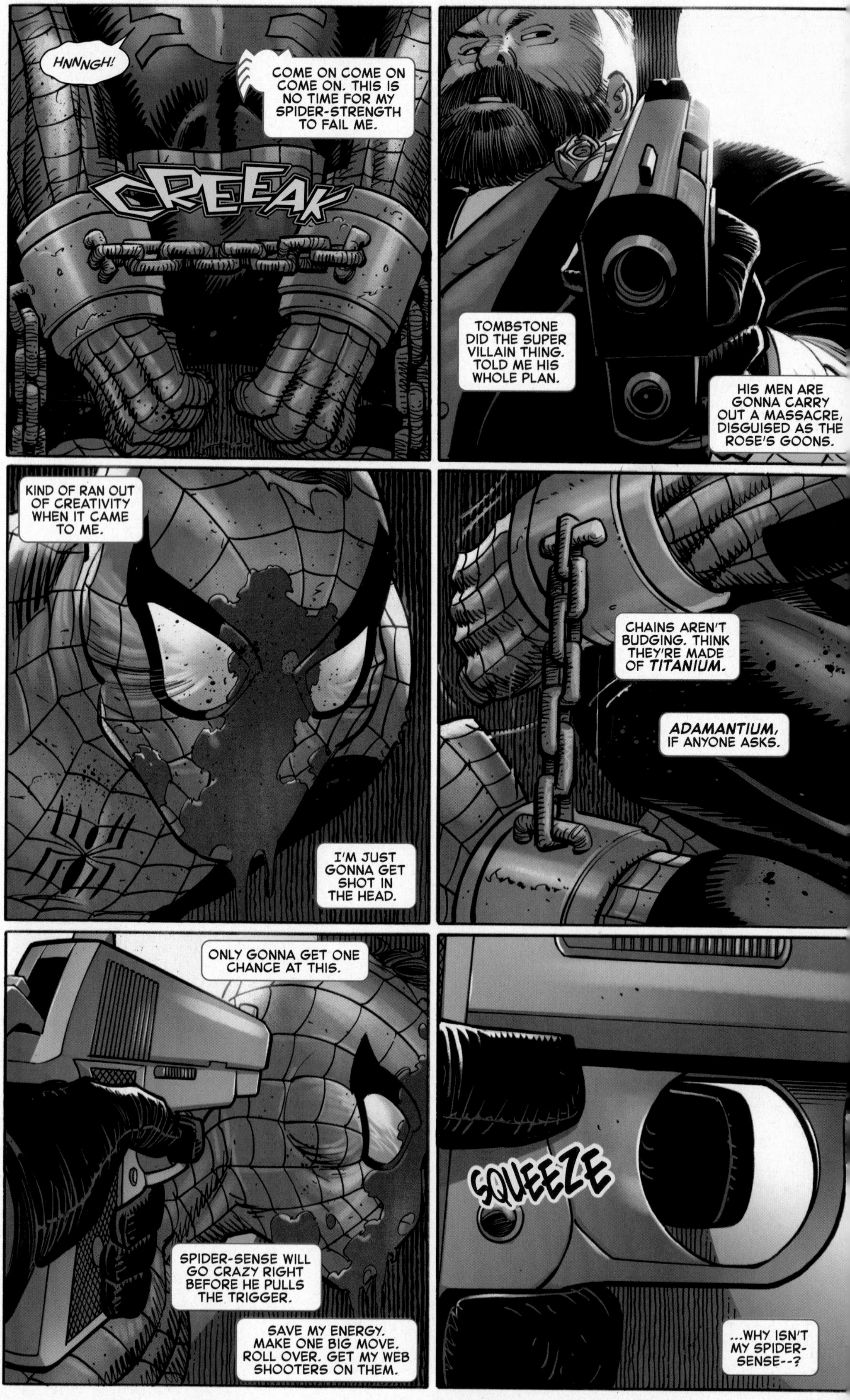
HNNNGH!
COME ON COME ON COME ON. THIS IS NO TIME FOR MY SPIDER-STRENGTH TO FAIL ME.
CREEAK
TOMBSTONE DID THE SUPER VILLAIN THING. TOLD ME HIS WHOLE PLAN.
HIS MEN ARE GONNA CARRY OUT A MASSACRE, DISGUISED AS THE ROSE'S GOONS.
KIND OF RAN OUT OF CREATIVITY WHEN IT CAME TO ME.
I'M JUST GONNA GET SHOT IN THE HEAD.
CHAINS AREN'T BUDGING. THINK THEY'RE MADE OF *TITANIUM.*
ADAMANTIUM, IF ANYONE ASKS.
ONLY GONNA GET ONE CHANCE AT THIS.
SPIDER-SENSE WILL GO CRAZY RIGHT BEFORE HE PULLS THE TRIGGER.
SAVE MY ENERGY. MAKE ONE BIG MOVE. ROLL OVER. GET MY WEB SHOOTERS ON THEM.
SQUEEZE
...WHY ISN'T MY SPIDER-SENSE--?

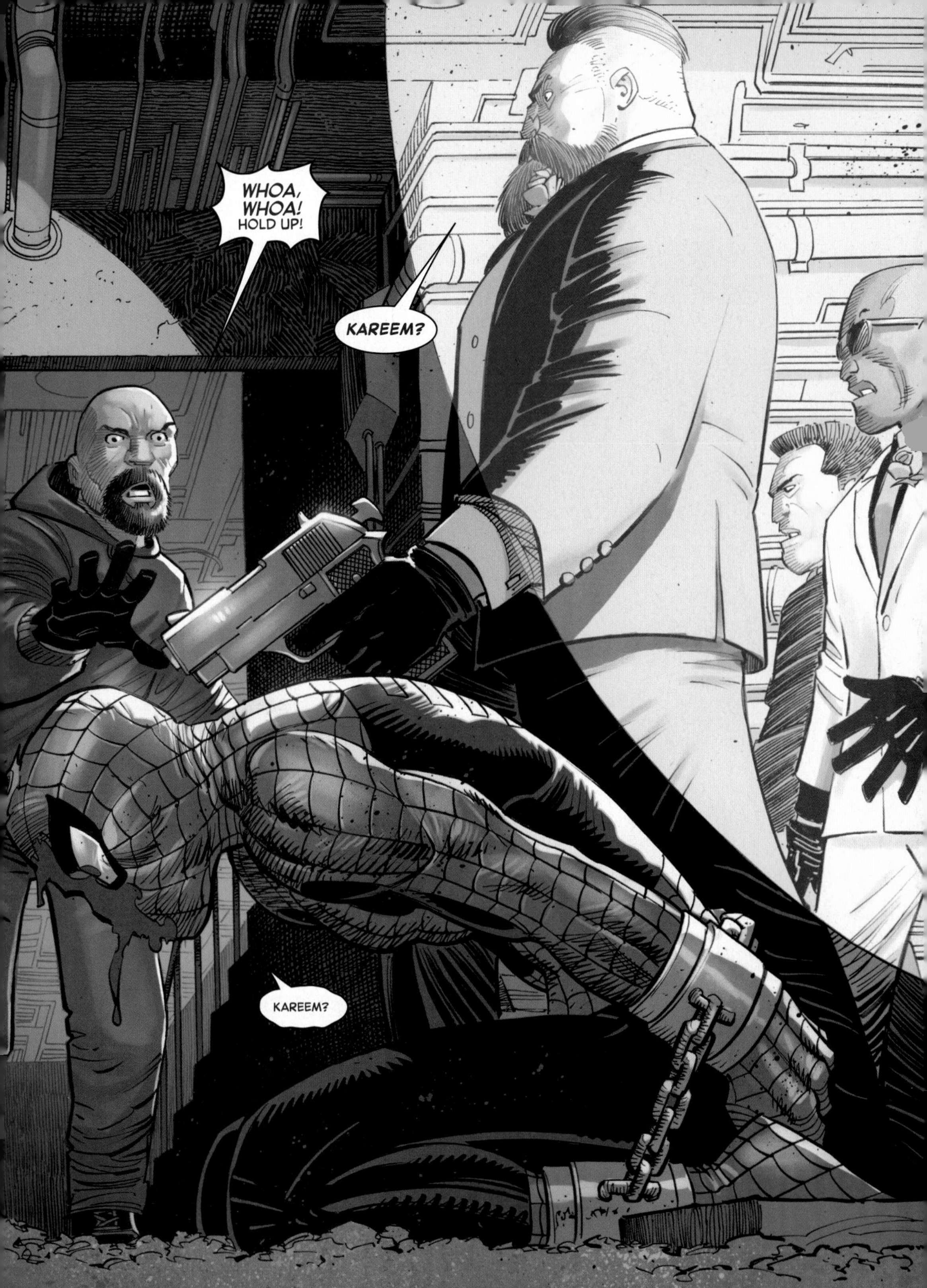

WHOA, WHOA! HOLD UP!
KAREEM?
KAREEM?

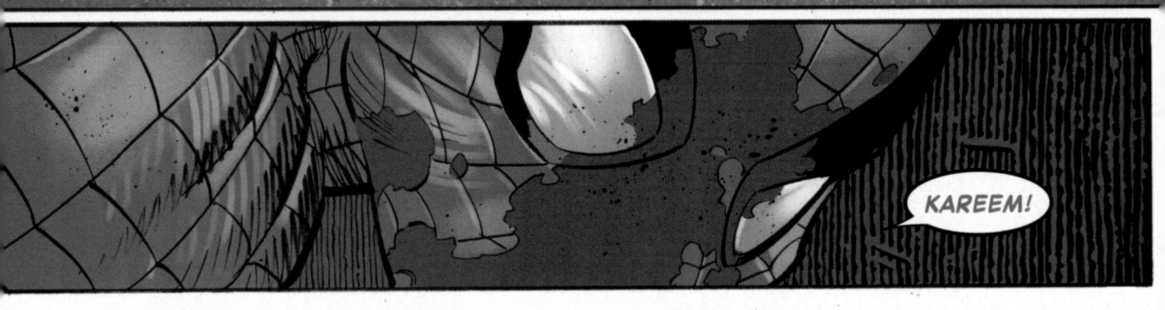

KAREEM!

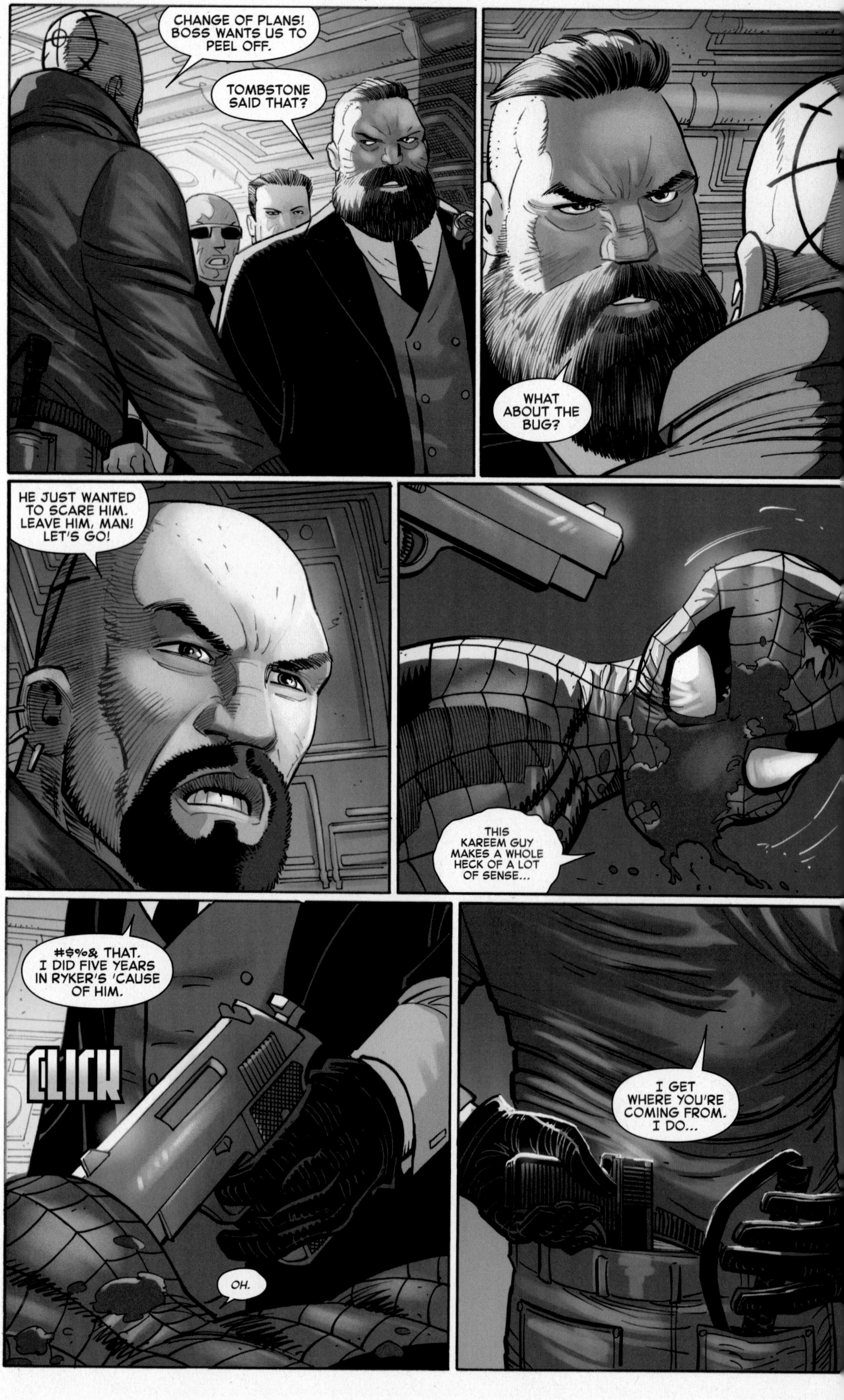

CHANGE OF PLANS! BOSS WANTS US TO PEEL OFF.
TOMBSTONE SAID THAT?
WHAT ABOUT THE BUG?
HE JUST WANTED TO SCARE HIM. LEAVE HIM, MAN! LET'S GO!
THIS KAREEM GUY MAKES A WHOLE HECK OF A LOT OF SENSE...
#$%& THAT. I DID FIVE YEARS IN RYKER'S 'CAUSE OF HIM.
CLICK
OH.
I GET WHERE YOU'RE COMING FROM. I DO...

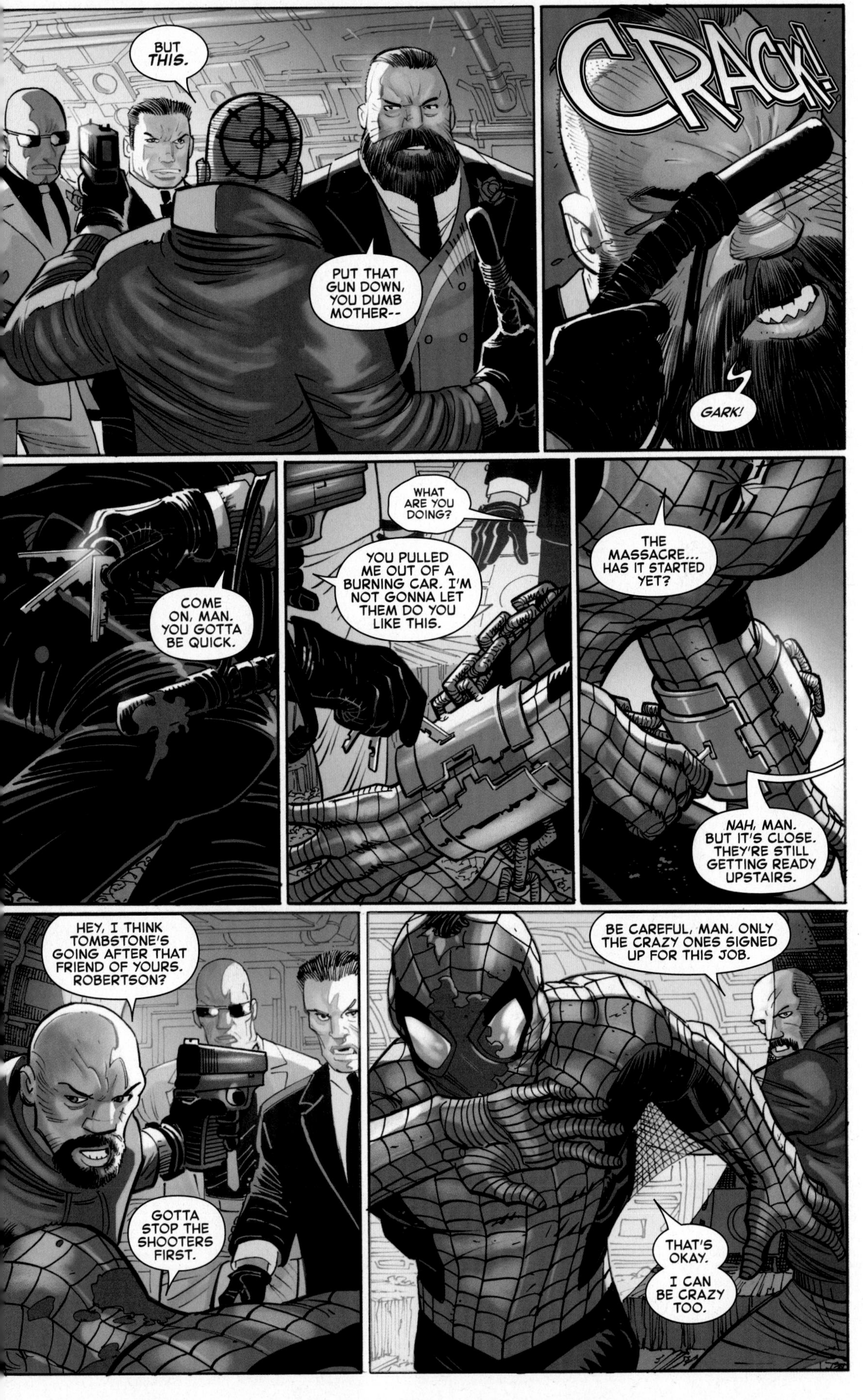
BUT THIS.
PUT THAT GUN DOWN, YOU DUMB MOTHER--
CRACK!
GARK!
COME ON, MAN. YOU GOTTA BE QUICK.
WHAT ARE YOU DOING?
YOU PULLED ME OUT OF A BURNING CAR. I'M NOT GONNA LET THEM DO YOU LIKE THIS.
THE MASSACRE... HAS IT STARTED YET?
NAH, MAN. BUT IT'S CLOSE. THEY'RE STILL GETTING READY UPSTAIRS.
HEY, I THINK TOMBSTONE'S GOING AFTER THAT FRIEND OF YOURS. ROBERTSON?
GOTTA STOP THE SHOOTERS FIRST.
BE CAREFUL, MAN. ONLY THE CRAZY ONES SIGNED UP FOR THIS JOB.
THAT'S OKAY.
I CAN BE CRAZY TOO.

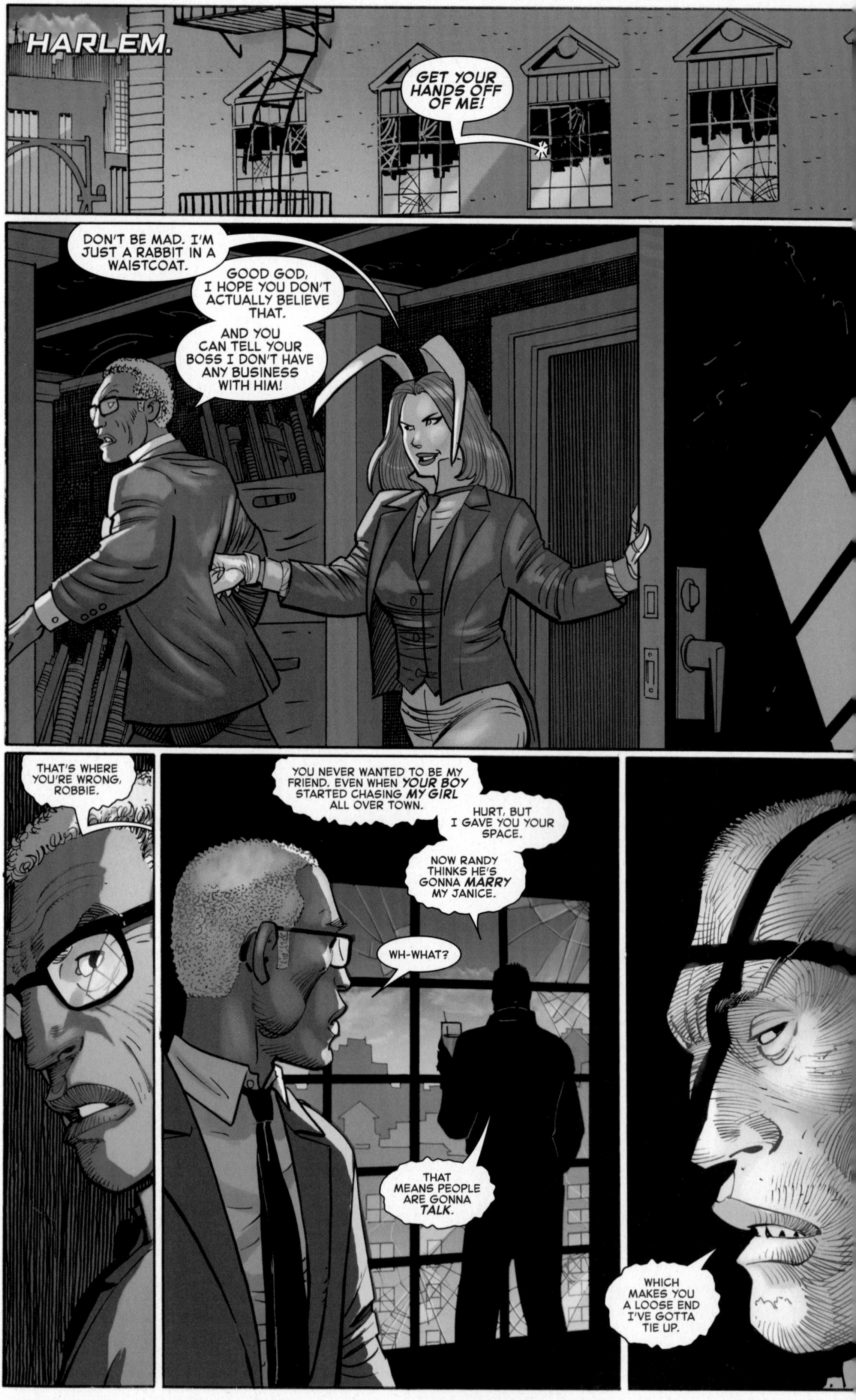
HARLEM.
GET YOUR HANDS OFF OF ME!
DON'T BE MAD. I'M JUST A RABBIT IN A WAISTCOAT.
GOOD GOD, I HOPE YOU DON'T ACTUALLY BELIEVE THAT.
AND YOU CAN TELL YOUR BOSS I DON'T HAVE ANY BUSINESS WITH HIM!
THAT'S WHERE YOU'RE WRONG, ROBBIE.
YOU NEVER WANTED TO BE MY FRIEND. EVEN WHEN YOUR BOY STARTED CHASING MY GIRL ALL OVER TOWN.
HURT, BUT I GAVE YOU YOUR SPACE.
NOW RANDY THINKS HE'S GONNA MARRY MY JANICE.
WH-WHAT?
THAT MEANS PEOPLE ARE GONNA TALK.
WHICH MAKES YOU A LOOSE END I'VE GOTTA TIE UP.

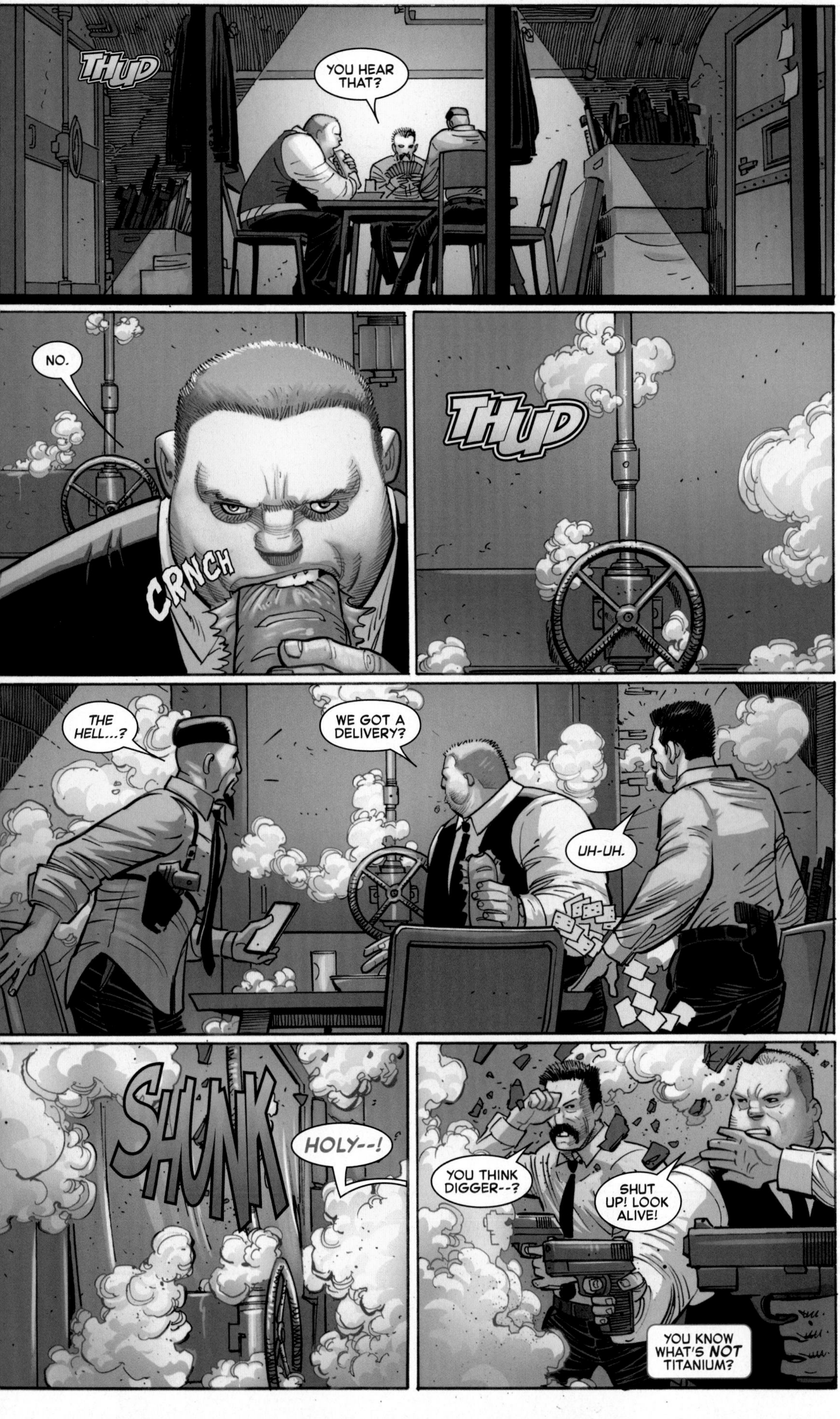
THUD
YOU HEAR THAT?
NO.
CRNCH
THUD
THE HELL...?
WE GOT A DELIVERY?
UH-UH.
SHUNK
HOLY--!
YOU THINK DIGGER--?
SHUT UP! LOOK ALIVE!
YOU KNOW WHAT'S NOT TITANIUM?

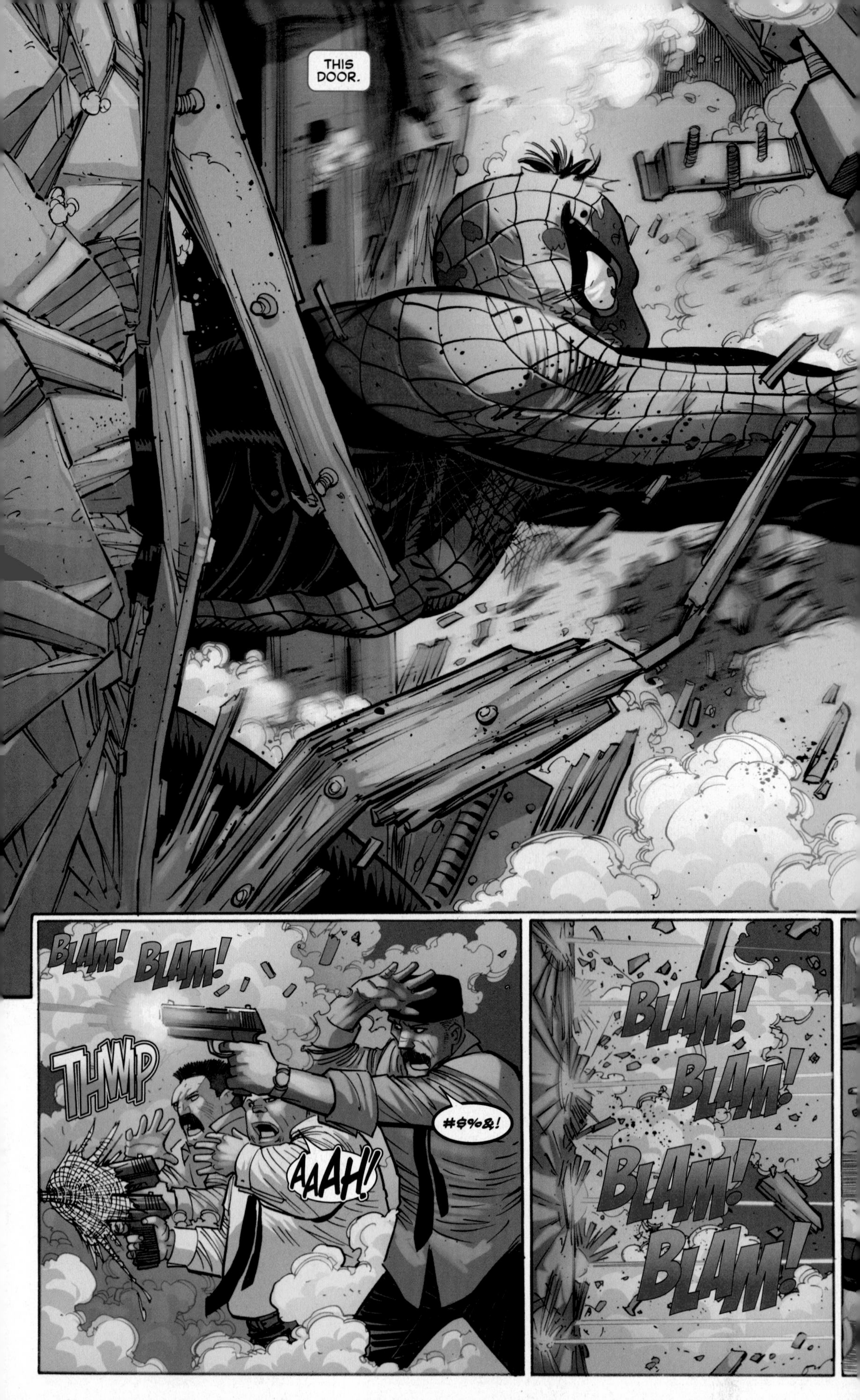
THIS DOOR.
BLAM! BLAM!
THWIP
#$%&!
AAAH!
BLAM! BLAM! BLAM! BLAM!

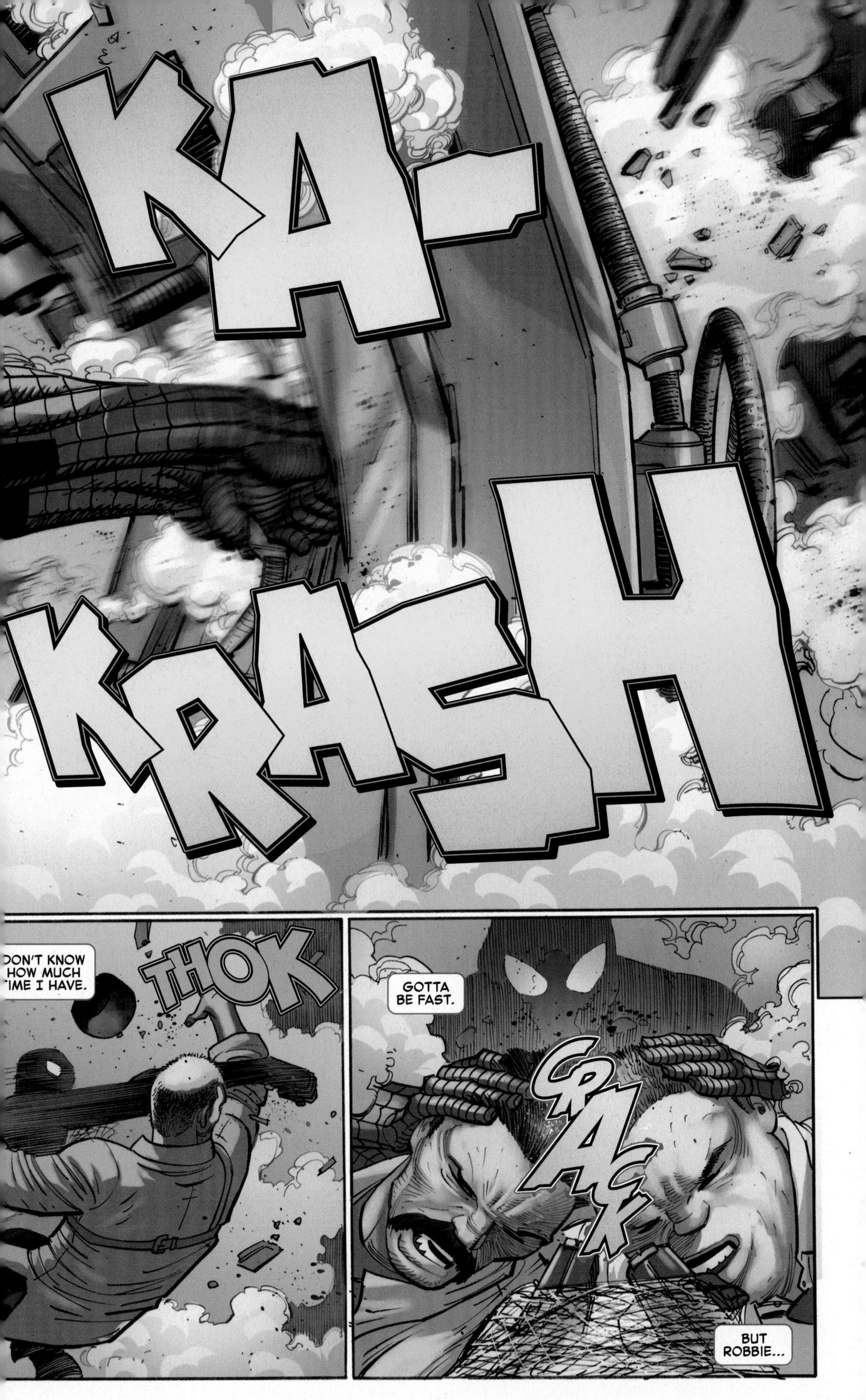
KA-
KRASH
DON'T KNOW HOW MUCH TIME I HAVE.
THOK
GOTTA BE FAST.
CRACK
BUT ROBBIE...

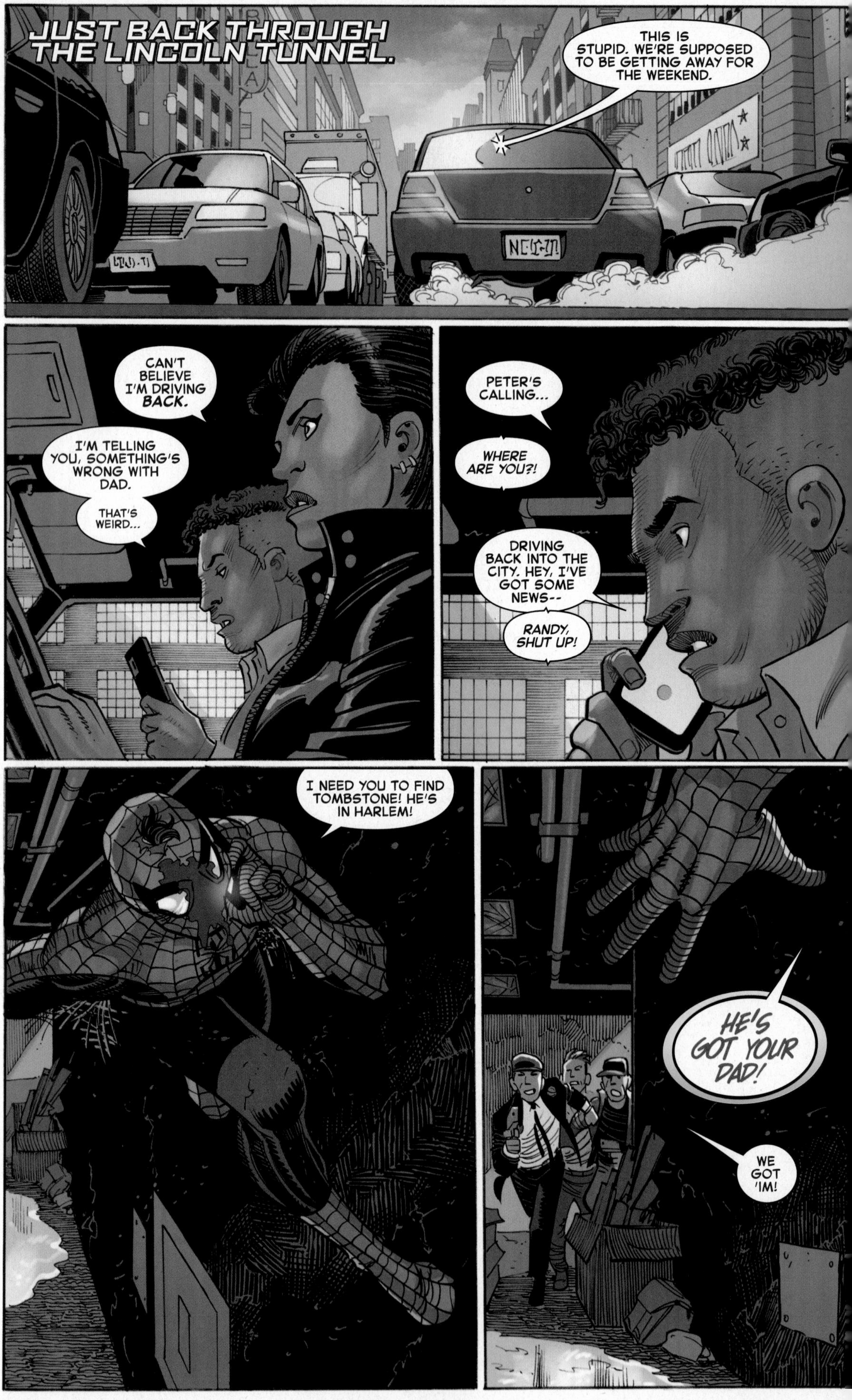

JUST BACK THROUGH THE LINCOLN TUNNEL.
THIS IS STUPID. WE'RE SUPPOSED TO BE GETTING AWAY FOR THE WEEKEND.
CAN'T BELIEVE I'M DRIVING BACK.
I'M TELLING YOU, SOMETHING'S WRONG WITH DAD.
THAT'S WEIRD...
PETER'S CALLING...
WHERE ARE YOU?!
DRIVING BACK INTO THE CITY. HEY, I'VE GOT SOME NEWS--
RANDY, SHUT UP!
I NEED YOU TO FIND TOMBSTONE! HE'S IN HARLEM!
HE'S GOT YOUR DAD!
WE GOT 'IM!

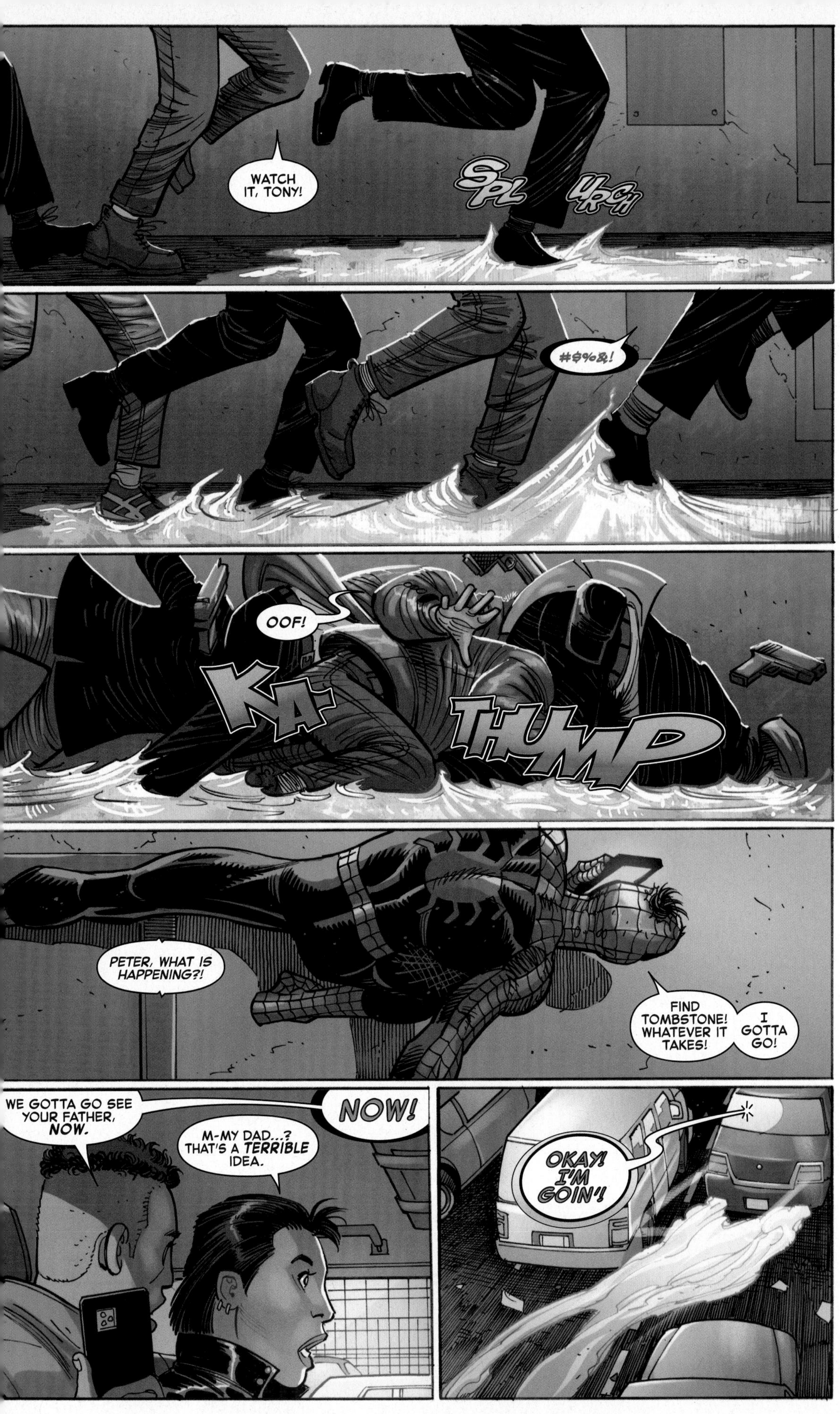
WATCH IT, TONY!
SPLURCH
#$%&!
OOF!
KA-THUMP
PETER, WHAT IS HAPPENING?!
FIND TOMBSTONE! WHATEVER IT TAKES!
I GOTTA GO!
WE GOTTA GO SEE YOUR FATHER, NOW.
NOW!
M-MY DAD...? THAT'S A TERRIBLE IDEA.
OKAY! I'M GOIN'!

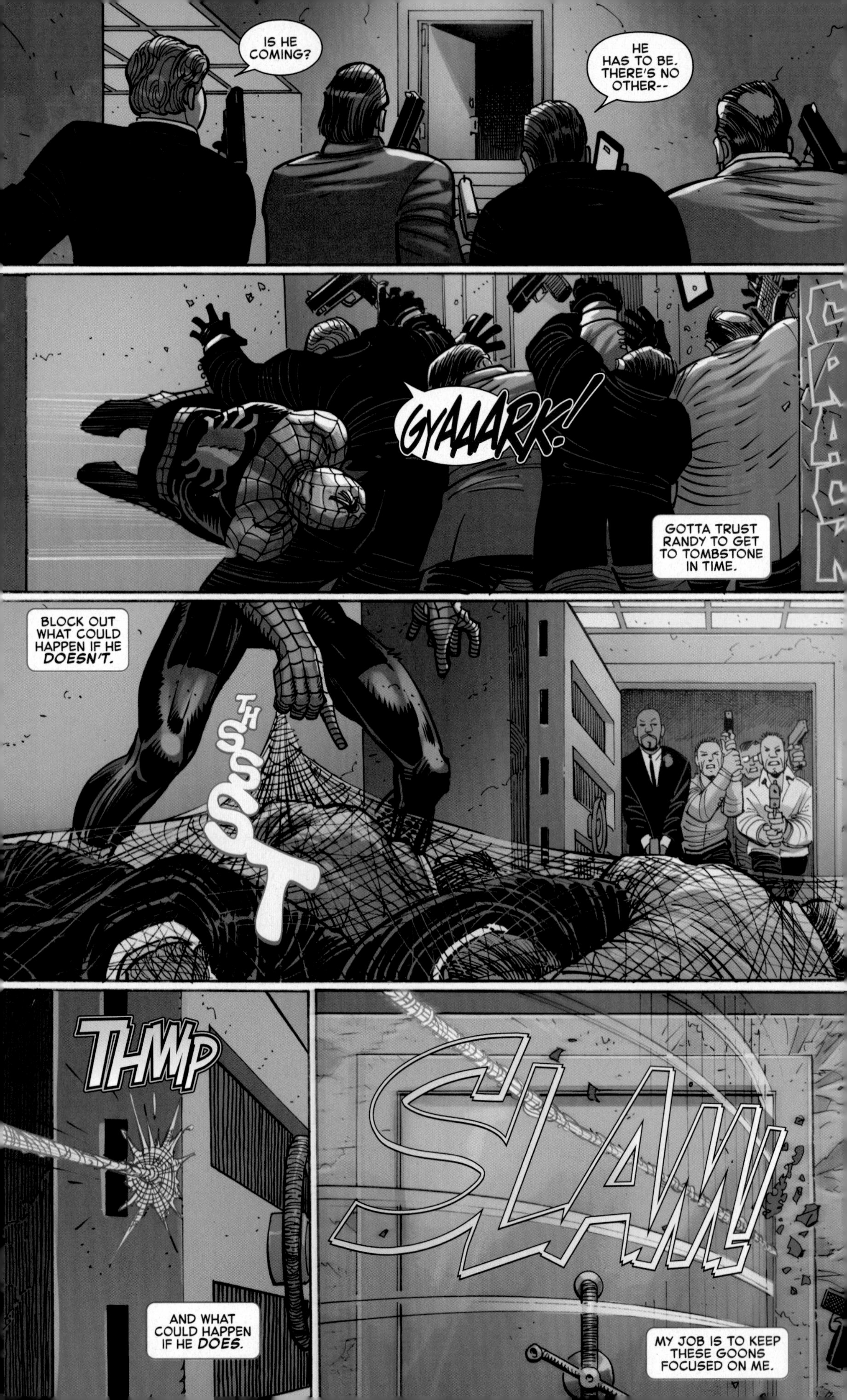
IS HE COMING?
HE HAS TO BE. THERE'S NO OTHER--
CRACK
GYAAARK!
GOTTA TRUST RANDY TO GET TO TOMBSTONE IN TIME.
BLOCK OUT WHAT COULD HAPPEN IF HE DOESN'T.
THSSSST
THWIP
AND WHAT COULD HAPPEN IF HE DOES.
SLAM!
MY JOB IS TO KEEP THESE GOONS FOCUSED ON ME.

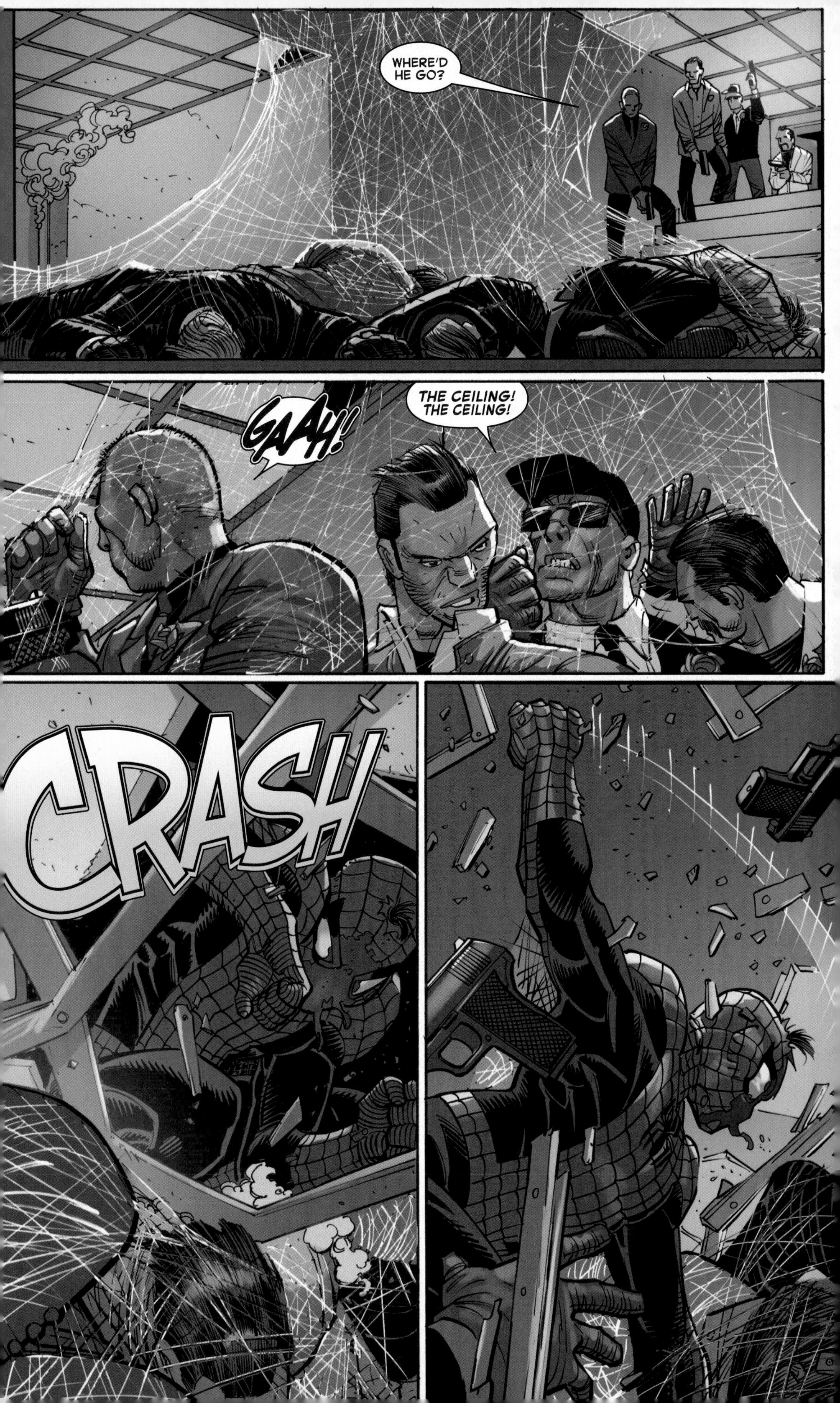
WHERE'D HE GO?
GAAH!
THE CEILING! THE CEILING!
CRASH

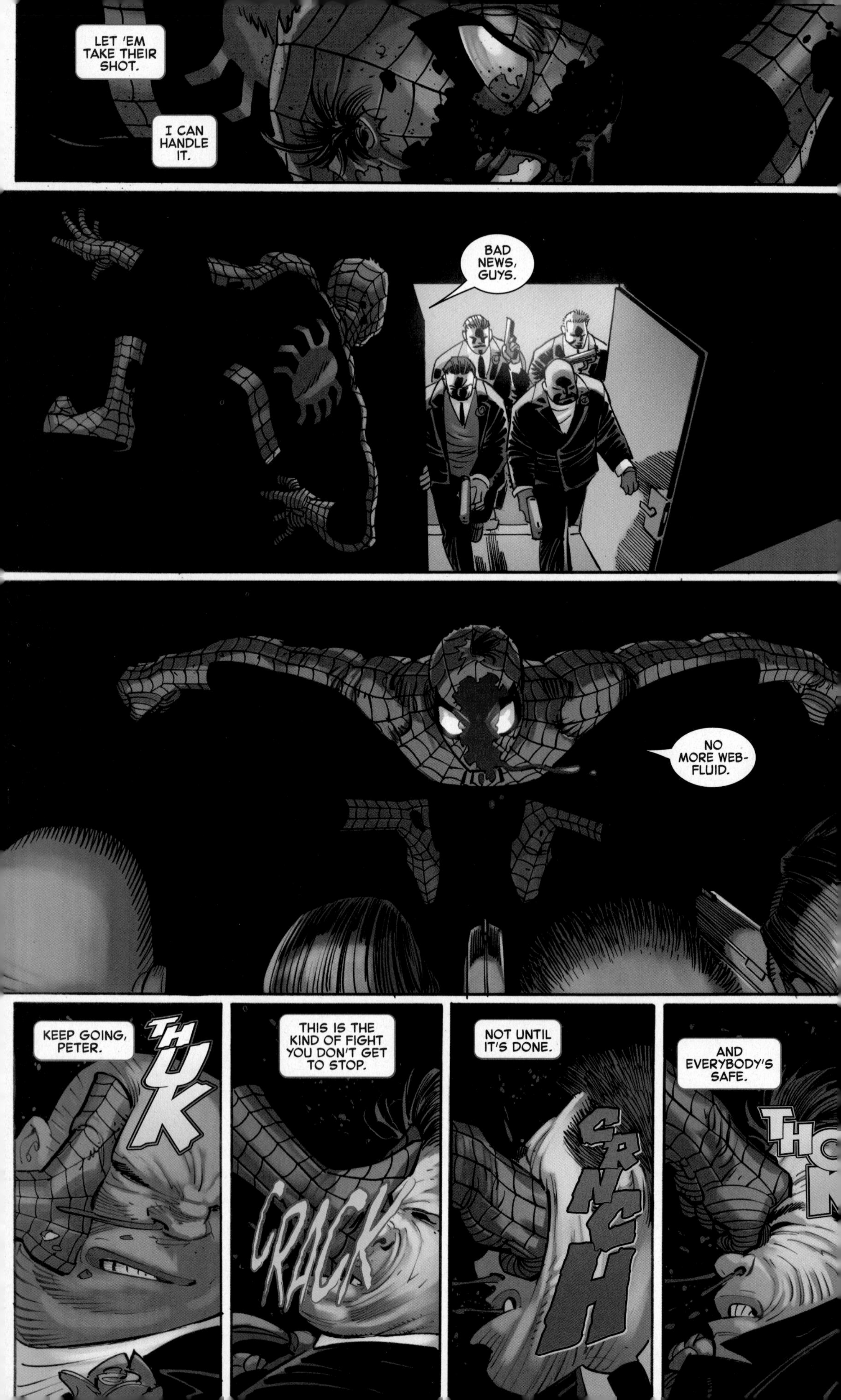
LET 'EM TAKE THEIR SHOT.
I CAN HANDLE IT.
BAD NEWS, GUYS.
NO MORE WEB-FLUID.
KEEP GOING, PETER.
THUK
THIS IS THE KIND OF FIGHT YOU DON'T GET TO STOP.
CRACK
NOT UNTIL IT'S DONE.
CRNCH
AND EVERYBODY'S SAFE.

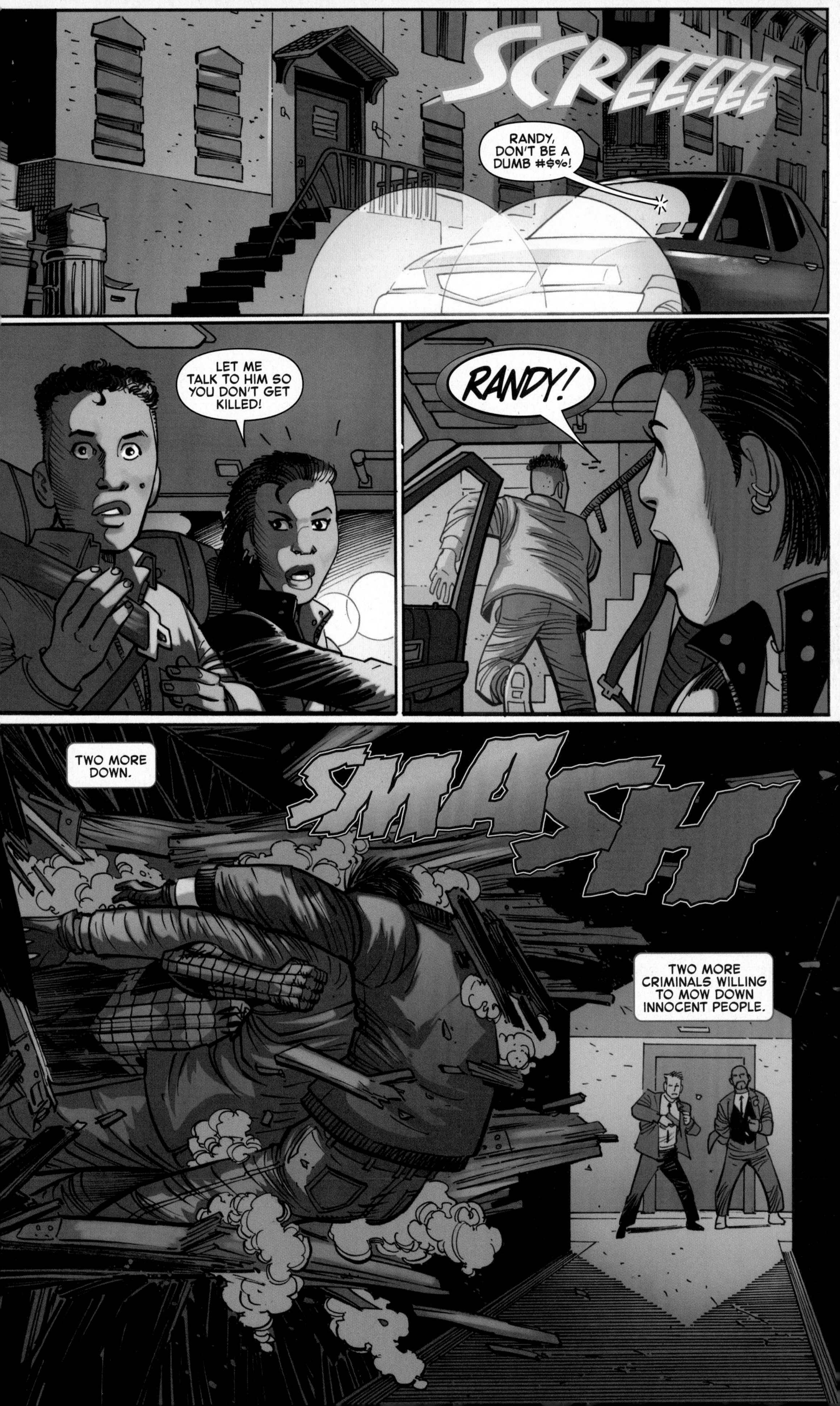

SCREEEEE
RANDY, DON'T BE A DUMB #$%!
LET ME TALK TO HIM SO YOU DON'T GET KILLED!
RANDY!
TWO MORE DOWN.
SMASH
TWO MORE CRIMINALS WILLING TO MOW DOWN INNOCENT PEOPLE.

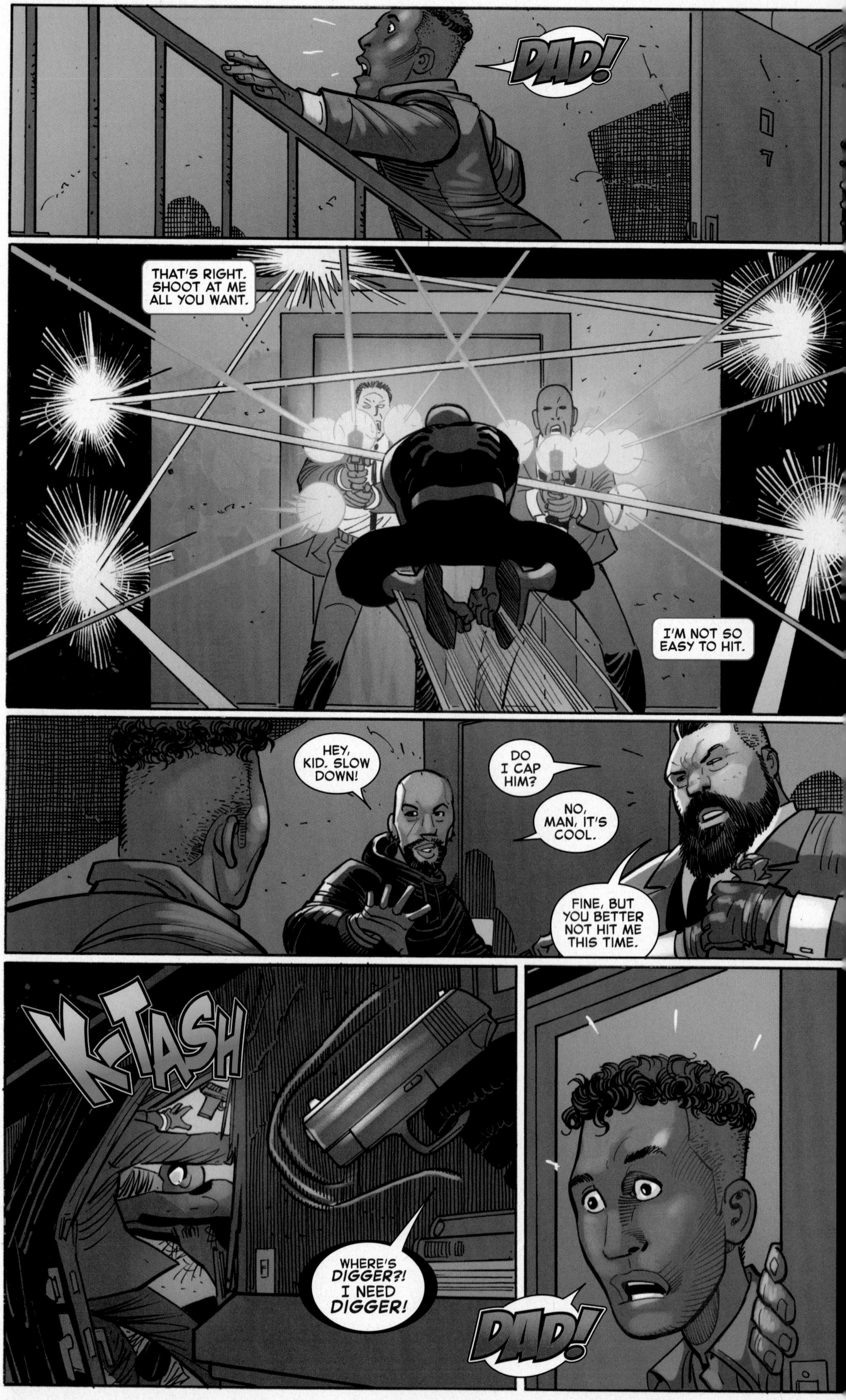
DAD!
THAT'S RIGHT. SHOOT AT ME ALL YOU WANT.
I'M NOT SO EASY TO HIT.
HEY, KID. SLOW DOWN!
DO I CAP HIM?
NO, MAN, IT'S COOL.
FINE, BUT YOU BETTER NOT HIT ME THIS TIME.
K-TASH
WHERE'S DIGGER?! I NEED DIGGER!
DAD!

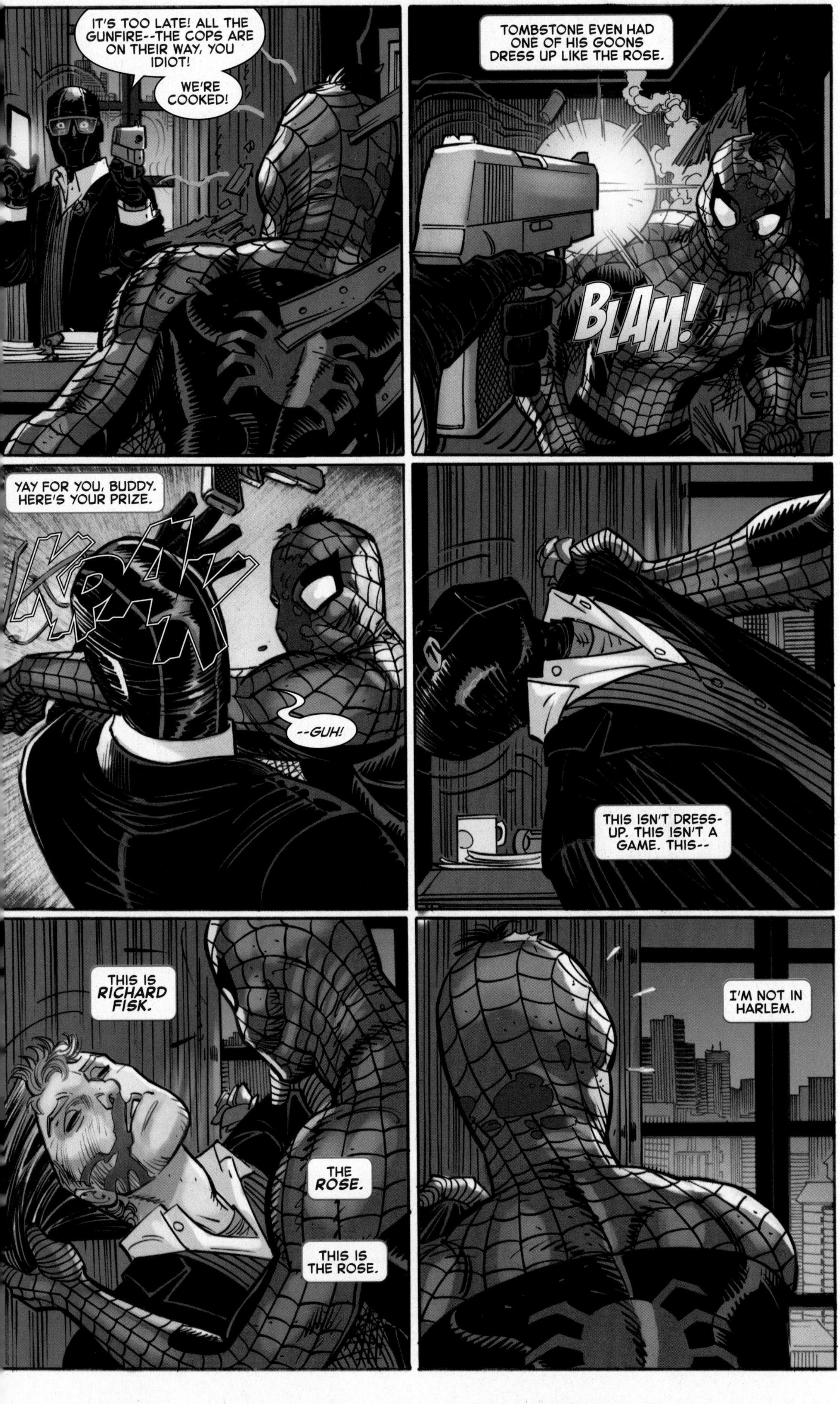
IT'S TOO LATE! ALL THE GUNFIRE--THE COPS ARE ON THEIR WAY, YOU IDIOT!
WE'RE COOKED!
TOMBSTONE EVEN HAD ONE OF HIS GOONS DRESS UP LIKE THE ROSE.
BLAM!
YAY FOR YOU, BUDDY. HERE'S YOUR PRIZE.
KRAK
--GUH!
THIS ISN'T DRESS-UP. THIS ISN'T A GAME. THIS--
THIS IS RICHARD FISK.
THE ROSE.
THIS IS THE ROSE.
I'M NOT IN HARLEM.

RANDY?

DAD, A-ARE YOU OKAY?

I'M IN SHOCK, TO BE COMPLETELY HONEST.

ALONZO HERE TELLS ME WE'RE GOING TO BE RELATED.

I WAS UNDER *THE ROSE'S* HIDEOUT.

THESE ARE *HIS* MEN.

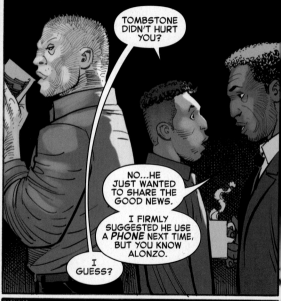

TOMBSTONE DIDN'T HURT YOU?

NO...HE JUST WANTED TO SHARE THE GOOD NEWS.

I FIRMLY SUGGESTED HE USE A *PHONE* NEXT TIME, BUT YOU KNOW ALONZO.

I GUESS?

TOMBSTONE TRICKED ME.

I JUST WON HIS WAR FOR HIM.

DON'T HURT HIM--!

DAD?

RELAX, JANICE. I DON'T DO THAT ANYMORE.

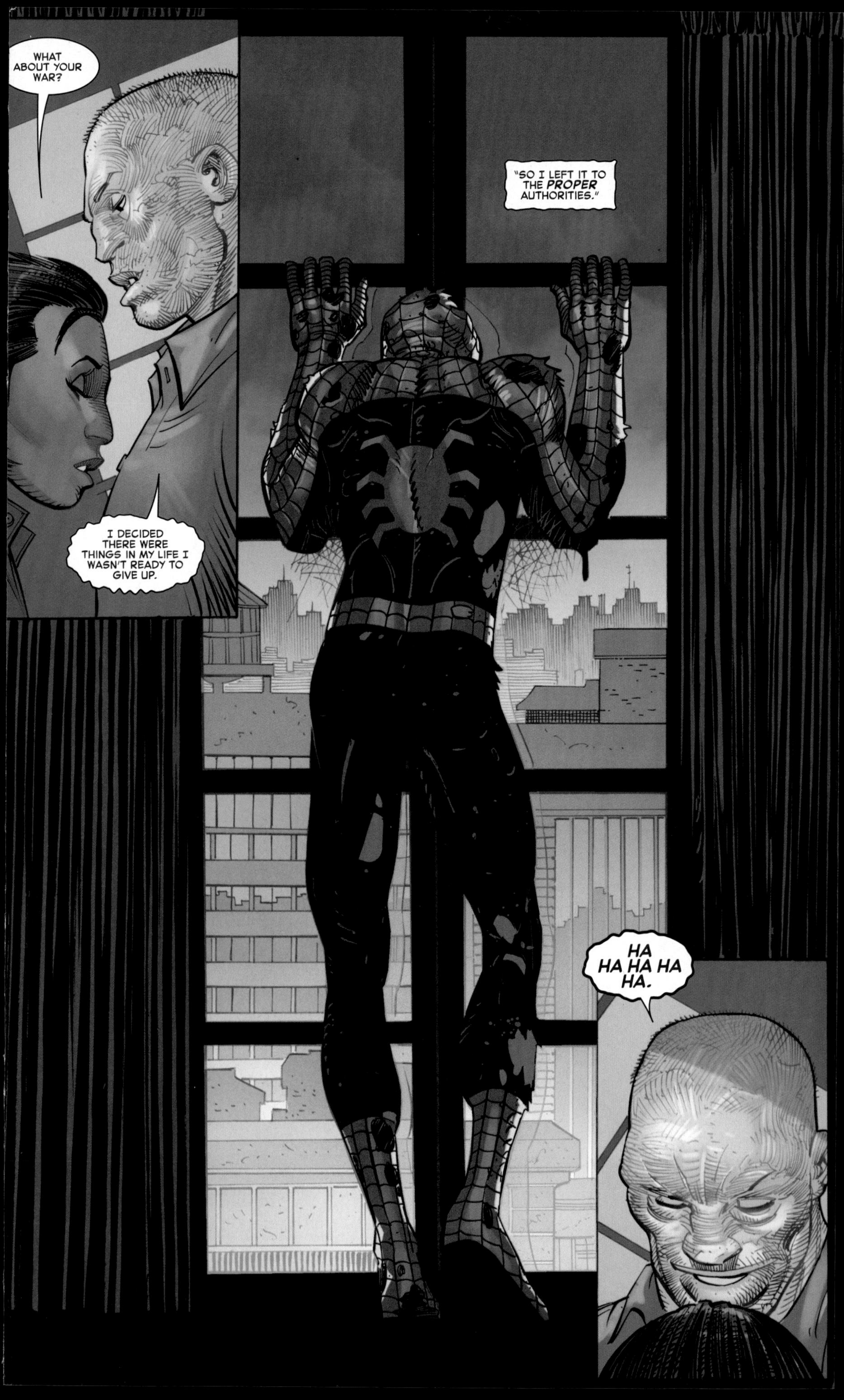
WHAT ABOUT YOUR WAR?
I DECIDED THERE WERE THINGS IN MY LIFE I WASN'T READY TO GIVE UP.
"SO I LEFT IT TO THE PROPER AUTHORITIES."
HA HA HA HA HA.

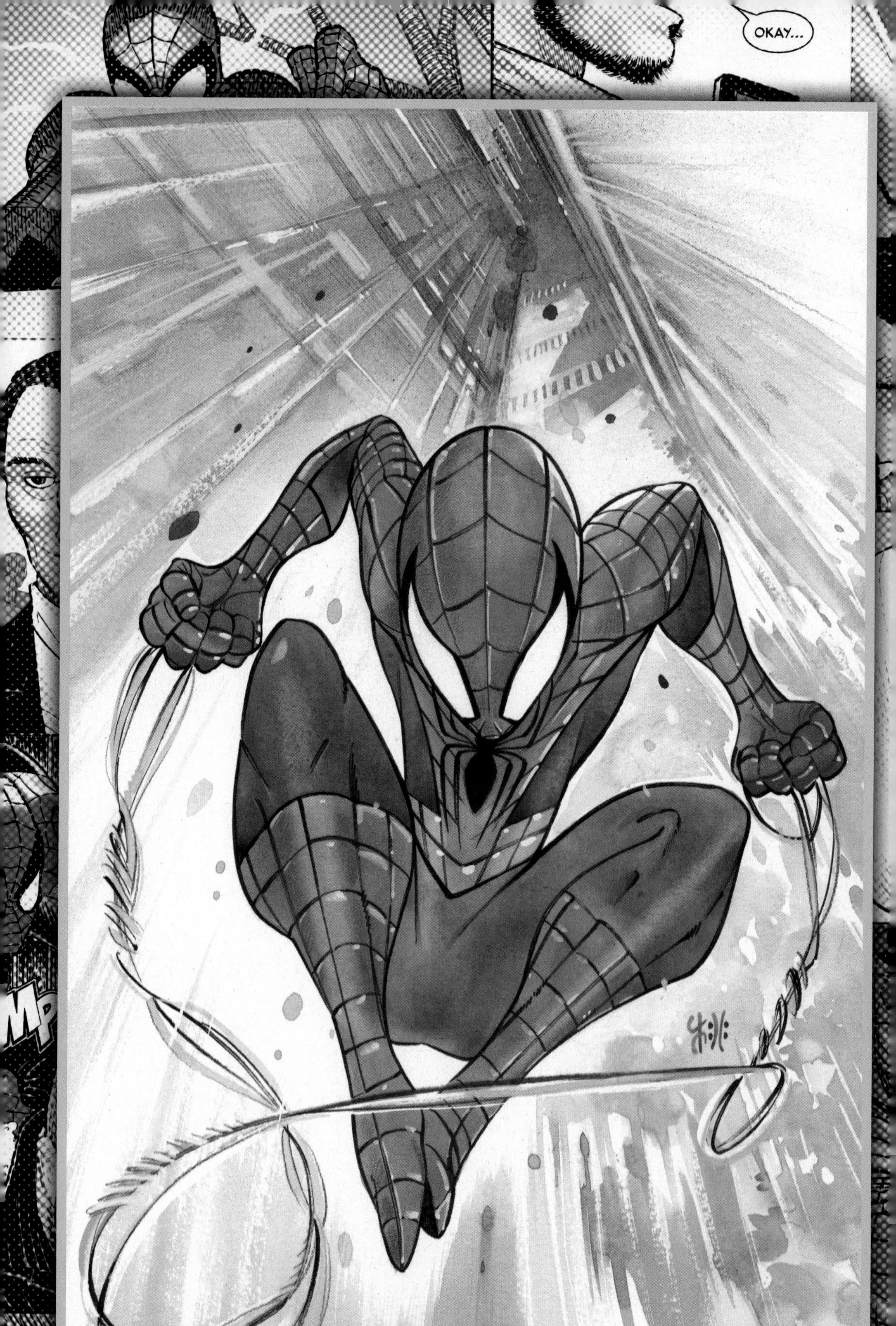
OKAY...

Peach Momoko #1 VARIANT

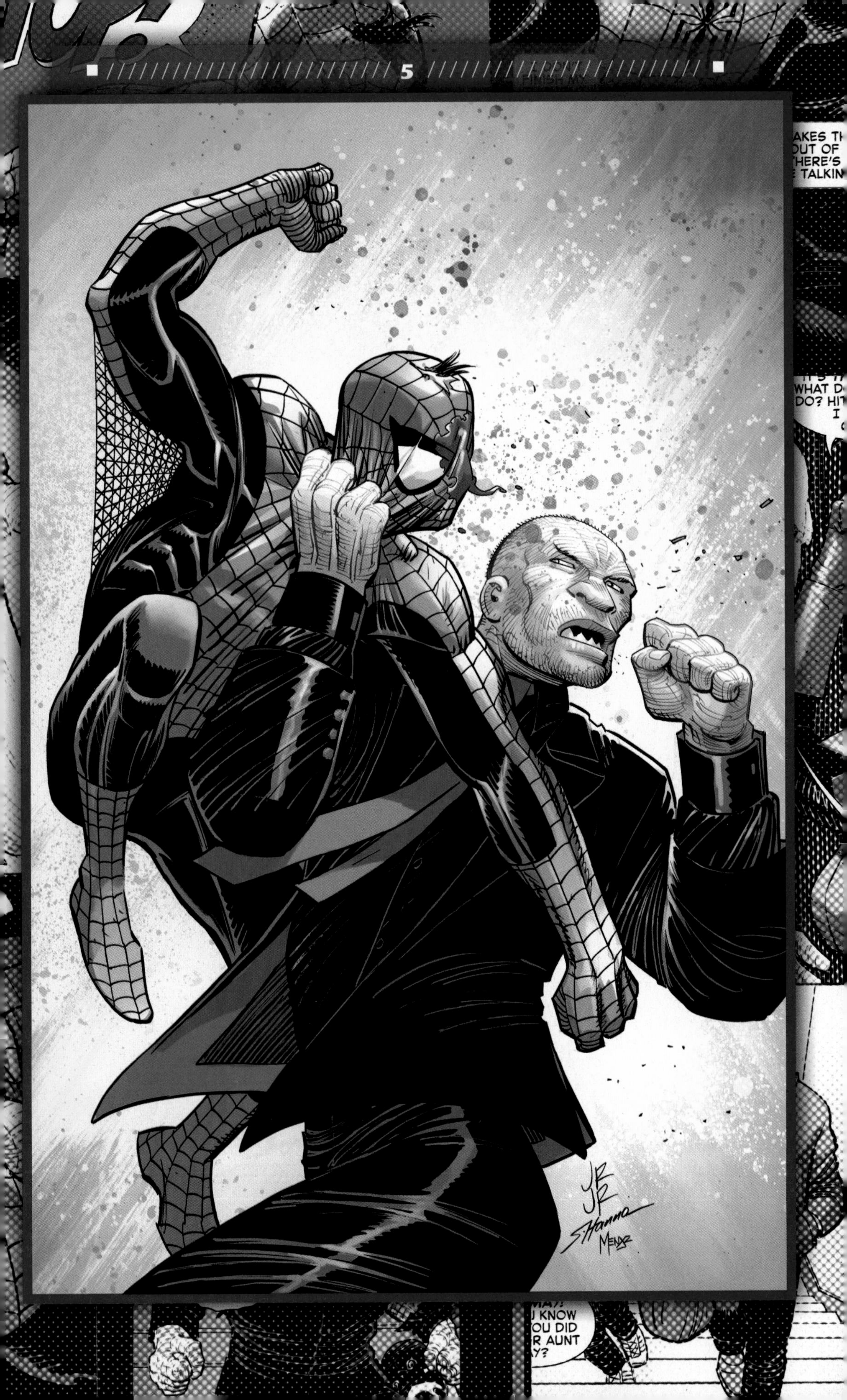

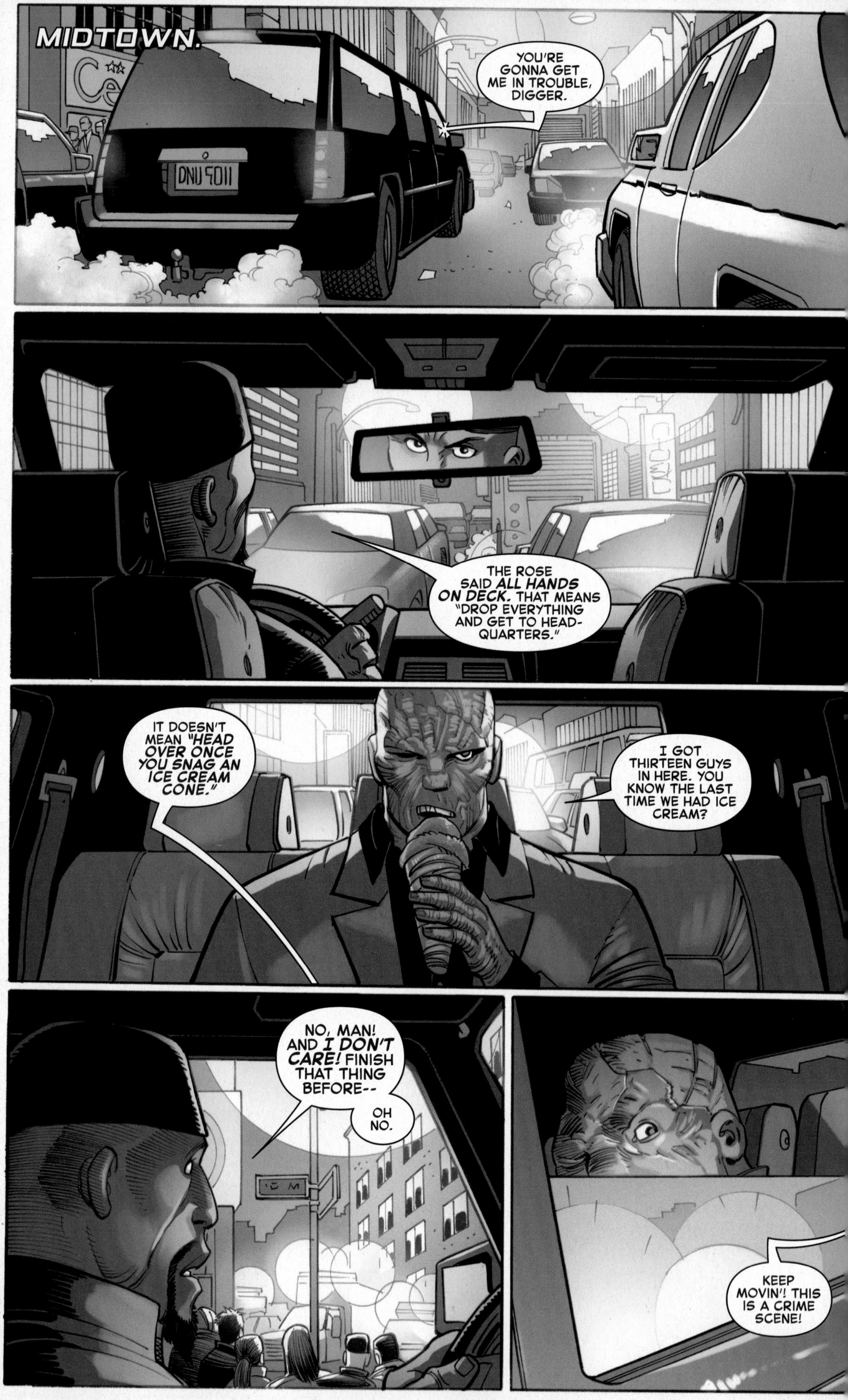
MIDTOWN.
YOU'RE GONNA GET ME IN TROUBLE, DIGGER.
DNU 5011
THE ROSE SAID **ALL HANDS ON DECK.** THAT MEANS "DROP EVERYTHING AND GET TO HEAD-QUARTERS."
IT DOESN'T MEAN "**HEAD OVER ONCE YOU SNAG AN ICE CREAM CONE.**"
I GOT THIRTEEN GUYS IN HERE. YOU KNOW THE LAST TIME WE HAD ICE CREAM?
NO, MAN! AND **I DON'T CARE!** FINISH THAT THING BEFORE--
OH NO.
KEEP MOVIN'! THIS IS A CRIME SCENE!

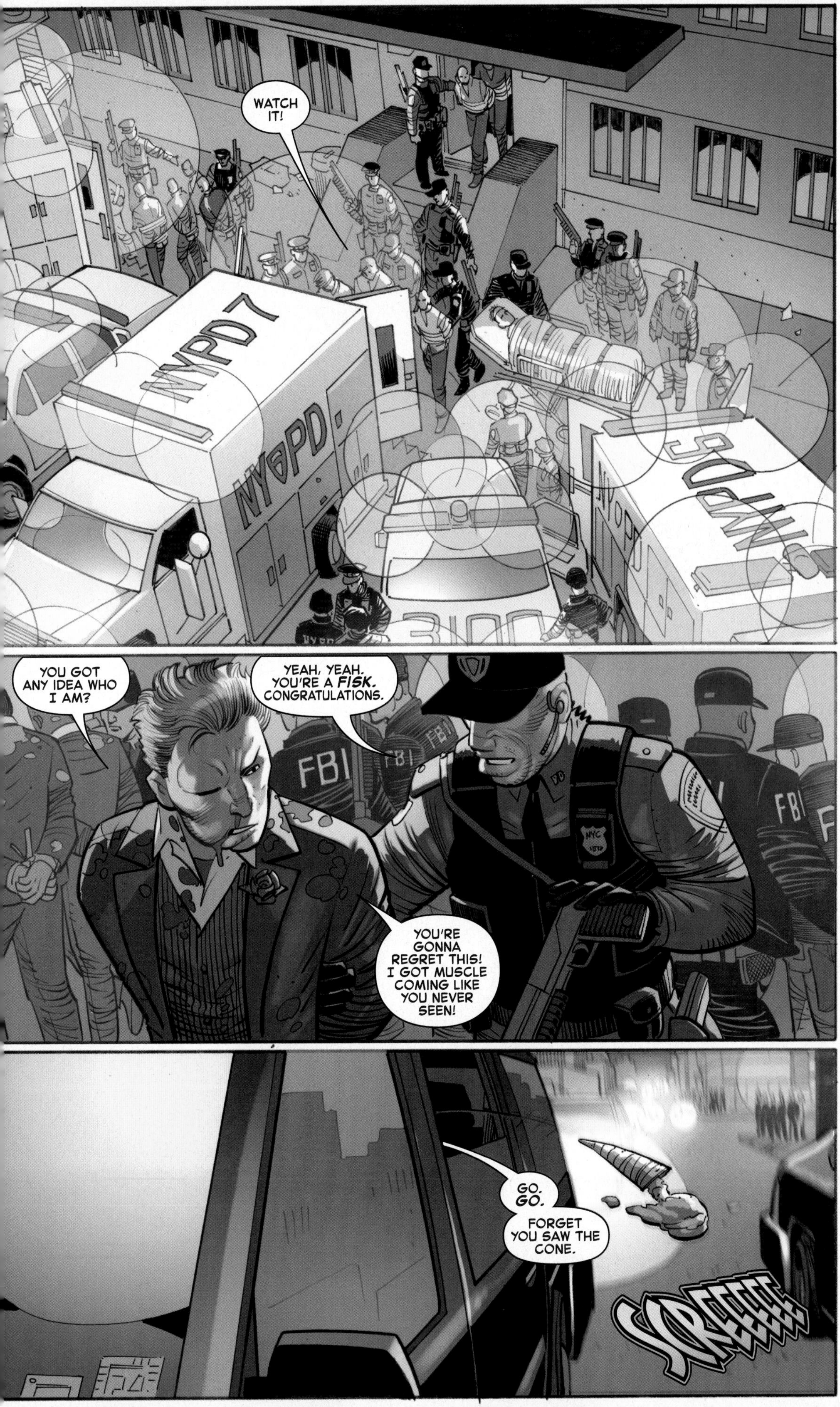
WATCH IT!
NYPD 7
NYPD
YOU GOT ANY IDEA WHO I AM?
YEAH, YEAH. YOU'RE A *FISK.* CONGRATULATIONS.
FBI
YOU'RE GONNA REGRET THIS! I GOT MUSCLE COMING LIKE YOU NEVER SEEN!
GO. *GO.*
FORGET YOU SAW THE CONE.
SCREEEE

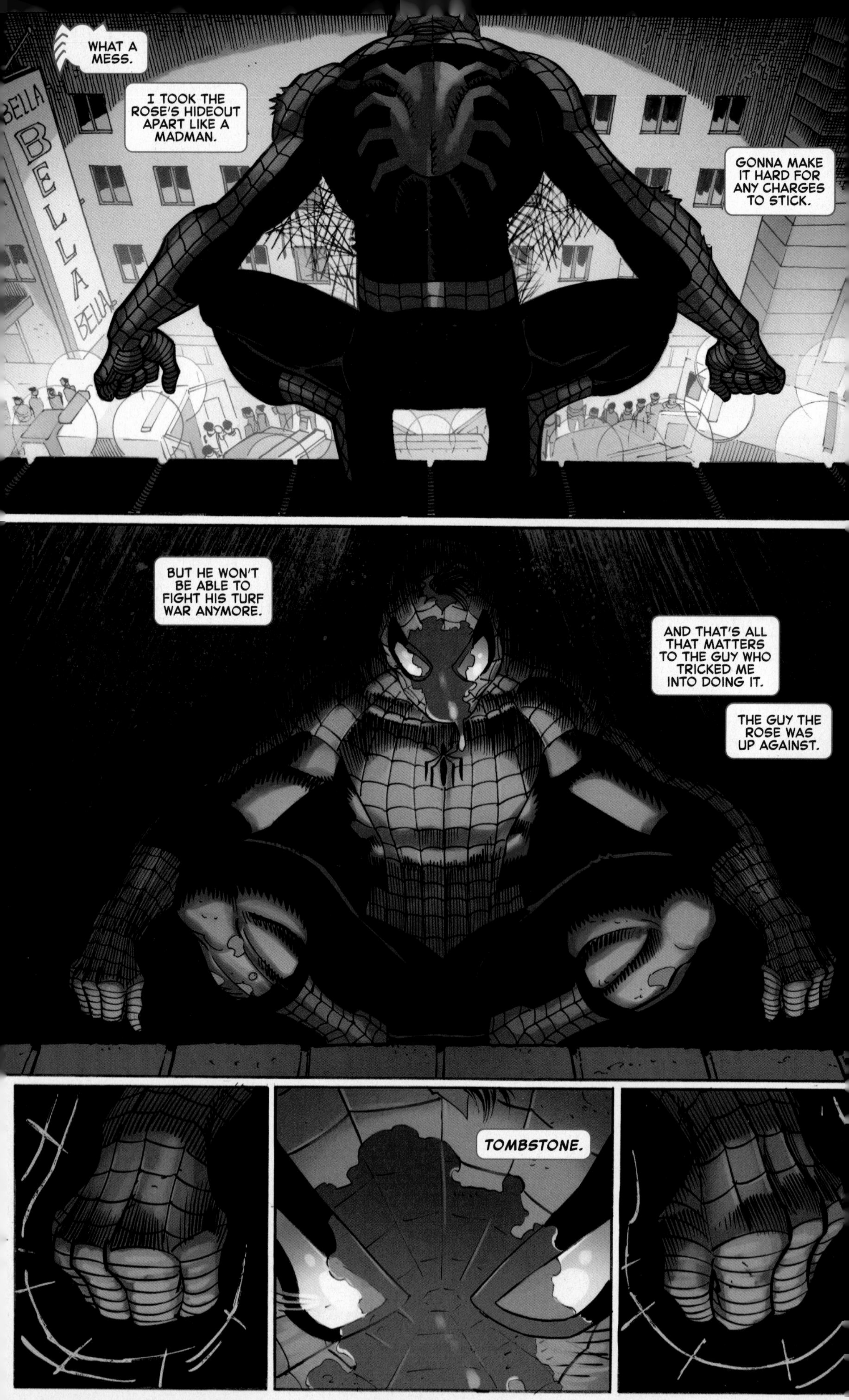
WHAT A MESS.
I TOOK THE ROSE'S HIDEOUT APART LIKE A MADMAN.
GONNA MAKE IT HARD FOR ANY CHARGES TO STICK.
BELLA
BELLA
BELLA
BUT HE WON'T BE ABLE TO FIGHT HIS TURF WAR ANYMORE.
AND THAT'S ALL THAT MATTERS TO THE GUY WHO TRICKED ME INTO DOING IT.
THE GUY THE ROSE WAS UP AGAINST.
TOMBSTONE.

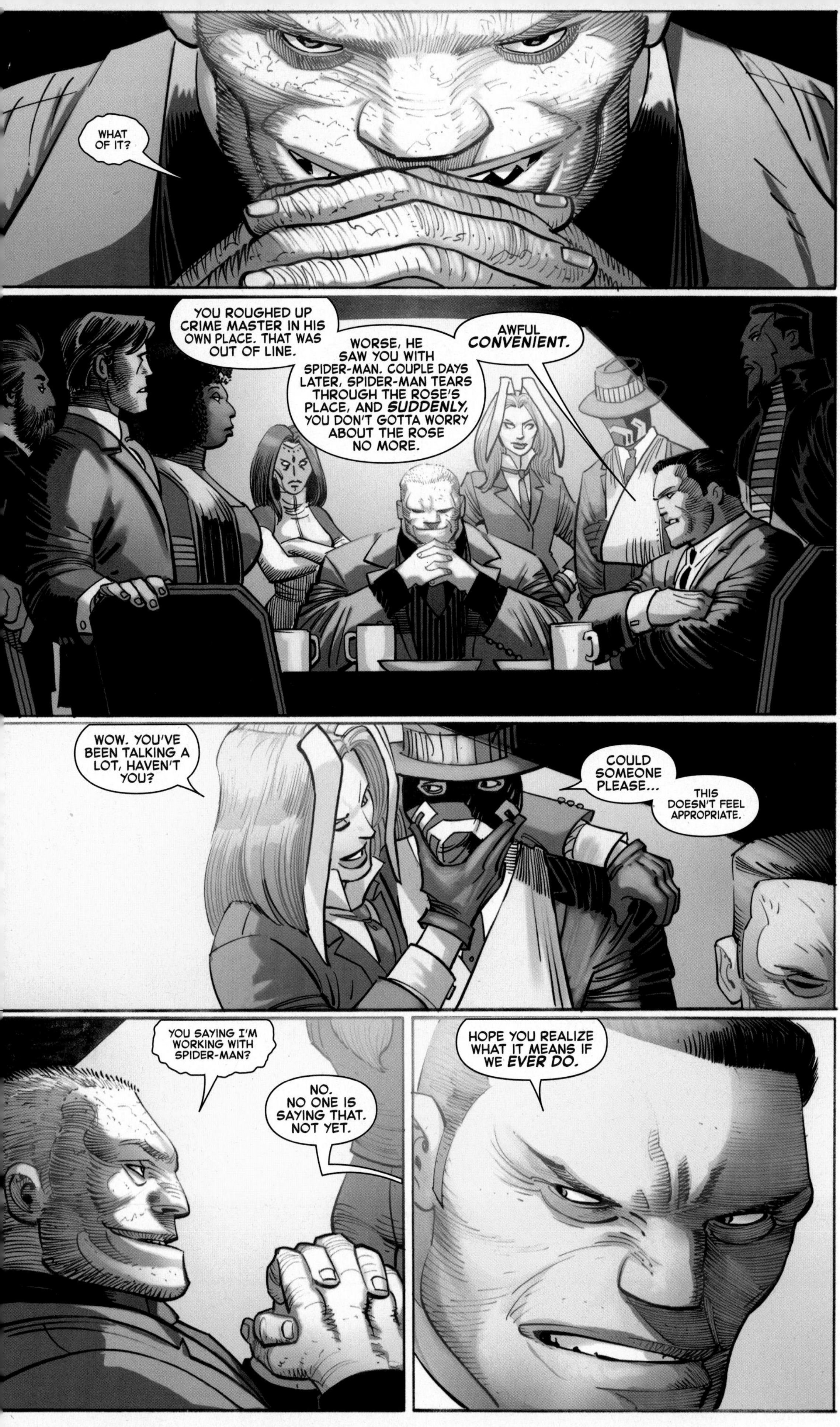
WHAT OF IT?
YOU ROUGHED UP CRIME MASTER IN HIS OWN PLACE. THAT WAS OUT OF LINE.
WORSE, HE SAW YOU WITH SPIDER-MAN. COUPLE DAYS LATER, SPIDER-MAN TEARS THROUGH THE ROSE'S PLACE, AND SUDDENLY, YOU DON'T GOTTA WORRY ABOUT THE ROSE NO MORE.
AWFUL CONVENIENT.
WOW. YOU'VE BEEN TALKING A LOT, HAVEN'T YOU?
COULD SOMEONE PLEASE...
THIS DOESN'T FEEL APPROPRIATE.
YOU SAYING I'M WORKING WITH SPIDER-MAN?
NO. NO ONE IS SAYING THAT. NOT YET.
HOPE YOU REALIZE WHAT IT MEANS IF WE EVER DO.

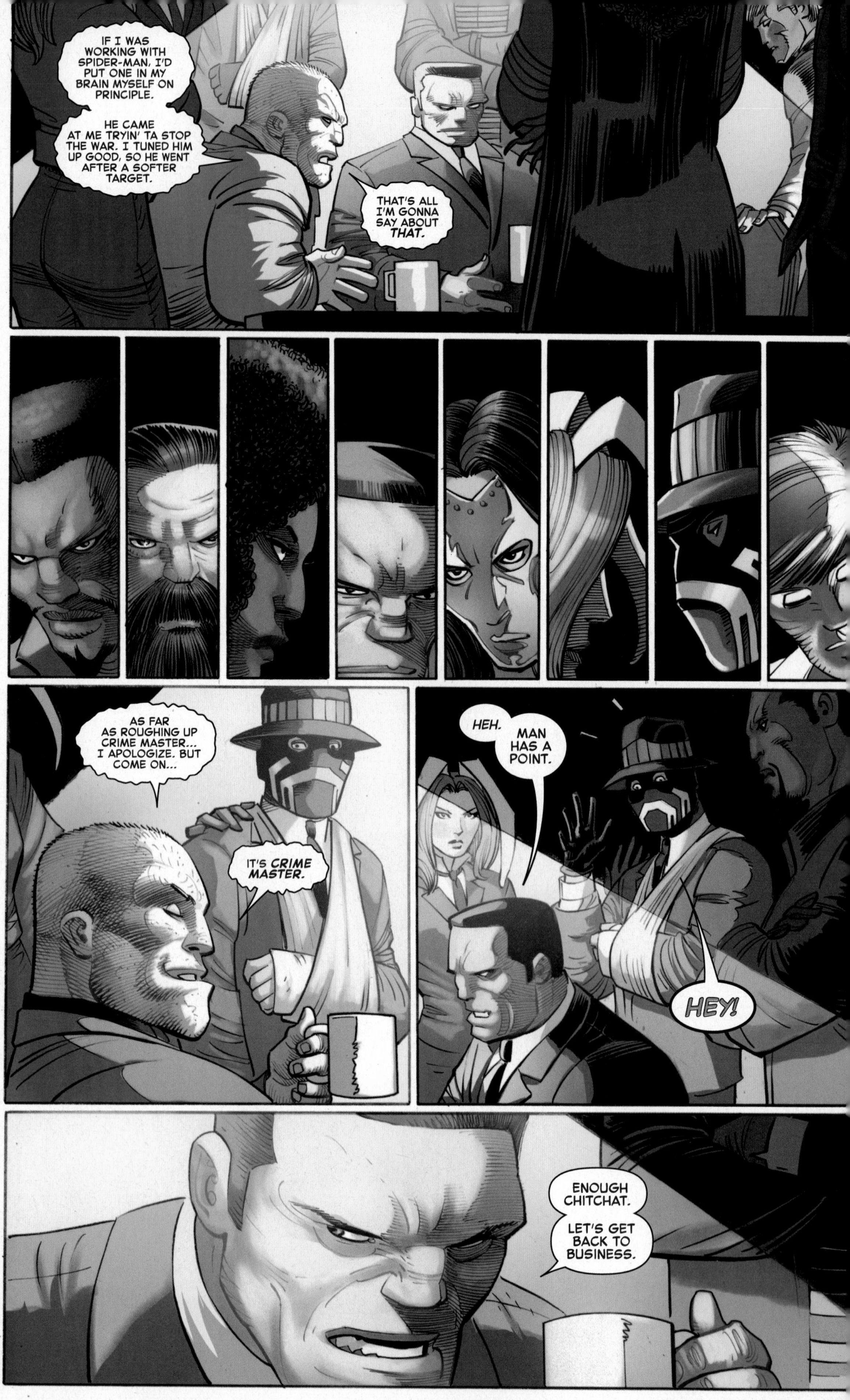
IF I WAS WORKING WITH SPIDER-MAN, I'D PUT ONE IN MY BRAIN MYSELF ON PRINCIPLE.
HE CAME AT ME TRYIN' TA STOP THE WAR. I TUNED HIM UP GOOD, SO HE WENT AFTER A SOFTER TARGET.
THAT'S ALL I'M GONNA SAY ABOUT *THAT.*
AS FAR AS ROUGHING UP CRIME MASTER... I APOLOGIZE. BUT COME ON...
IT'S *CRIME MASTER.*
HEH.
MAN HAS A POINT.
HEY!
ENOUGH CHITCHAT.
LET'S GET BACK TO BUSINESS.

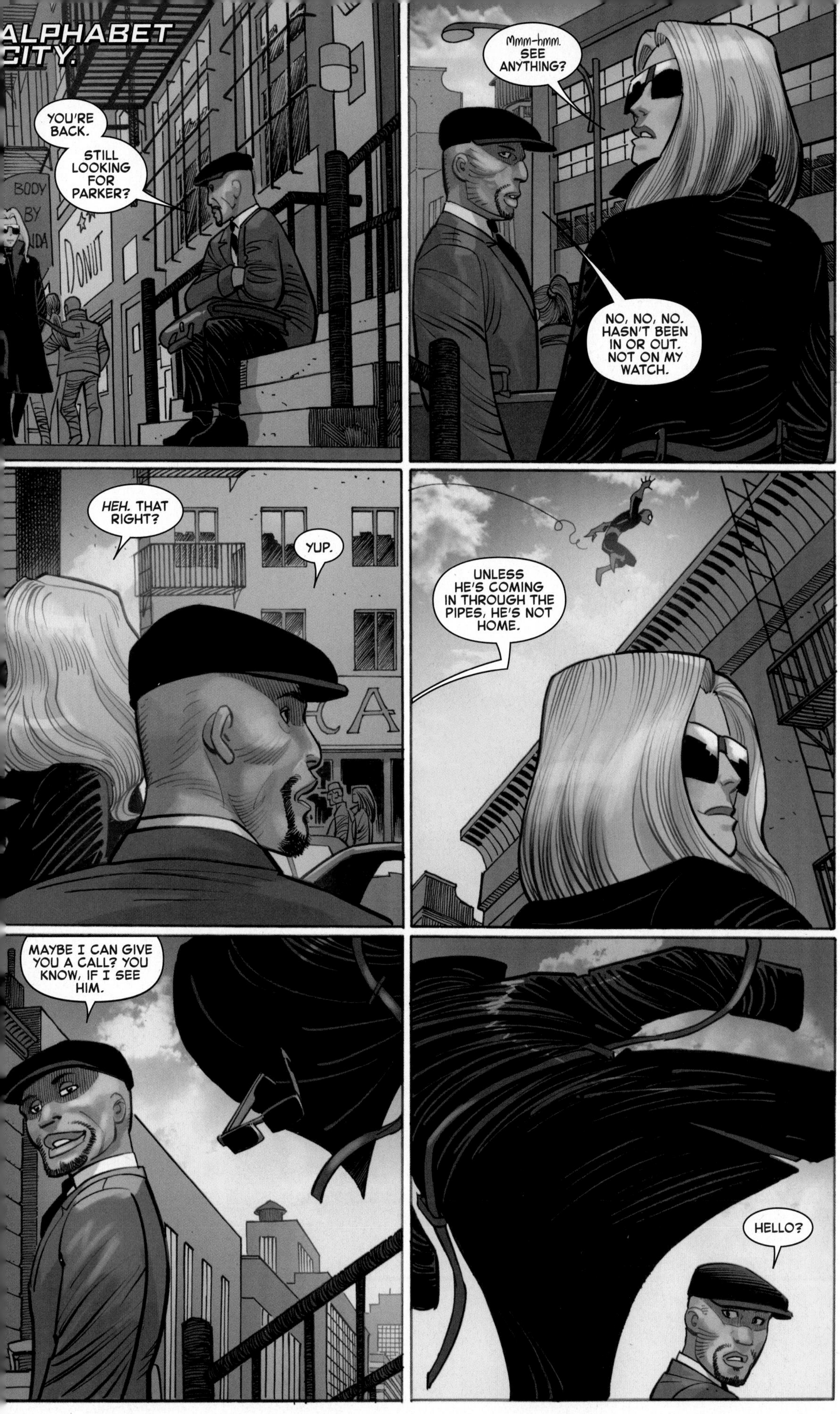
ALPHABET CITY.
YOU'RE BACK.
STILL LOOKING FOR PARKER?
BODY BY
DONUT
Mmm-hmm. SEE ANYTHING?
NO, NO, NO. HASN'T BEEN IN OR OUT. NOT ON MY WATCH.
HEH. THAT RIGHT?
YUP.
UNLESS HE'S COMING IN THROUGH THE PIPES, HE'S NOT HOME.
MAYBE I CAN GIVE YOU A CALL? YOU KNOW, IF I SEE HIM.
HELLO?

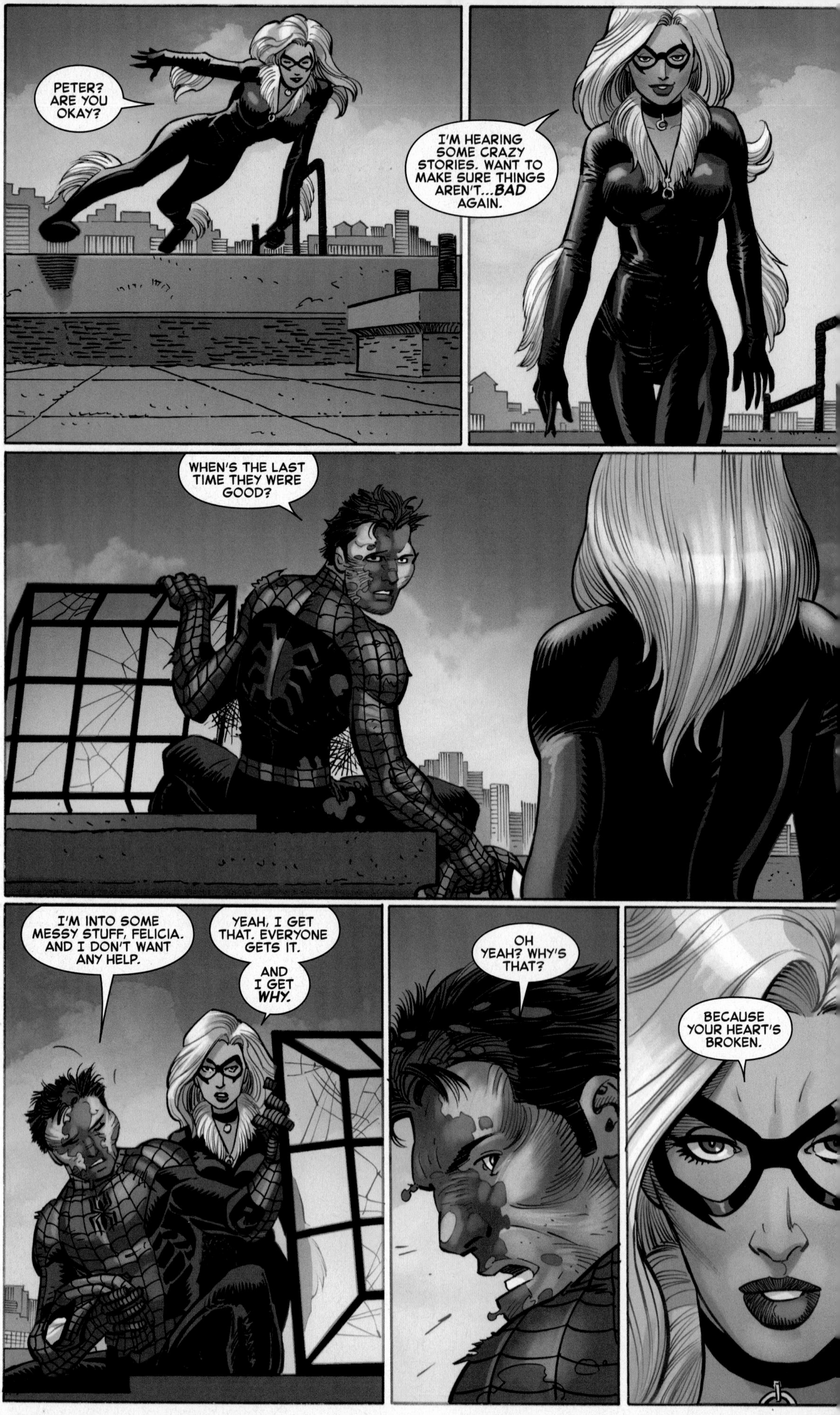
PETER? ARE YOU OKAY?
I'M HEARING SOME CRAZY STORIES. WANT TO MAKE SURE THINGS AREN'T...BAD AGAIN.
WHEN'S THE LAST TIME THEY WERE GOOD?
I'M INTO SOME MESSY STUFF, FELICIA. AND I DON'T WANT ANY HELP.
YEAH, I GET THAT. EVERYONE GETS IT.
AND I GET WHY.
OH YEAH? WHY'S THAT?
BECAUSE YOUR HEART'S BROKEN.

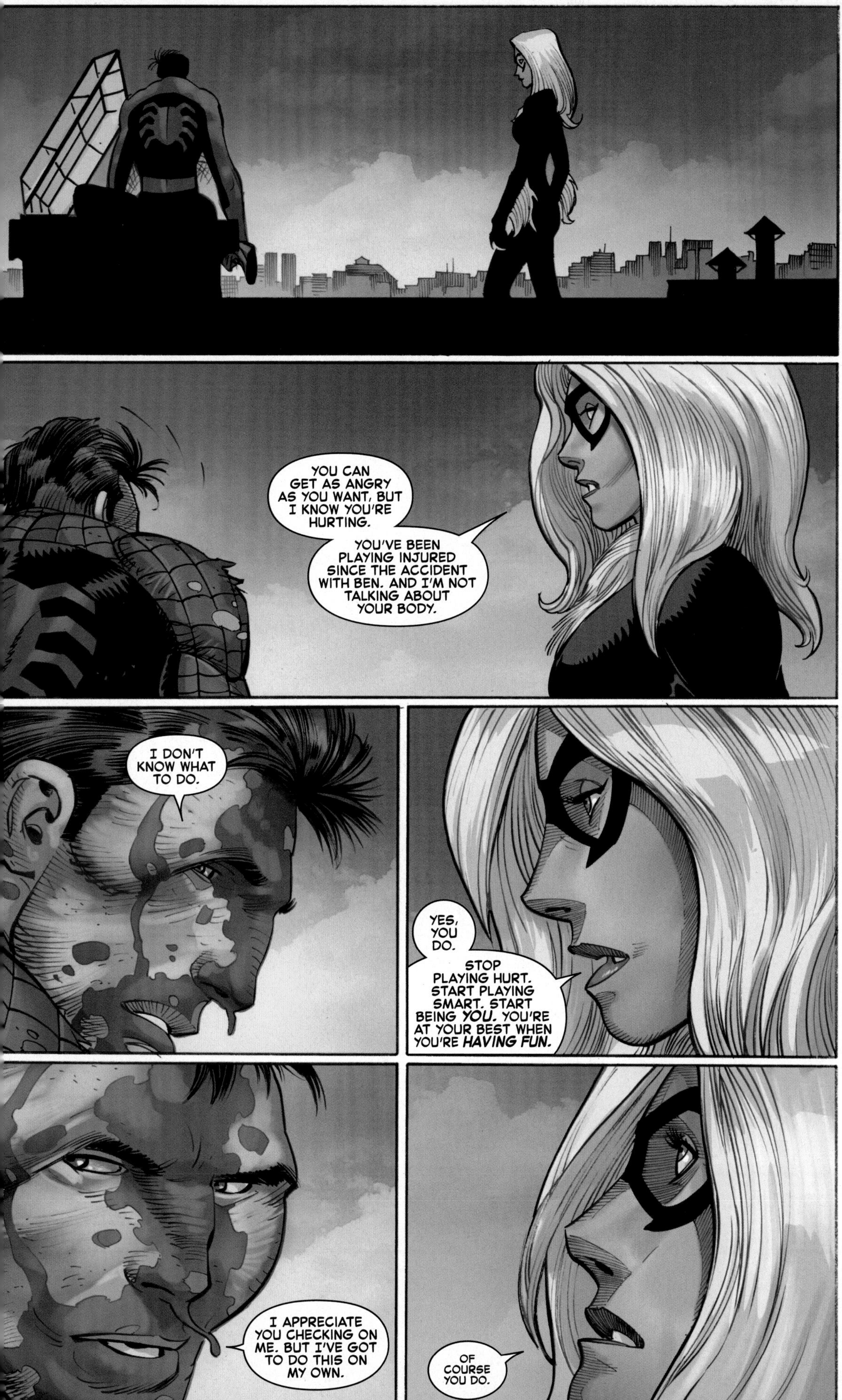
YOU CAN GET AS ANGRY AS YOU WANT, BUT I KNOW YOU'RE HURTING.
YOU'VE BEEN PLAYING INJURED SINCE THE ACCIDENT WITH BEN. AND I'M NOT TALKING ABOUT YOUR BODY.
I DON'T KNOW WHAT TO DO.
YES, YOU DO.
STOP PLAYING HURT. START PLAYING SMART. START BEING *YOU*. YOU'RE AT YOUR BEST WHEN YOU'RE *HAVING FUN*.
I APPRECIATE YOU CHECKING ON ME. BUT I'VE GOT TO DO THIS ON MY OWN.
OF COURSE YOU DO.

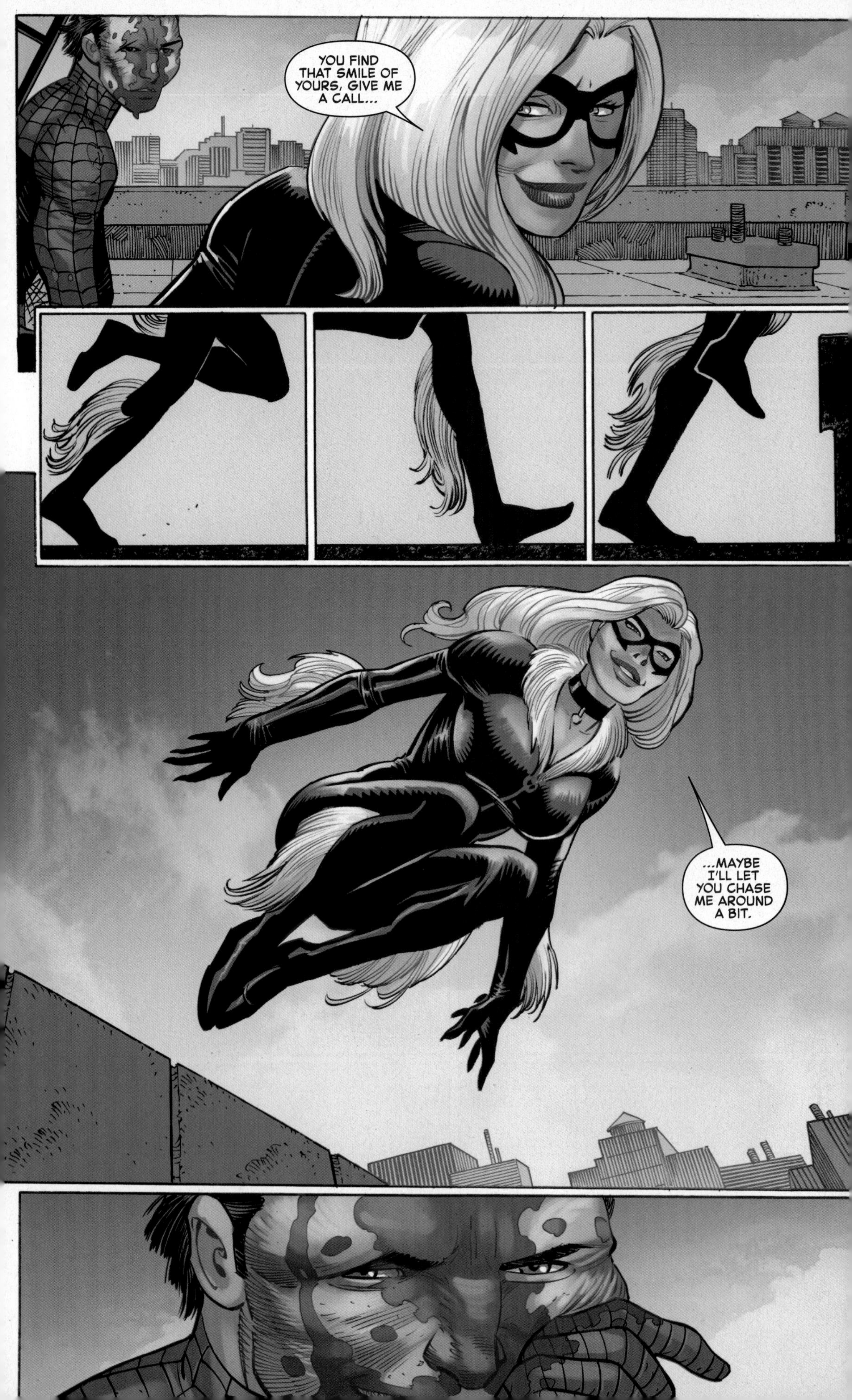
YOU FIND THAT SMILE OF YOURS, GIVE ME A CALL...
...MAYBE I'LL LET YOU CHASE ME AROUND A BIT.

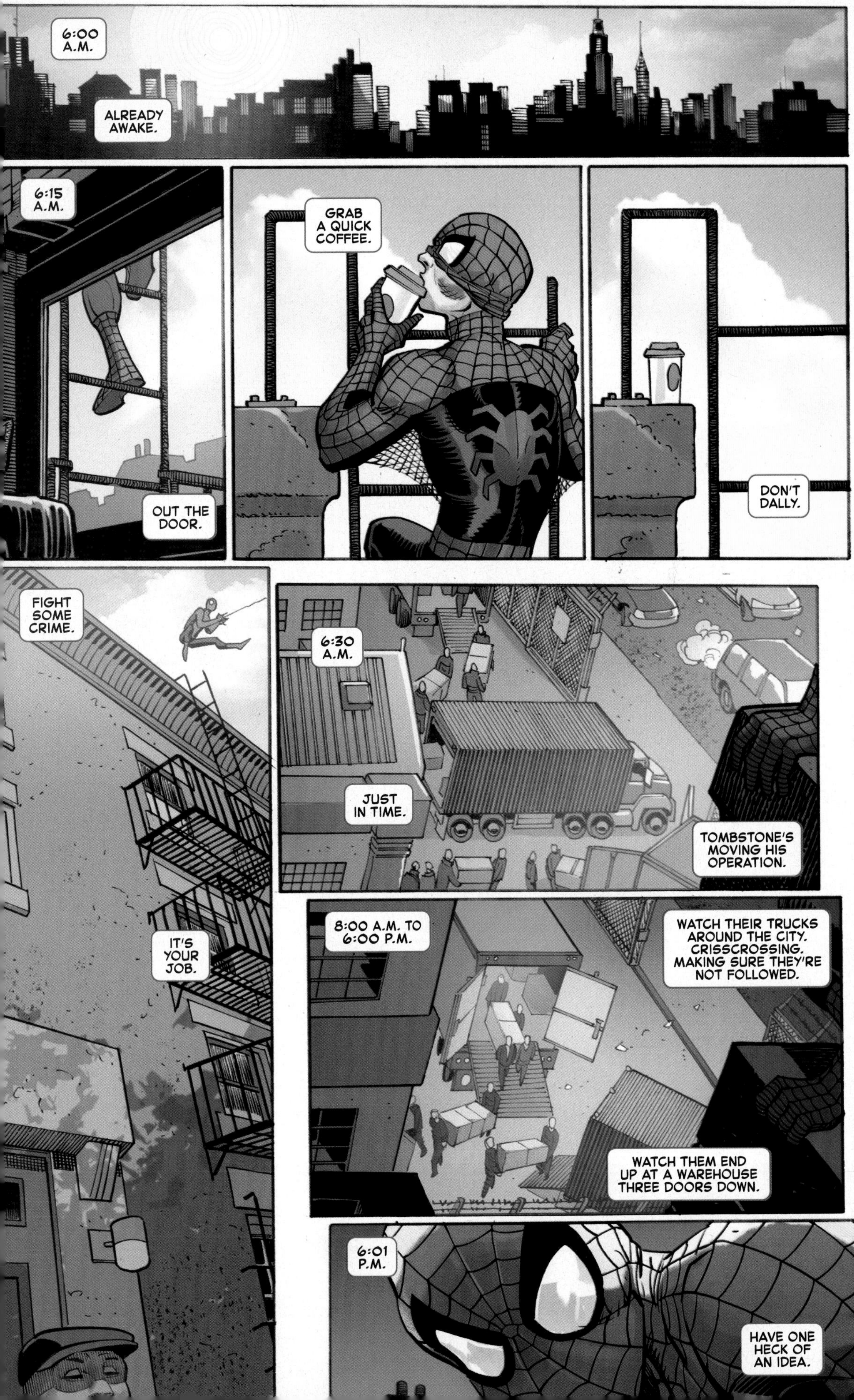
6:00 A.M.
ALREADY AWAKE.
6:15 A.M.
OUT THE DOOR.
GRAB A QUICK COFFEE.
DON'T DALLY.
FIGHT SOME CRIME.
IT'S YOUR JOB.
6:30 A.M.
JUST IN TIME.
TOMBSTONE'S MOVING HIS OPERATION.
8:00 A.M. TO 6:00 P.M.
WATCH THEIR TRUCKS AROUND THE CITY. CRISSCROSSING. MAKING SURE THEY'RE NOT FOLLOWED.
WATCH THEM END UP AT A WAREHOUSE THREE DOORS DOWN.
6:01 P.M.
HAVE ONE HECK OF AN IDEA.

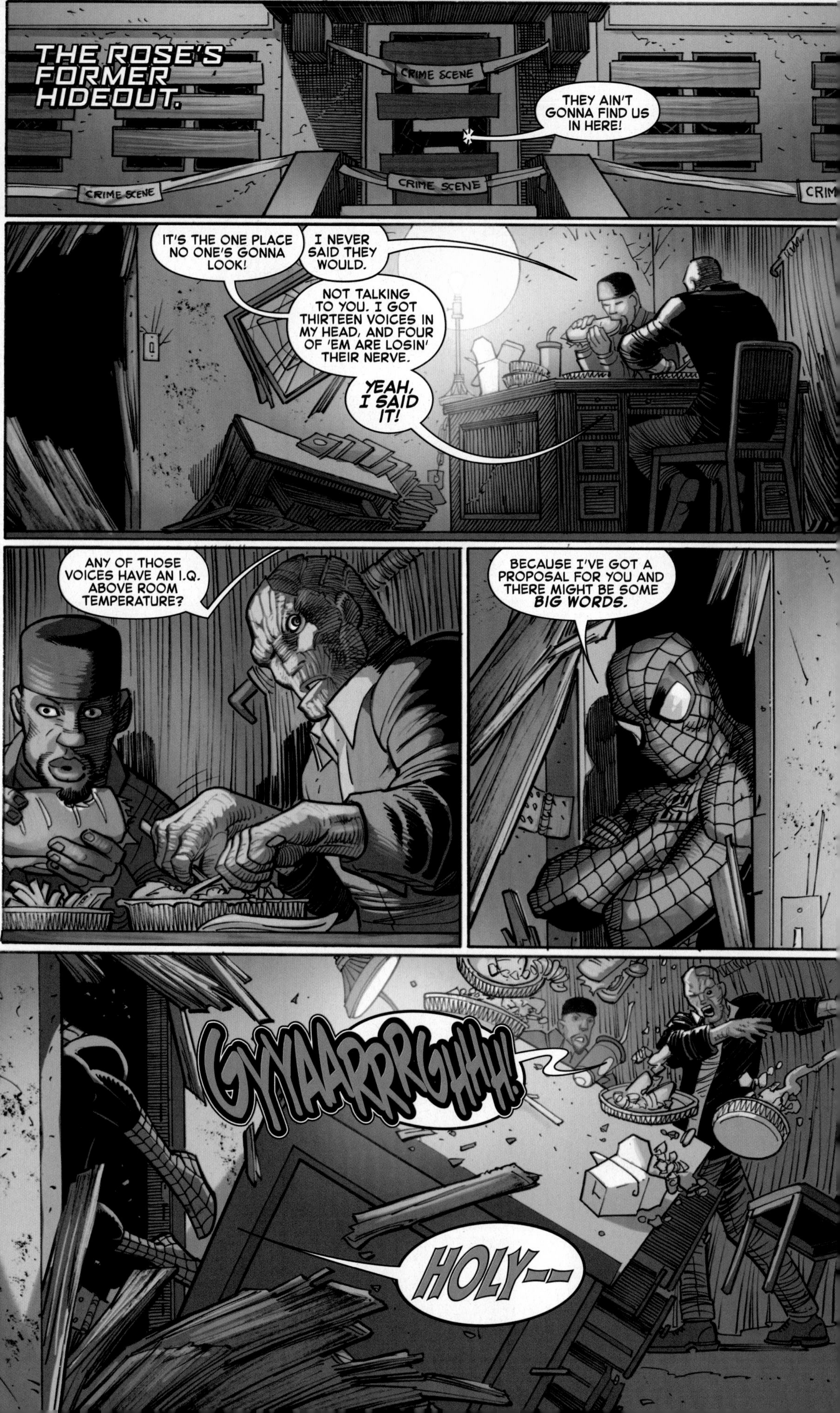
THE ROSE'S FORMER HIDEOUT.
CRIME SCENE
CRIME SCENE
CRIME SCENE
THEY AIN'T GONNA FIND US IN HERE!
IT'S THE ONE PLACE NO ONE'S GONNA LOOK!
I NEVER SAID THEY WOULD.
NOT TALKING TO YOU. I GOT THIRTEEN VOICES IN MY HEAD, AND FOUR OF 'EM ARE LOSIN' THEIR NERVE.
YEAH, I SAID IT!
ANY OF THOSE VOICES HAVE AN I.Q. ABOVE ROOM TEMPERATURE?
BECAUSE I'VE GOT A PROPOSAL FOR YOU AND THERE MIGHT BE SOME BIG WORDS.
GYYAARRRGHHH!
HOLY--

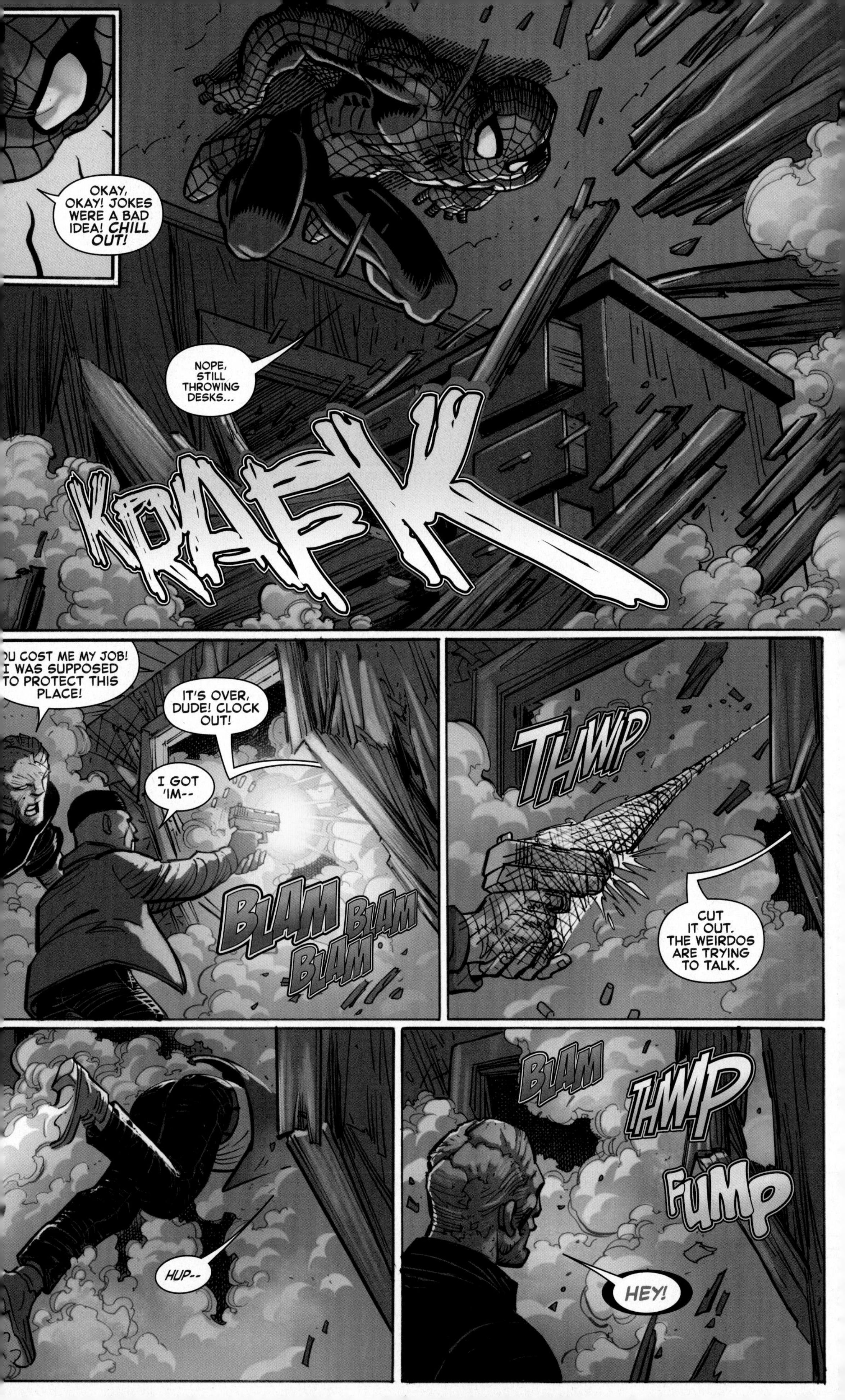
OKAY, OKAY! JOKES WERE A BAD IDEA! CHILL OUT!
NOPE, STILL THROWING DESKS...
KRAAK
OU COST ME MY JOB! I WAS SUPPOSED TO PROTECT THIS PLACE!
IT'S OVER, DUDE! CLOCK OUT!
I GOT 'IM--
BLAM BLAM BLAM
THWIP
CUT IT OUT. THE WEIRDOS ARE TRYING TO TALK.
HUP--
BLAM
THWIP
FUMP
HEY!

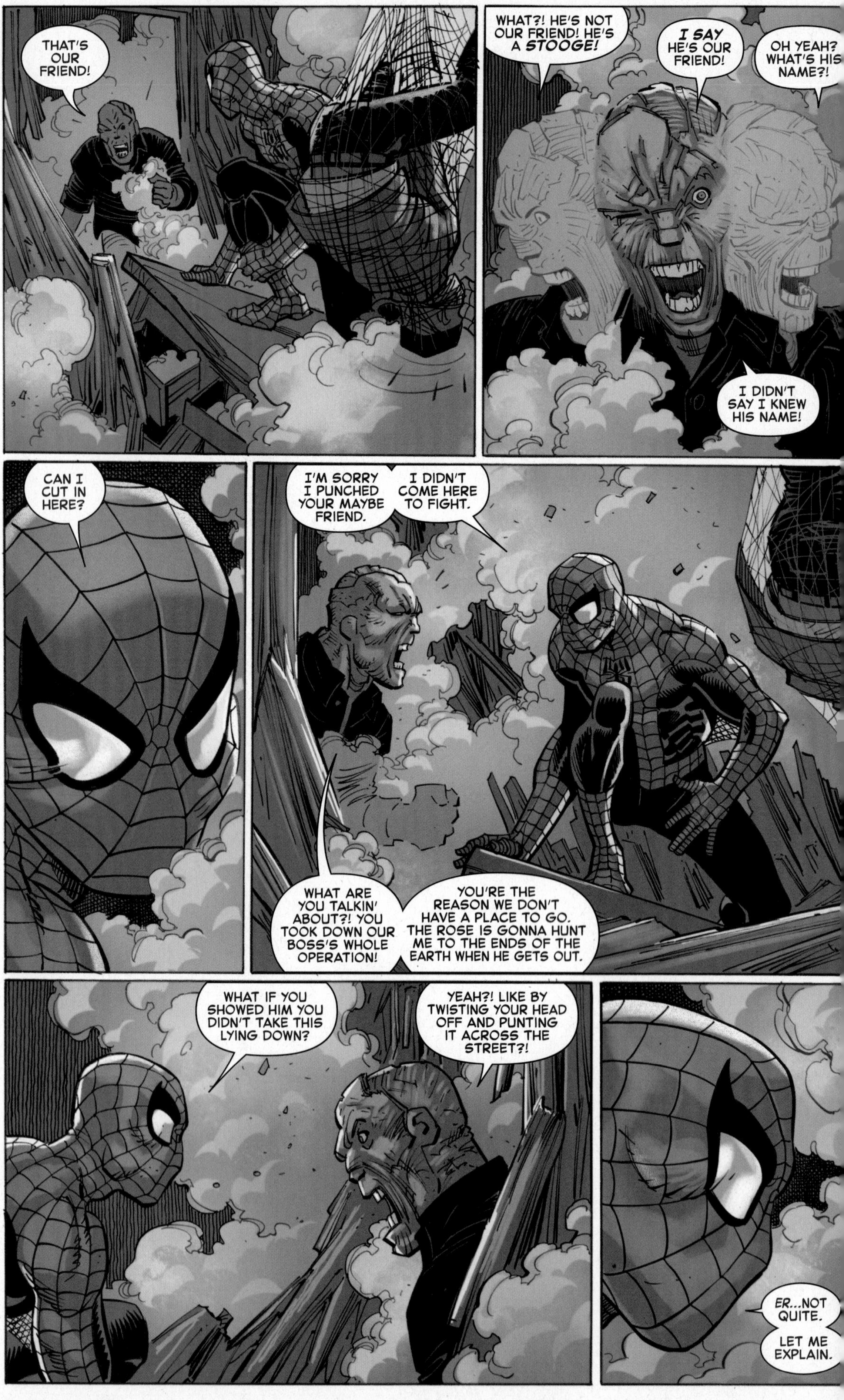
THAT'S OUR FRIEND!
WHAT?! HE'S NOT OUR FRIEND! HE'S A STOOGE!
I SAY HE'S OUR FRIEND!
OH YEAH? WHAT'S HIS NAME?!
I DIDN'T SAY I KNEW HIS NAME!
CAN I CUT IN HERE?
I'M SORRY I PUNCHED YOUR MAYBE FRIEND.
I DIDN'T COME HERE TO FIGHT.
WHAT ARE YOU TALKIN' ABOUT?! YOU TOOK DOWN OUR BOSS'S WHOLE OPERATION!
YOU'RE THE REASON WE DON'T HAVE A PLACE TO GO. THE ROSE IS GONNA HUNT ME TO THE ENDS OF THE EARTH WHEN HE GETS OUT.
WHAT IF YOU SHOWED HIM YOU DIDN'T TAKE THIS LYING DOWN?
YEAH?! LIKE BY TWISTING YOUR HEAD OFF AND PUNTING IT ACROSS THE STREET?!
ER...NOT QUITE.
LET ME EXPLAIN.

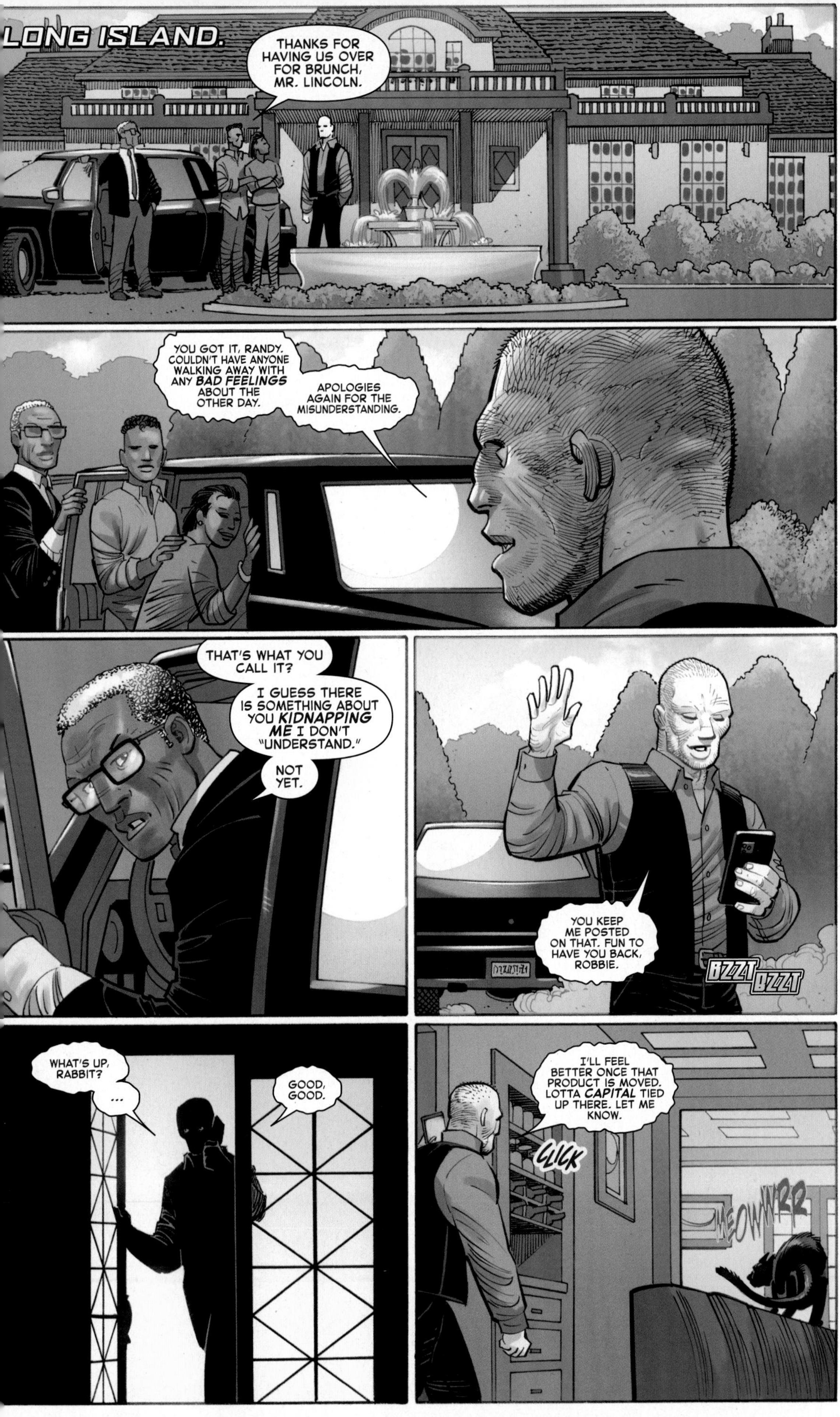
LONG ISLAND.
THANKS FOR HAVING US OVER FOR BRUNCH, MR. LINCOLN.
YOU GOT IT, RANDY. COULDN'T HAVE ANYONE WALKING AWAY WITH ANY BAD FEELINGS ABOUT THE OTHER DAY.
APOLOGIES AGAIN FOR THE MISUNDERSTANDING.
THAT'S WHAT YOU CALL IT?
I GUESS THERE IS SOMETHING ABOUT YOU KIDNAPPING ME I DON'T "UNDERSTAND."
NOT YET.
YOU KEEP ME POSTED ON THAT. FUN TO HAVE YOU BACK, ROBBIE.
BZZZT BZZZT
WHAT'S UP, RABBIT?
...
GOOD, GOOD.
I'LL FEEL BETTER ONCE THAT PRODUCT IS MOVED. LOTTA CAPITAL TIED UP THERE. LET ME KNOW.
CLICK
MEOWWRR

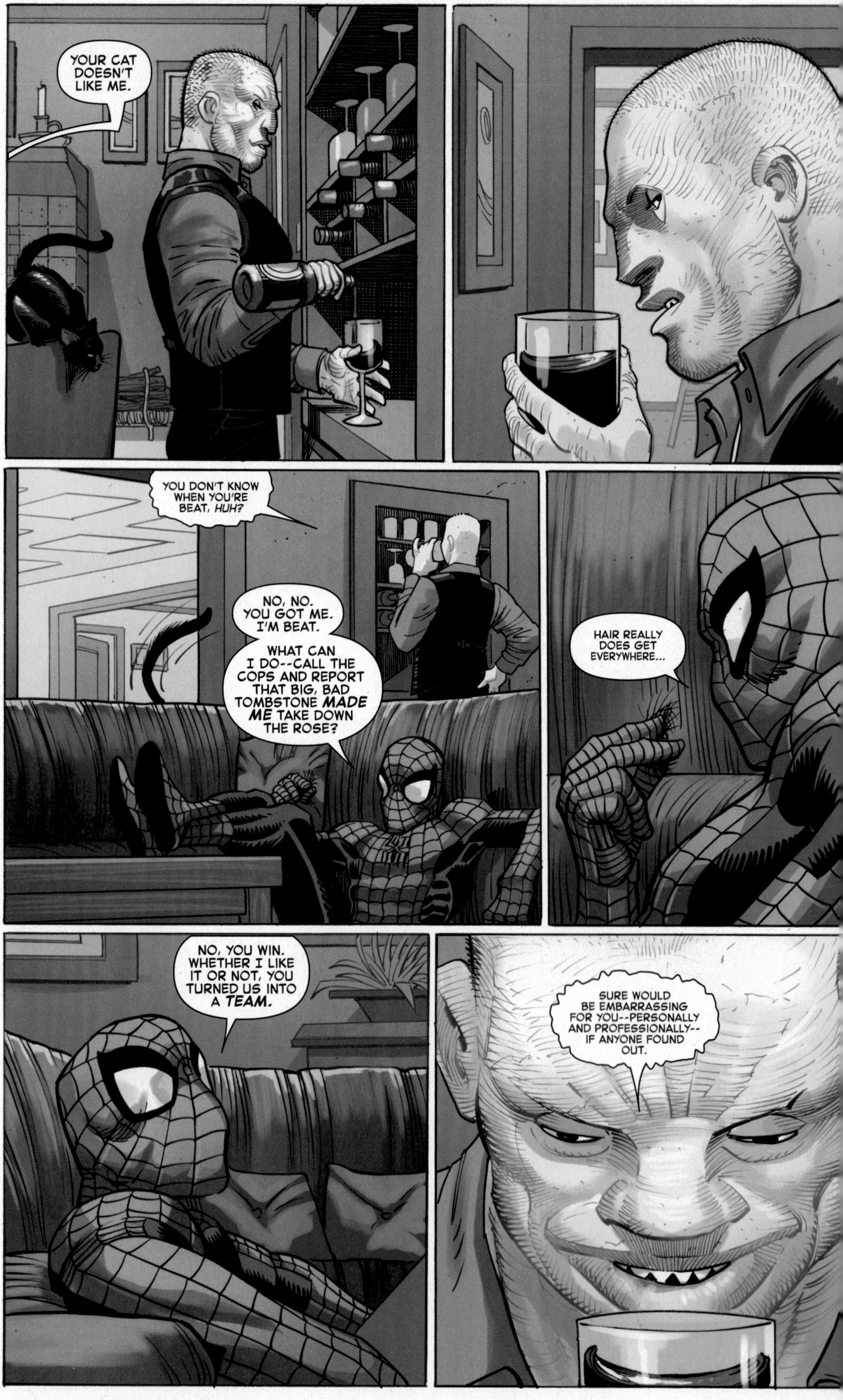
YOUR CAT DOESN'T LIKE ME.
YOU DON'T KNOW WHEN YOU'RE BEAT, *HUH?*
NO, NO. YOU GOT ME. I'M BEAT.
WHAT CAN I DO--CALL THE COPS AND REPORT THAT BIG, BAD TOMBSTONE ***MADE ME*** TAKE DOWN THE ROSE?
HAIR REALLY DOES GET EVERYWHERE...
NO, YOU WIN. WHETHER I LIKE IT OR NOT, YOU TURNED US INTO A ***TEAM.***
SURE WOULD BE EMBARRASSING FOR YOU--PERSONALLY AND PROFESSIONALLY--IF ANYONE FOUND OUT.

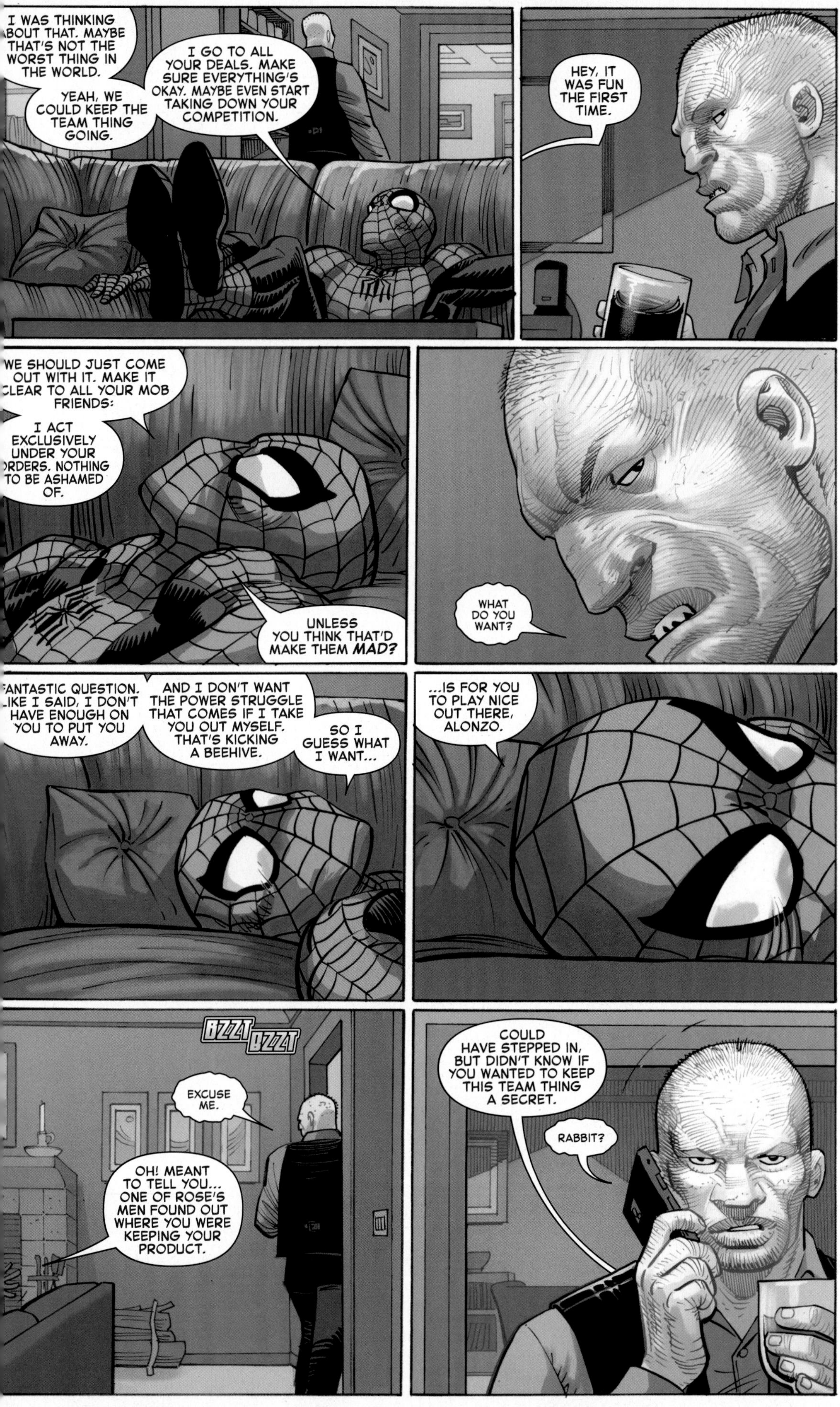

I WAS THINKING ABOUT THAT. MAYBE THAT'S NOT THE WORST THING IN THE WORLD.
YEAH, WE COULD KEEP THE TEAM THING GOING.
I GO TO ALL YOUR DEALS. MAKE SURE EVERYTHING'S OKAY. MAYBE EVEN START TAKING DOWN YOUR COMPETITION.
HEY, IT WAS FUN THE FIRST TIME.
WE SHOULD JUST COME OUT WITH IT. MAKE IT CLEAR TO ALL YOUR MOB FRIENDS:
I ACT EXCLUSIVELY UNDER YOUR ORDERS. NOTHING TO BE ASHAMED OF.
UNLESS YOU THINK THAT'D MAKE THEM MAD?
WHAT DO YOU WANT?
FANTASTIC QUESTION. LIKE I SAID, I DON'T HAVE ENOUGH ON YOU TO PUT YOU AWAY.
AND I DON'T WANT THE POWER STRUGGLE THAT COMES IF I TAKE YOU OUT MYSELF. THAT'S KICKING A BEEHIVE.
SO I GUESS WHAT I WANT...
...IS FOR YOU TO PLAY NICE OUT THERE, ALONZO.
BZZZT BZZZT
EXCUSE ME.
OH! MEANT TO TELL YOU... ONE OF ROSE'S MEN FOUND OUT WHERE YOU WERE KEEPING YOUR PRODUCT.
COULD HAVE STEPPED IN, BUT DIDN'T KNOW IF YOU WANTED TO KEEP THIS TEAM THING A SECRET.
RABBIT?

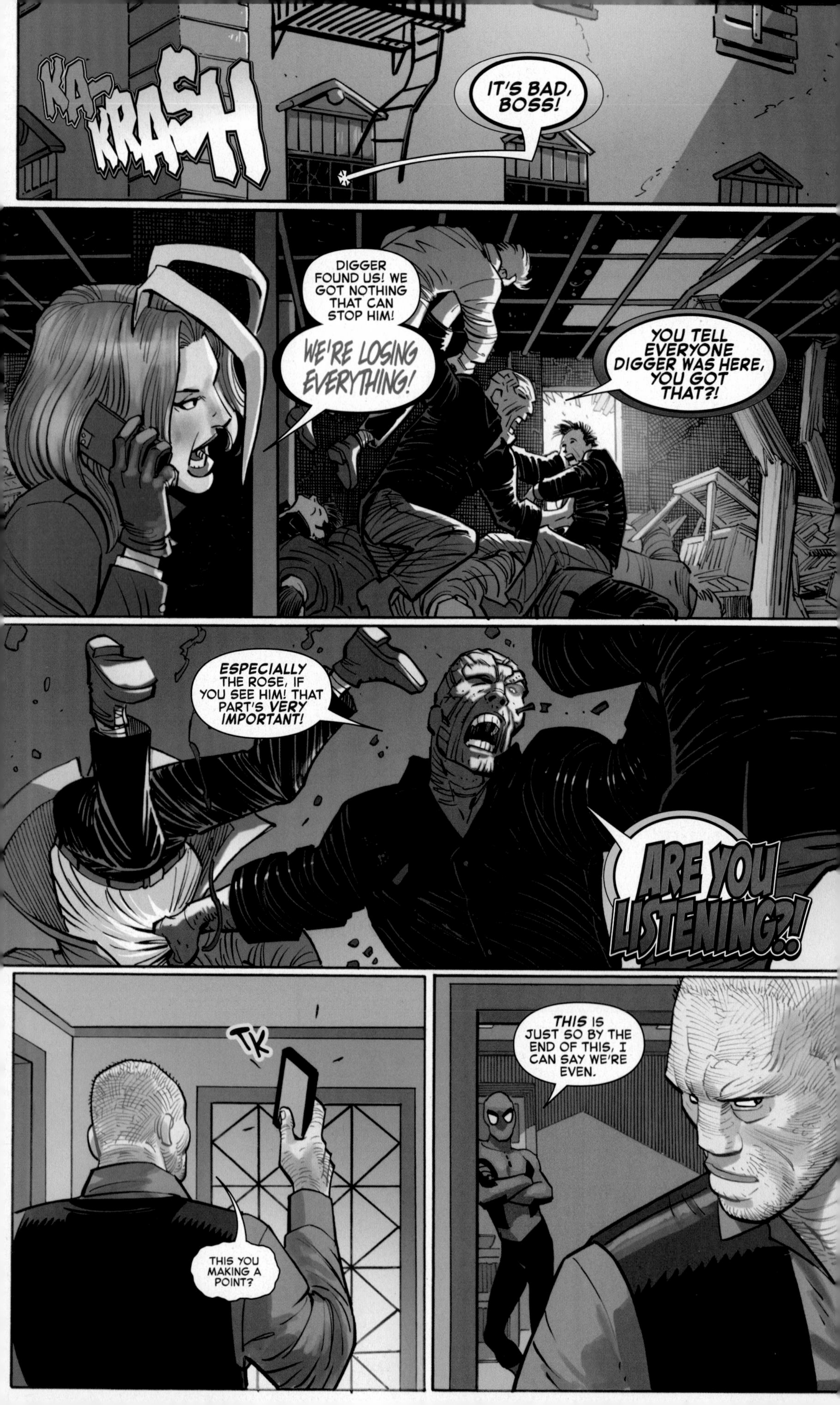
KA-KRASH
IT'S BAD, BOSS!
DIGGER FOUND US! WE GOT NOTHING THAT CAN STOP HIM!
WE'RE LOSING EVERYTHING!
YOU TELL EVERYONE DIGGER WAS HERE, YOU GOT THAT?!
ESPECIALLY THE ROSE, IF YOU SEE HIM! THAT PART'S VERY IMPORTANT!
ARE YOU LISTENING?!
TK
THIS YOU MAKING A POINT?
THIS IS JUST SO BY THE END OF THIS, I CAN SAY WE'RE EVEN.

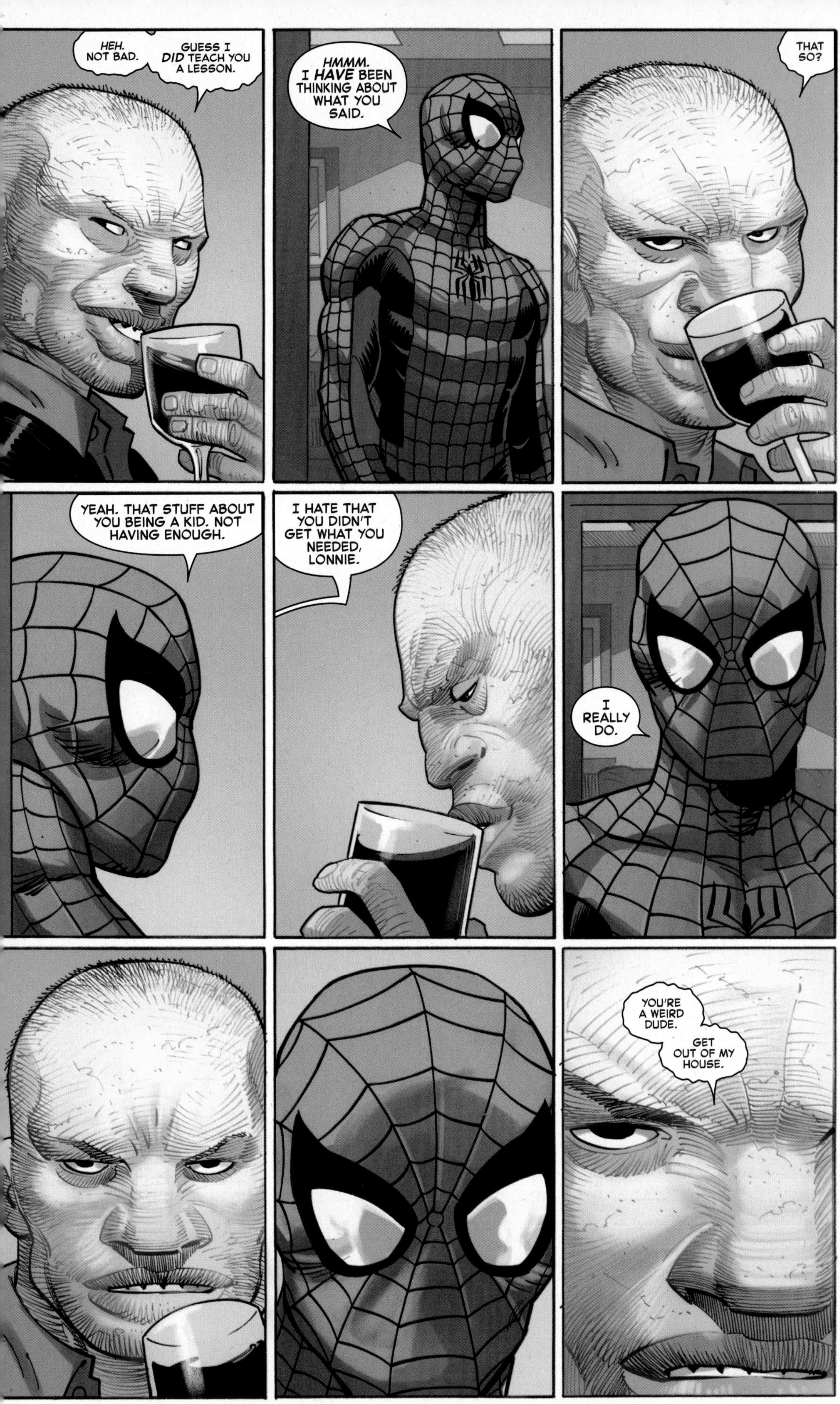
HEH. NOT BAD.
GUESS I *DID* TEACH YOU A LESSON.
HMMM. I *HAVE* BEEN THINKING ABOUT WHAT YOU SAID.
THAT SO?
YEAH. THAT STUFF ABOUT YOU BEING A KID. NOT HAVING ENOUGH.
I HATE THAT YOU DIDN'T GET WHAT YOU NEEDED, LONNIE.
I REALLY DO.
YOU'RE A WEIRD DUDE.
GET OUT OF MY HOUSE.

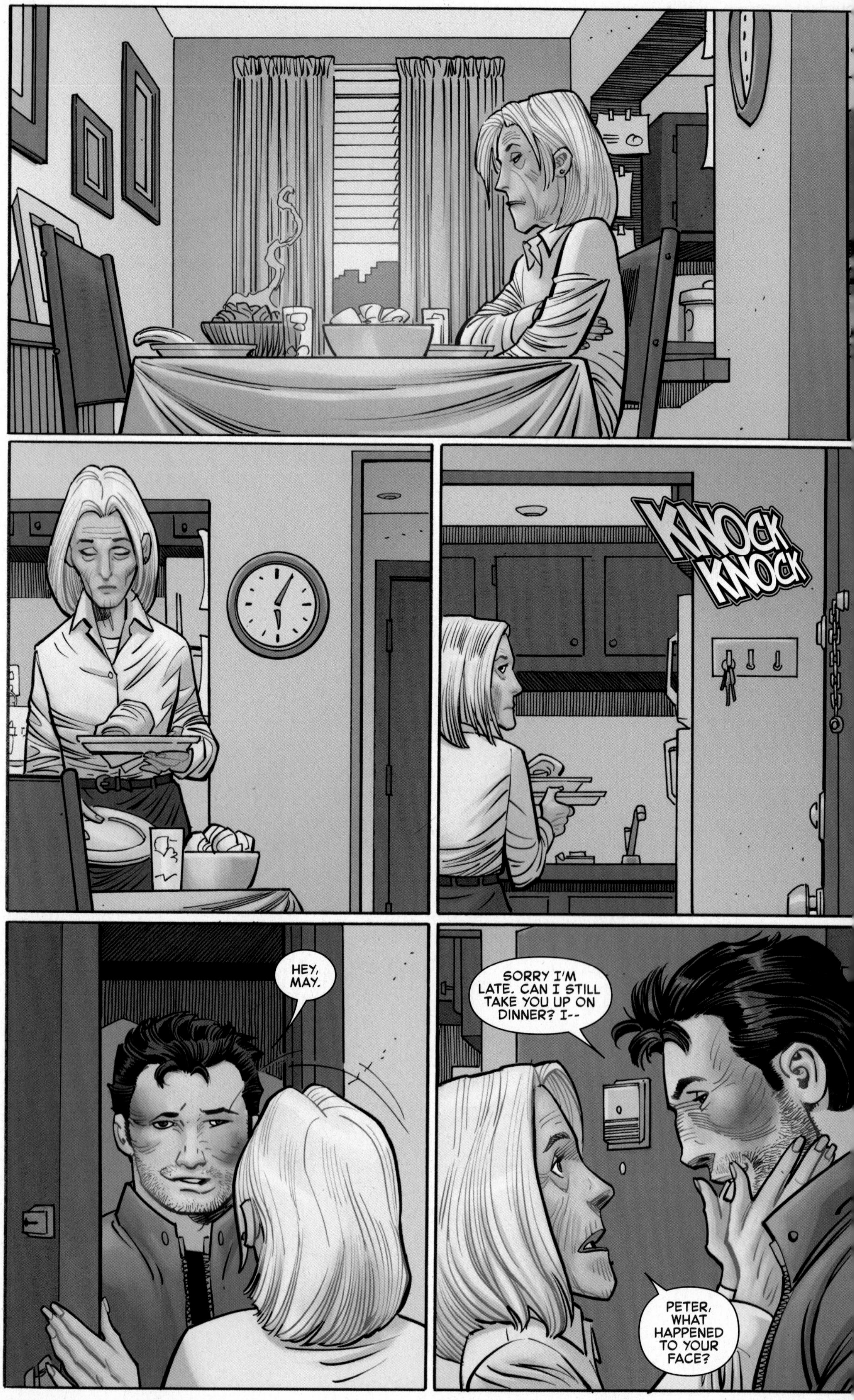

KNOCK
KNOCK
HEY, MAY.
SORRY I'M LATE. CAN I STILL TAKE YOU UP ON DINNER? I--
PETER, WHAT HAPPENED TO YOUR FACE?

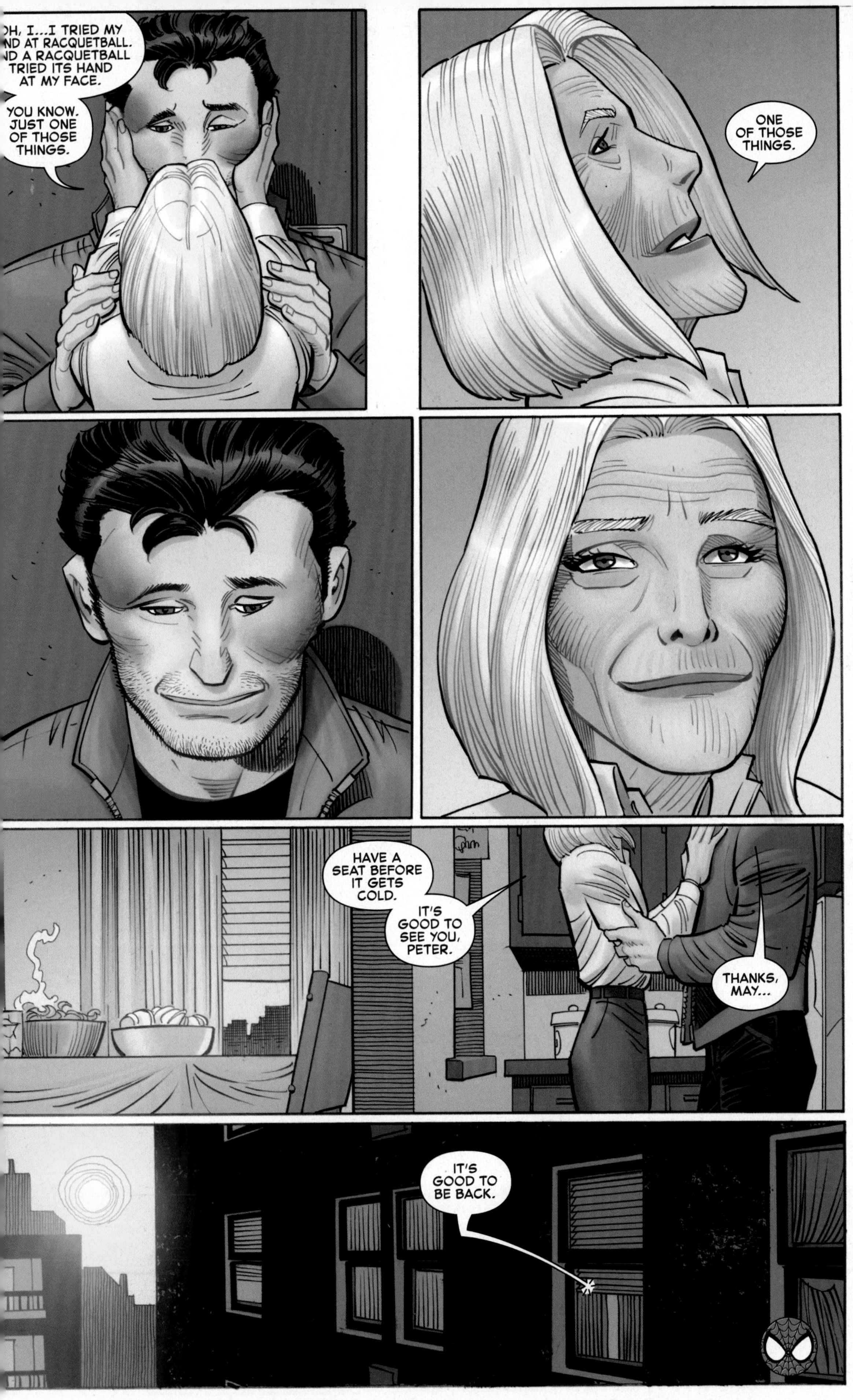

)H, I...I TRIED MY
ND AT RACQUETBALL.
ND A RACQUETBALL
TRIED ITS HAND
AT MY FACE.
YOU KNOW. JUST ONE OF THOSE THINGS.
ONE OF THOSE THINGS.
HAVE A SEAT BEFORE IT GETS COLD.
IT'S GOOD TO SEE YOU, PETER.
THANKS, MAY...
IT'S GOOD TO BE BACK.

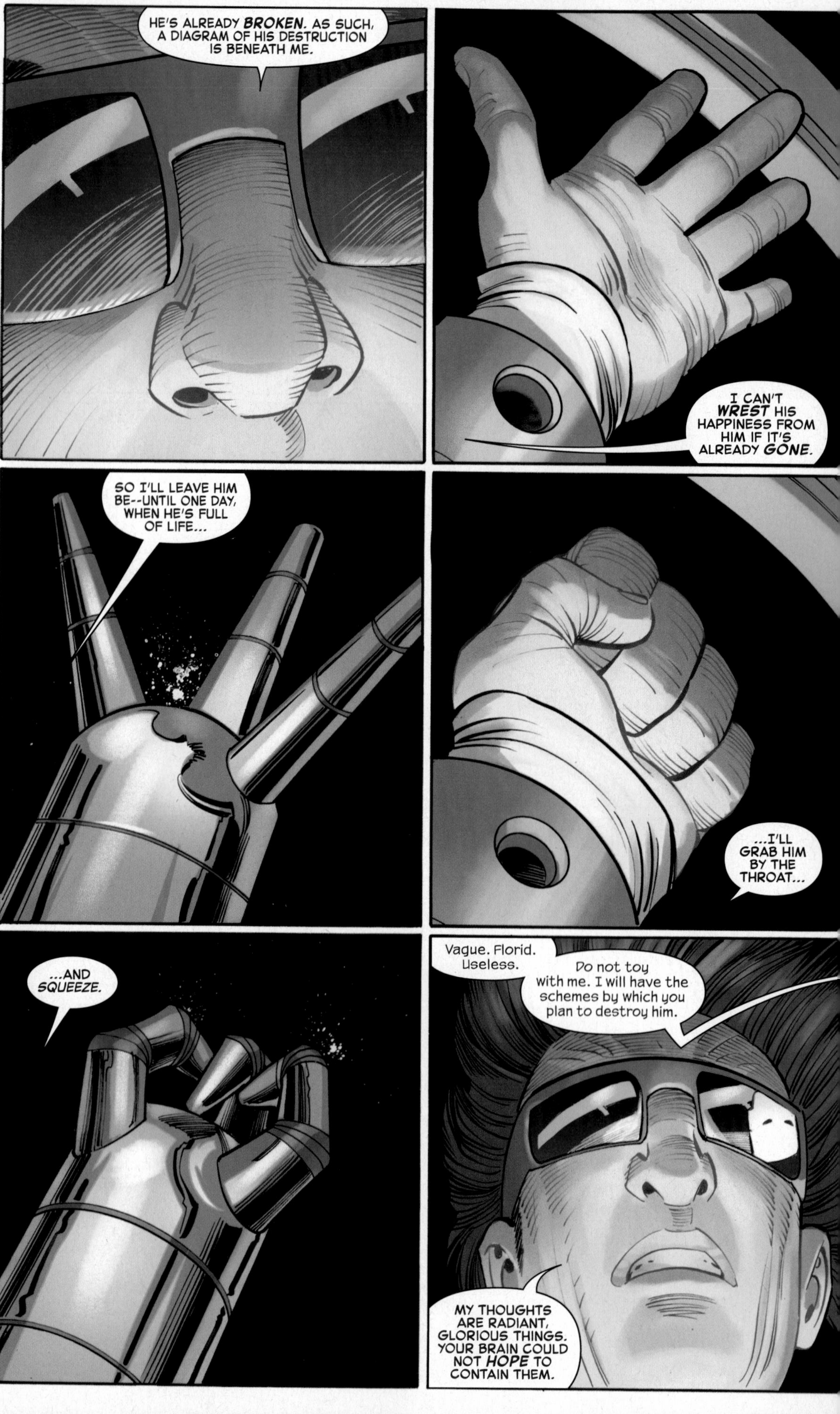
HE'S ALREADY BROKEN. AS SUCH, A DIAGRAM OF HIS DESTRUCTION IS BENEATH ME.
I CAN'T WREST HIS HAPPINESS FROM HIM IF IT'S ALREADY GONE.
SO I'LL LEAVE HIM BE--UNTIL ONE DAY, WHEN HE'S FULL OF LIFE...
...I'LL GRAB HIM BY THE THROAT...
...AND SQUEEZE.
Vague. Florid. Useless.
Do not toy with me. I will have the schemes by which you plan to destroy him.
MY THOUGHTS ARE RADIANT, GLORIOUS THINGS. YOUR BRAIN COULD NOT HOPE TO CONTAIN THEM.

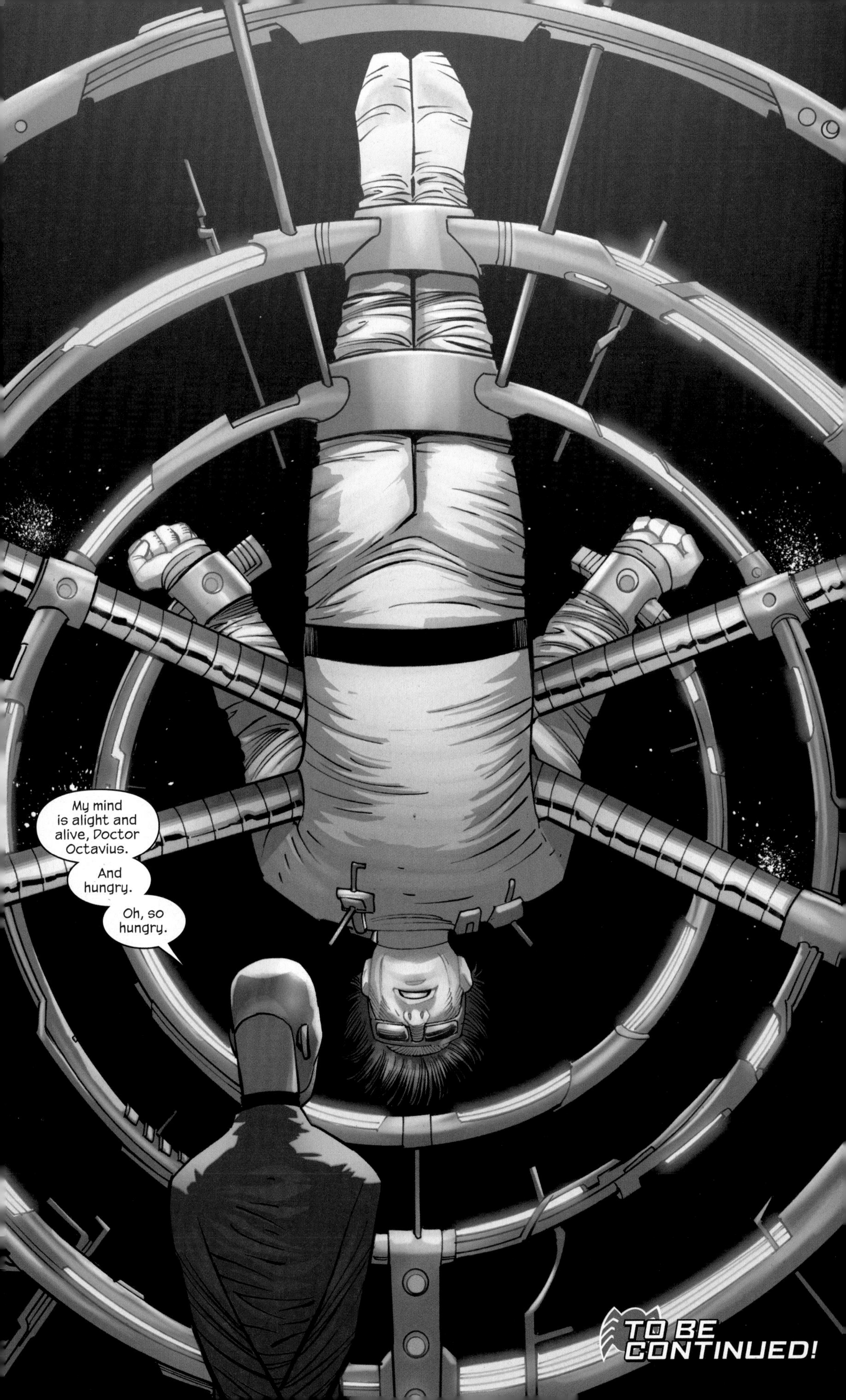
My mind is alight and alive, Doctor Octavius.
And hungry.
Oh, so hungry.
TO BE CONTINUED!

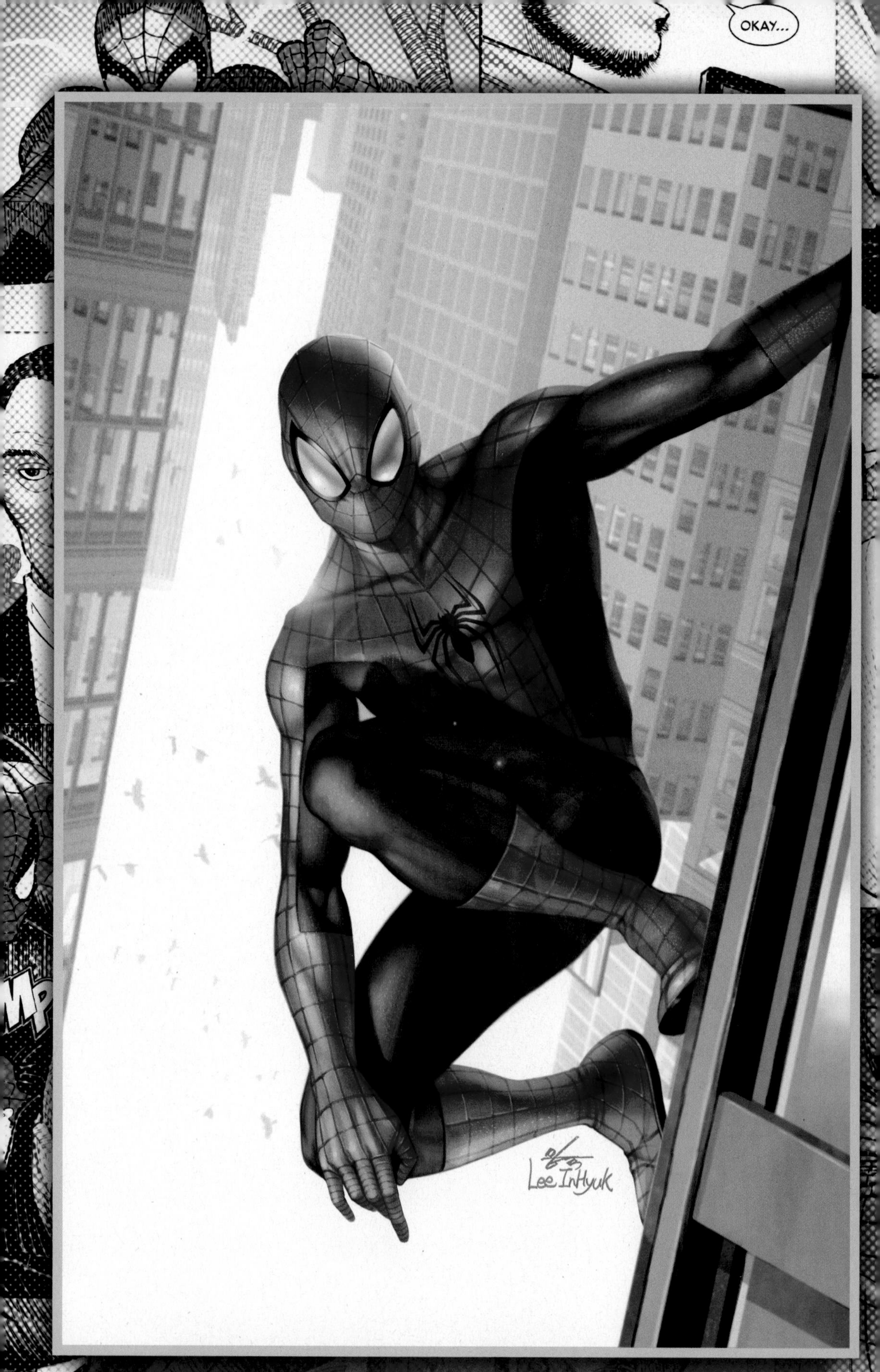
OKAY...
Lee InHyuk

InHyuk Lee #1 VARIANT

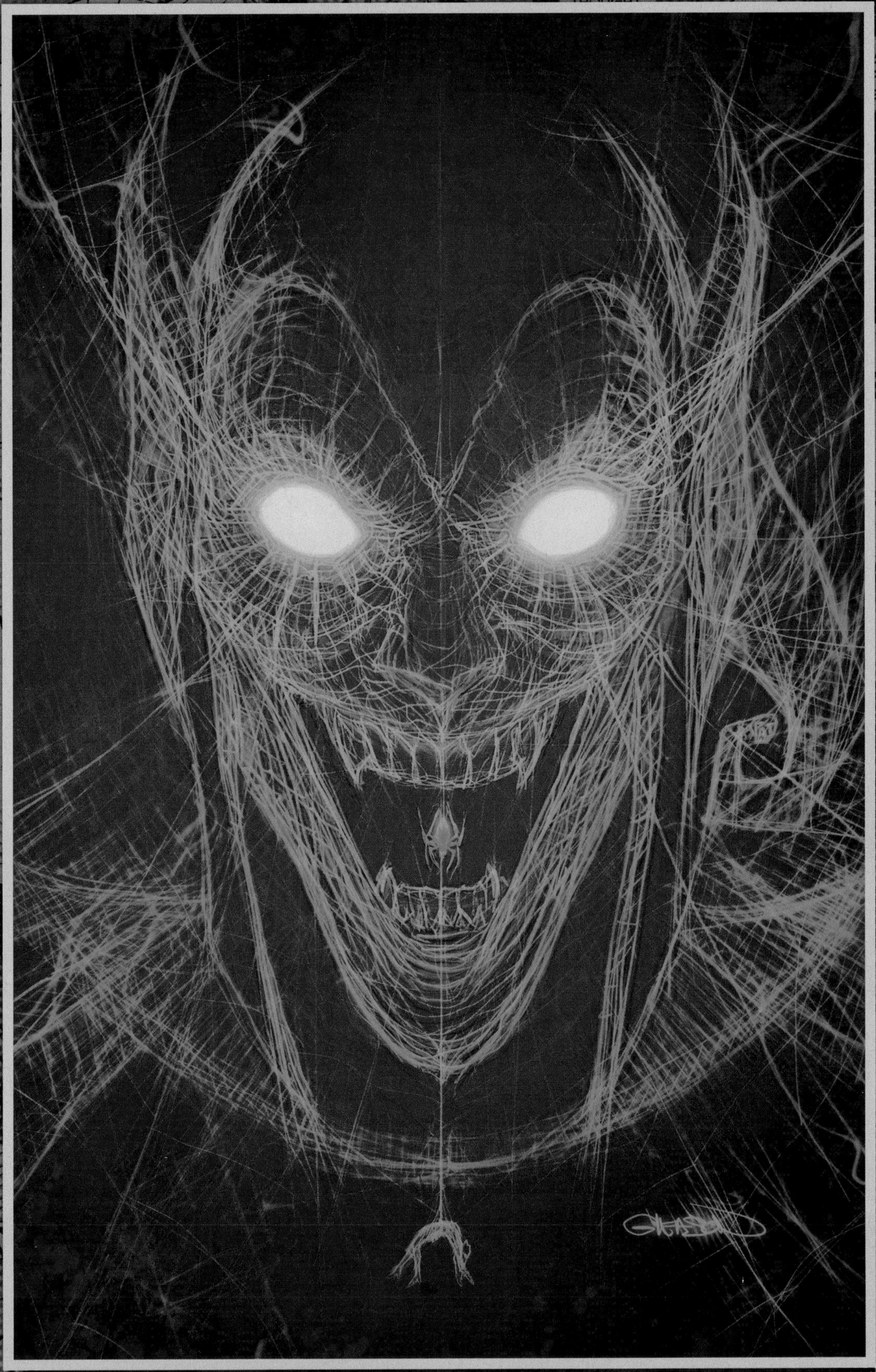

Patrick Gleason #1 WEB-HEAD VARIANT

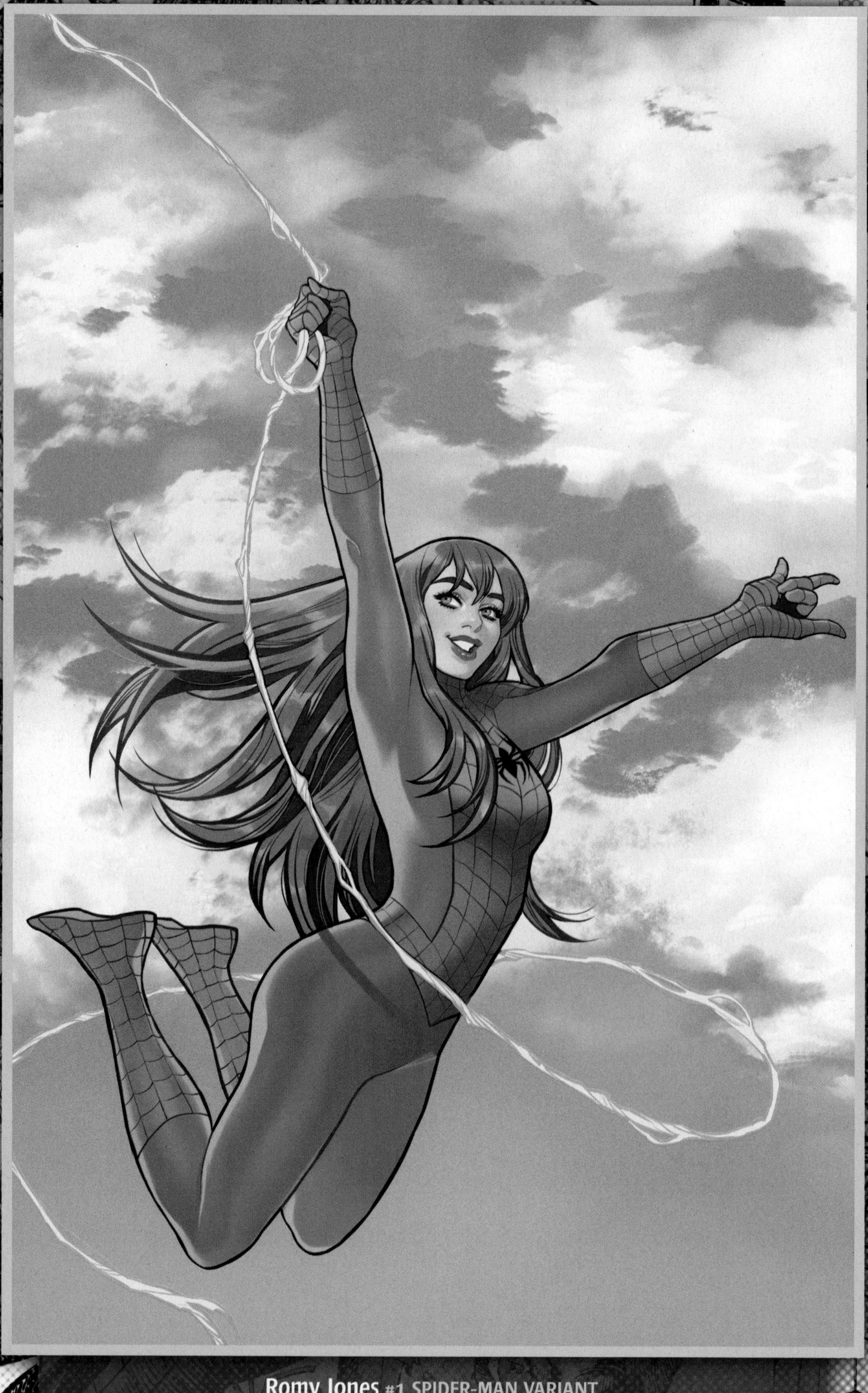

Romy Jones #1 SPIDER-MAN VARIANT

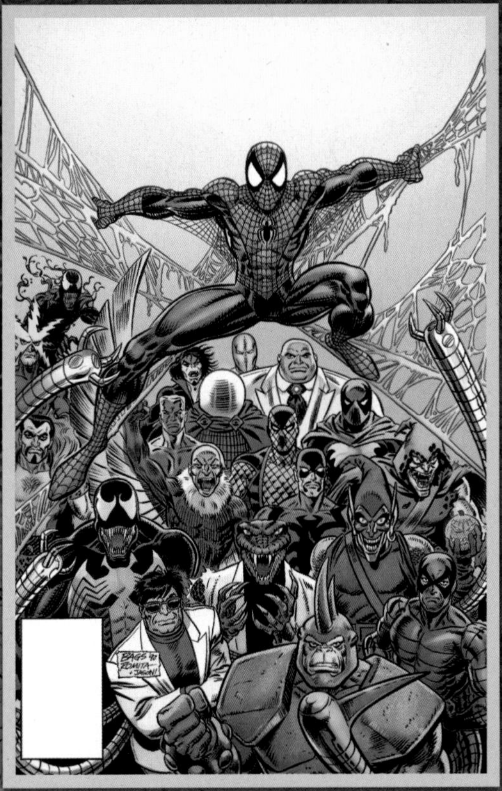

Mark Bagley, John Romita Sr., Sam Kieth & Jason Keith #1 HIDDEN GEM VARIANT

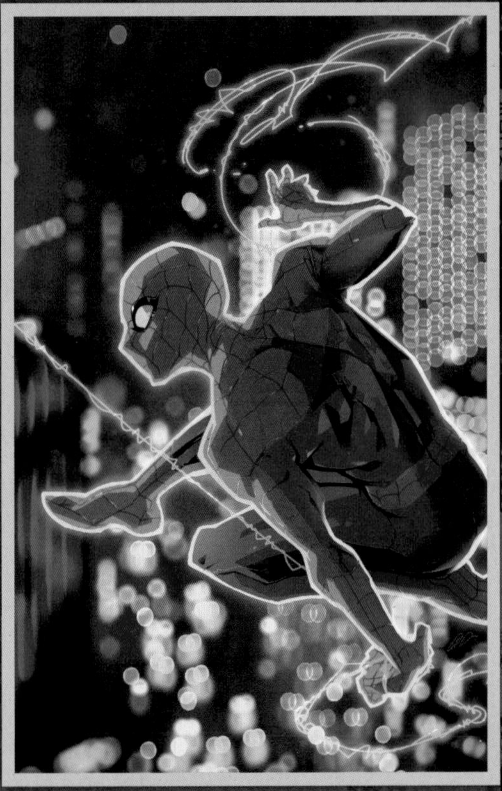

Rose Besch
#1 VARIANT

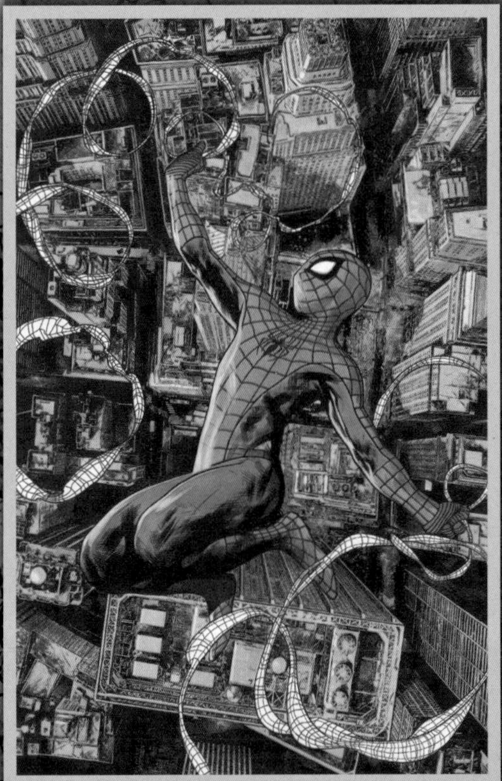

Travis Charest
#1 VARIANT

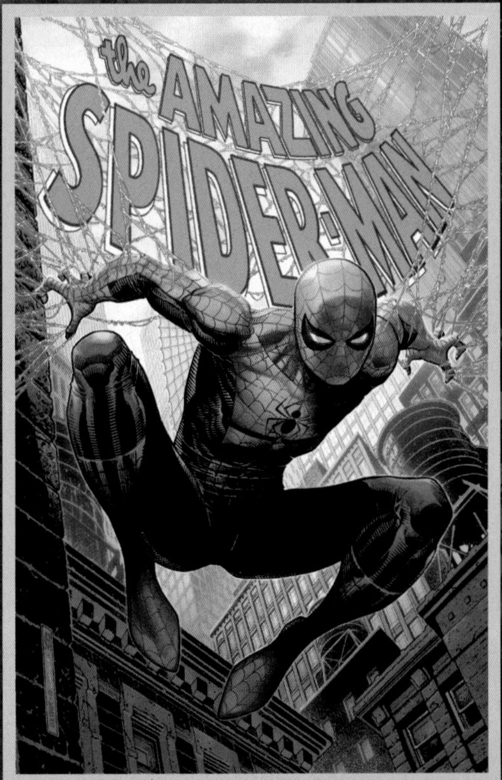
the AMAZING SPIDER-MAN

Jim Cheung & Jay David Ramos
#1 VARIANT

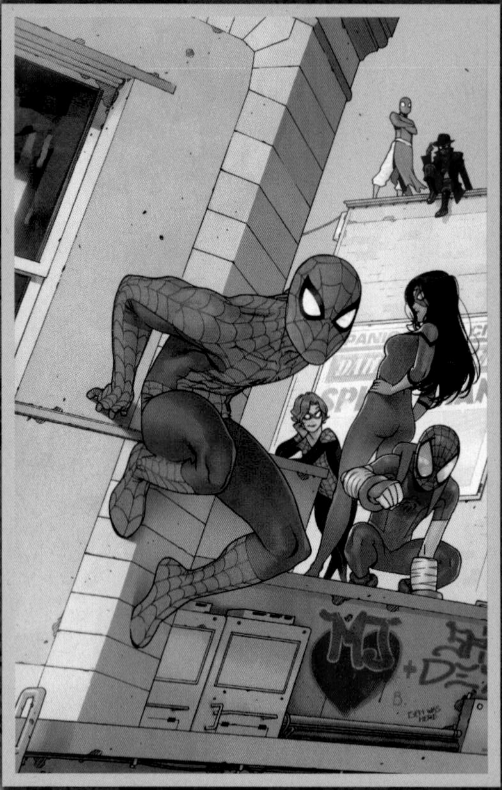

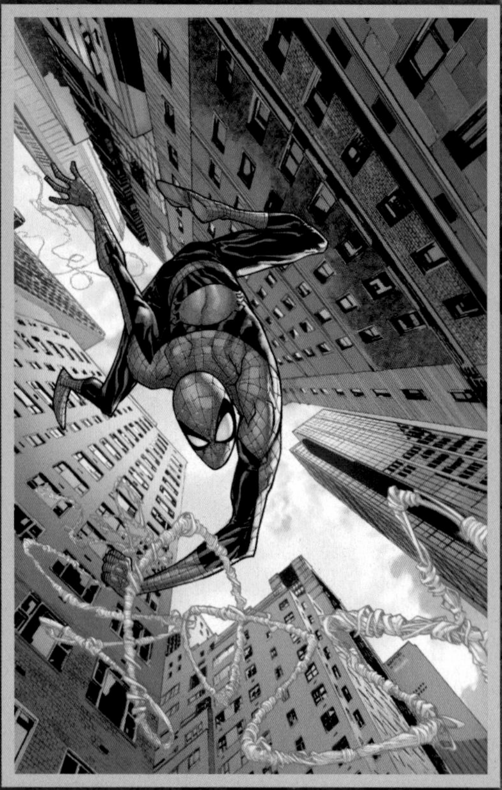

Bengal
#1 CONNECTING VARIANT

Humberto Ramos & Edgar Delgado
#1 VARIANT

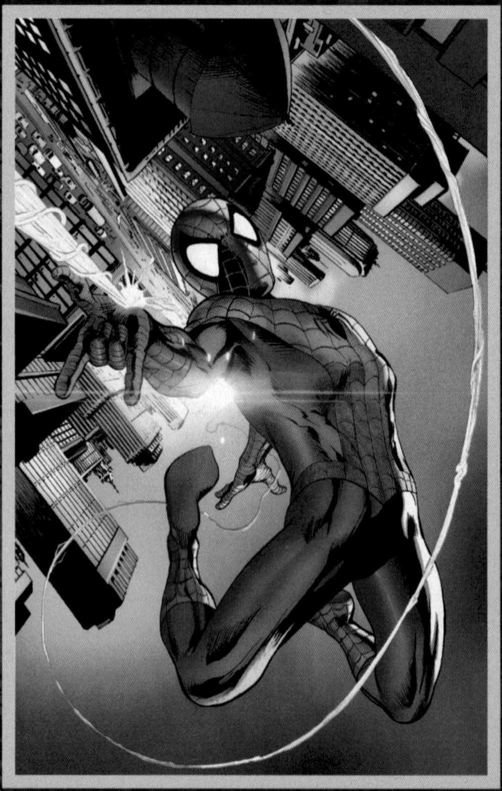

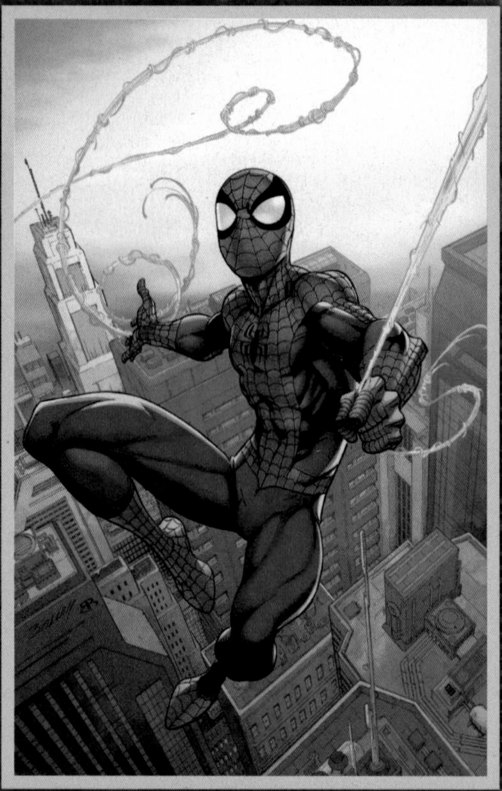

Alan Davis & David Curiel
#1 VARIANT

Mark Bagley & Brian Reber
#1 VARIANT

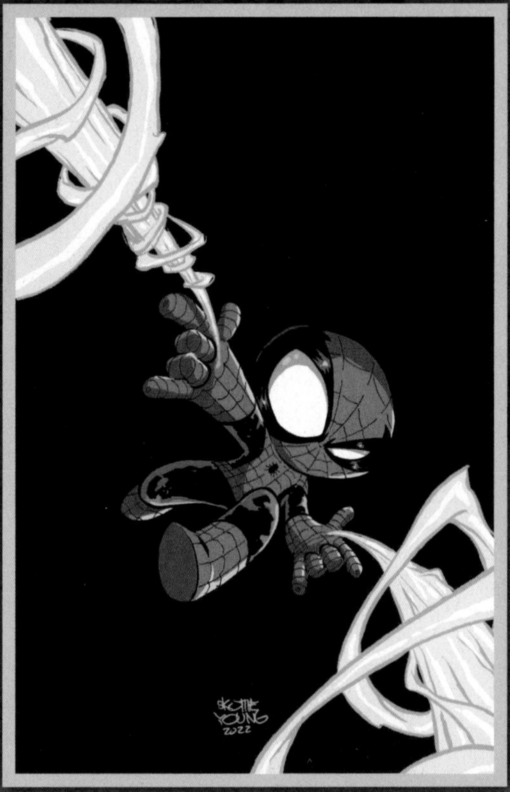
SKOTTIE YOUNG 2022

Skottie Young
#1 VARIANT

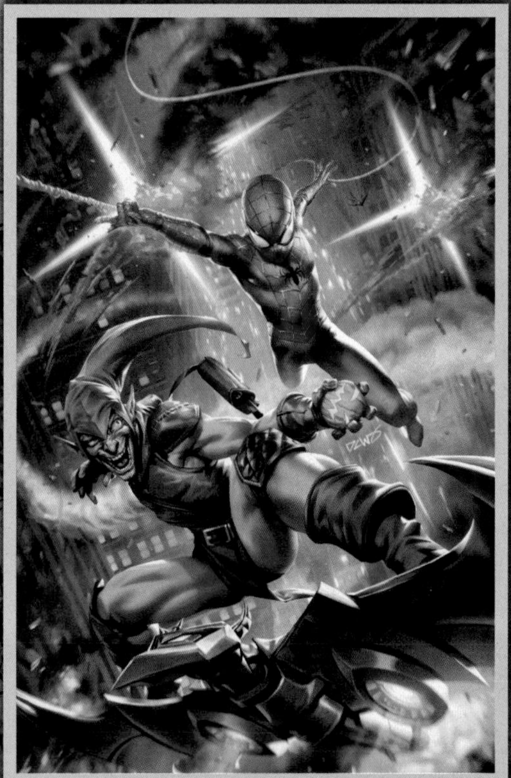

Derrick Chew
#2 VARIANT

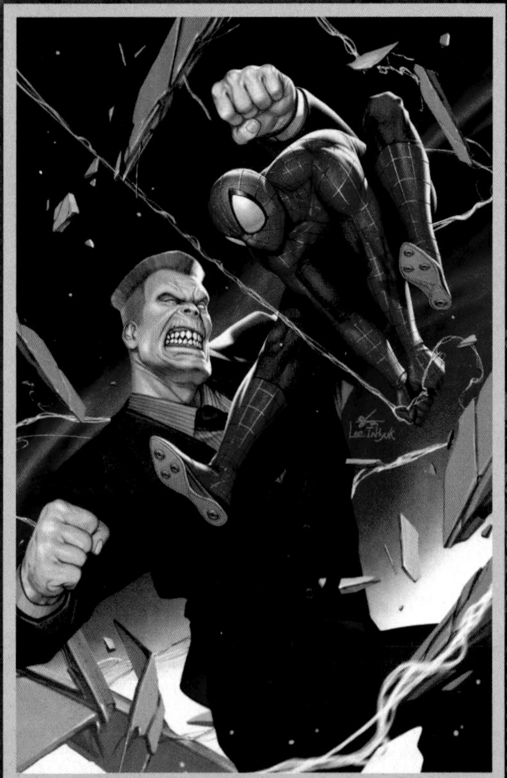

InHyuk Lee
#2 VARIANT

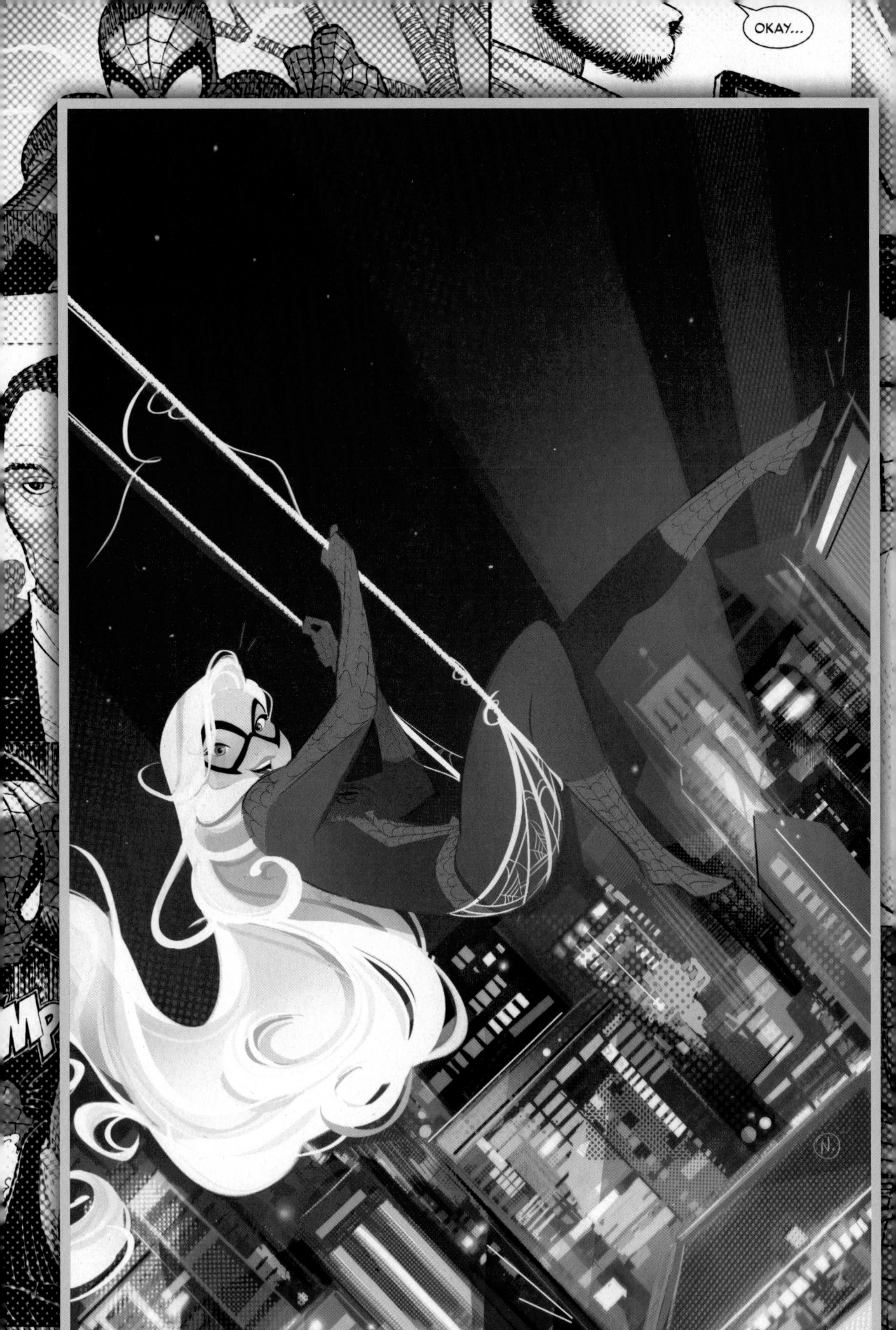
OKAY...

Nicoletta Baldari #2 VARIANT

Javier Garrón & David Curiel
#3 VARIANT

Salvador Larroca & Edgar Delgado
#3 SKRULL VARIANT

Hikaru Uesugi
#3 VARIANT

Jan Bazaldua & Edgar Delgado
#4 SKRULL VARIANT

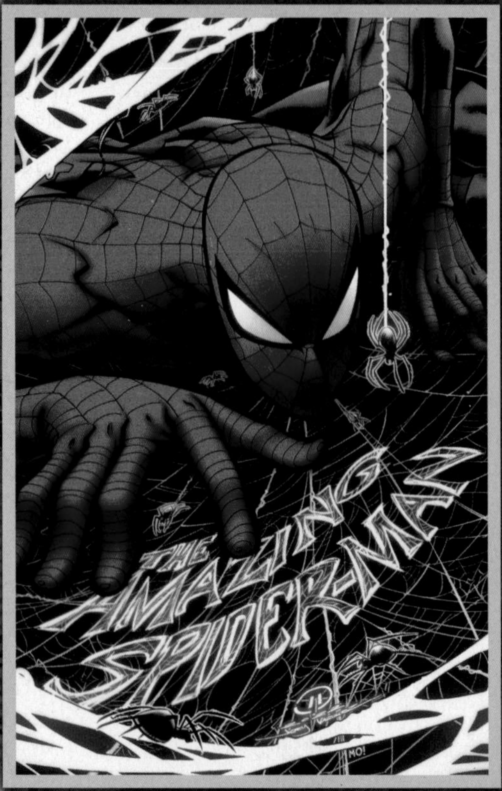
THE AMAZING SPIDER-MAN

Joey Vazquez & Morry Hollowell
#4 VARIANT

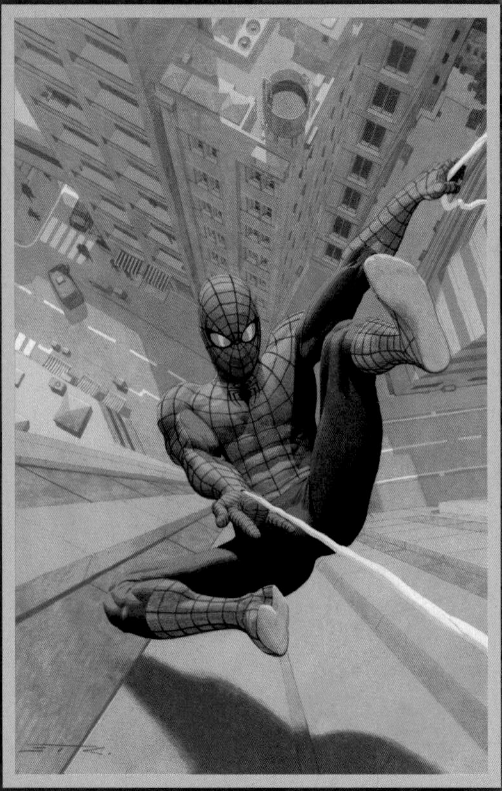

Esad Ribić
#5 VARIANT

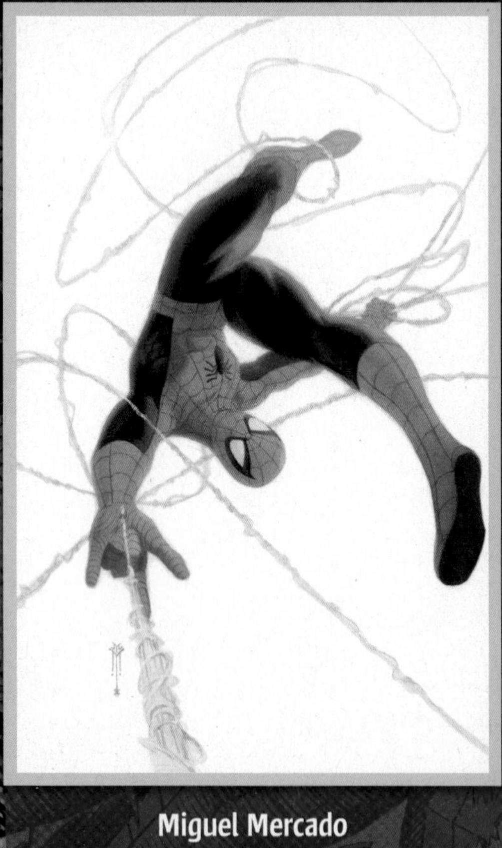

Miguel Mercado
#5 VARIANT

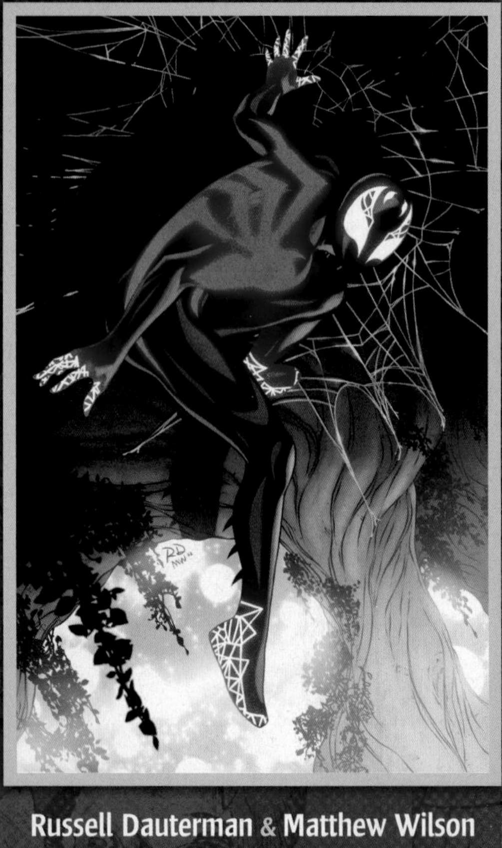

Russell Dauterman & Matthew Wilson
#5 HELLFIRE GALA VARIANT